# The Revolution That Wasn't

# SPENCER JAKAB

PORTFOLIO / PENGUIN

# The Revolution That Wasn't

## GameStop, Reddit, and the Fleecing of Small Investors

Portfolio/Penguin
An imprint of Penguin Random House LLC
penguinrandomhouse.com

Copyright © 2022 by Spencer Jakab

Most Portfolio books are available at a discount when purchased in quantity for sales promotions or corporate use. Special editions, which include personalized covers, excerpts, and corporate imprints, can be created when purchased in large quantities. For more information, please call (212) 572-2232 or e-mail specialmarkets @penguinrandomhouse.com. Your local bookstore can also assist with discounted bulk purchases using the Penguin Random House corporate Business-to-Business program. For assistance in locating a participating retailer, e-mail B2B@penguinrandomhouse.com.

ISBN: 9780593421154 (hardcover)
ISBN: 9780593421161 (ebook)

Printed in the United States of America
1st Printing

BOOK DESIGN BY CHRIS WELCH

To my three apes,

Jonah, Elliott, and Danny

# Contents

# Introduction

'll never forget the day I found out that my sons were degenerates.

    With my newsroom shut by COVID-19, I was working from home the morning of January 25, 2021, when I stopped editing a column for the next day's *Wall Street Journal* midsentence to see what they had been up to on the internet. After less than ten minutes of scrolling, I began to draft an email. It wasn't to their mom or their principal or even a child psychologist. It was to the publisher of the book you're holding in your hands.

    My oldest boy, a college senior, and my youngest, a high school freshman, were members of a "subreddit" called r/wallstreetbets whose members call one another degenerates, apes, and some even less flattering names. I had been aware of social networking site Reddit's freewheeling stock market forum for about a year at that point—an irreverent alternative to its older, more buttoned-down r/investing board. In the months before the pandemic, with the market booming, every week or so some random stock would jump on heavy volume because its members had started to buy it en masse. As far as I was concerned, it was an amped-up version of the infamous Yahoo stock message boards of the late 1990s. I would soon learn that I had woefully underestimated modern social media and the power of the latest smartphone-based, commission-free trading apps.

When the economy ground to a halt and stocks plunged as the world grasped the severity of the pandemic, older, grayer investors once again failed to follow their own advice about buying when others were panicking. Not the degenerates, though—maybe because they didn't know any better. The amateurs plunged in, and soon they were running circles around investing legends like Warren Buffett. But they were doing dumb things too like buying the shares of bankrupt companies or snapping up stocks with names that *sounded* like ones mentioned on Twitter by Elon Musk but that actually were worthless shells. Traders and fund managers thought it was hilarious. From what I saw and heard that morning, though, Wall Street wouldn't be laughing anymore.

My oldest son had prompted my deep dive into the subreddit by asking whether I was writing something about GameStop. The reason was that a friend of his, a bright boy I had known since they were both in kindergarten, had bought shares in the video game retailer after reading about it on WallStreetBets (WSB) and had nearly doubled his money in a couple of days. When I said he should count himself lucky and sell and he said he absolutely wouldn't, I was intrigued and began to read the forum.

With three sons, I was all too familiar with GameStop. I had driven them there countless times as they bought discs and then later traded them in for different ones. From editing columns about the chain over the years and from my sons' recent preference for bypassing the store and buying digital games online, I knew it was a dying business—sort of like Blockbuster Video after Netflix really started to take off. This was so obvious that it seemed like every hedge fund manager on Wall Street had piled into a bet that its share price was eventually headed to zero.

But the pros suddenly found themselves facing a group that wasn't interested in cash flows or when the next Xbox was coming out. If a stock went up for a week, or a day, or even a few hours and they sold it in time, the degenerates were happy. Over the past year or so, they had noticed that some stocks rose simply because they and a lot of strangers they had met on Reddit bought them. There was power in numbers.

Now they were playing a new and dangerous game—ruining the lives of hedge fund bosses. There were more than two million members of WallStreetBets by that day, and the group's membership would quadruple within a couple of weeks as they shocked the financial establishment.

Some users had grasped that investment funds were exposed to unlimited losses because they had engaged in a technique called "short selling," which allowed them to profit if stock prices fell—the opposite of what most investors do. The funds' bet against GameStop was so popular that it had left them with a very narrow escape hatch if the price started to rise sharply for some reason. With brokers like Robinhood allowing inexperienced traders to buy stocks using borrowed money and to employ derivatives that acted like a force multiplier, the amateurs had the means to do some serious damage.

They also had the motive. There was a lot of resentment in America at wealth inequality and what seemed like two sets of rules—one for the rich and connected and another for everybody else. Their formative experiences had included struggling to repay student loans and seeing their parents struggle during the financial crisis. What had started out as a way to have fun and make some money gained a special frisson: exacting revenge on the architects of a rigged system.

Intuitive, colorful apps made it surprisingly easy for a generation that had grown up glued to their phones. Bored and stuck at home during the pandemic, they found speculating on the stock market and comparing notes with strangers online even more exciting than betting on sports and, in a bull market, a whole lot more lucrative too. With nearly every stock going up, the challenge wasn't to pick a winner but to find a trade that would make it rain money. Meme-loving influencers who were rich, but the *good* kind of rich, were all too happy to make suggestions.

The new class of investors didn't trust traditional Wall Street advice, yet many were more than willing to take their cues from those influencers, and from fellow Redditors. Now some members of WallStreetBets who seemed to know a lot about arcane financial subjects like short selling and derivatives were talking about an investing opportunity that was a twofer—a way to make a bundle and to send some people who were the bad kind of rich to the poorhouse. The only thing was that you needed "diamond hands"—to hold on no matter how high the stock went. That was why my son's friend wouldn't sell.

Secretly setting up a stock market corner in which you squeeze a short seller dry by snapping up all the available shares was the sort of thing that happened all the time in 1921, but not in 2021. It has long been illegal. But what if, instead of a few rich people doing it behind closed doors, a few million strangers with small accounts did it in full public view? Even if regulators cried foul, what on earth were they going to do about it?

Not that they were paying attention as the wave was gathering strength. Neither were big fund managers. They were too busy staring at their Bloomberg terminals to waste time scrolling through memes on Reddit. If they had, they would have seen newly minted speculators with chips on their shoulders writing entries like "the biggest short squeeze of your life" and "Bankrupting Institutional Investors for Dummies." Some of these managers would even have seen their own names as the degenerates perused public securities filings. Instead of taking their lumps when GameStop shares kept rising, at first the pros saw a lot of weak hands and pushed even more chips into the pot. As Hemingway once described going broke, the force that would threaten to bankrupt some of the biggest players on Wall Street hit "gradually and then suddenly."

And then it got weirder. As cascading losses and surging volume threatened to overwhelm not just those funds but the very plumbing of the financial system, the game was put on hold. Suddenly brokers like Robinhood suspended the ability to buy more of the stocks that were on everybody's lips. No such restrictions were placed on the fat cats, though. The game was rigged!

But it always has been.

I was the director of the stock research department of a major bank before leaving high finance behind to write about it. In those twenty-eight combined years, I have never seen something happen in the market that created as much public buzz and controversy. Everyone read into it what they wanted to, and most were sympathetic to the little guy. I was too, but not because an army of retail traders wasn't allowed to buy as many GameStop shares as it wanted—it was because this was no revolution.

The reason Wall Street had to briefly circle the wagons was mostly technical, not a conspiracy. Aside from a handful of funds that lost big, the financial sector was loving it. David and Goliath stories are music to the industry's ears. A meme-loving retail-investor army putting one over on the big guys? People posting screenshots of their brokerage statements showing 5,000 percent gains and million-dollar balances? The attractive young couple with a grand total of five months' trading experience in a raucous bull market putting up instructional TikTok videos about how they don't have to work anymore because they only buy stocks that rise?

Wall Street feels about as badly about someone walking away with millions of dollars of "its" money and crowing about it as Las Vegas does—not at all. It is why lights and sirens go off when someone hits the jackpot and the person who wins the Powerball lottery is asked to pose for reporters with a giant check. Retail brokers had long been putting out commercials such as one with "the dumbest kid in your high school" partying with models on his superyacht after playing the market. But this? This was the sort of advertising that money couldn't buy.

When something crazy is happening in real life, I often think it's just like some movie. I guess I'm not alone because a lot of people compared WallStreetBets' supposedly turning the tables on greedy financiers to the plot of *Trading Places*, in which the down-and-out Billy Ray Valentine outwits the corrupt Duke brothers and bankrupts them in the futures market. "Sell, Mortimer! Sell!"

I love that movie, but what first came to my mind was the more serious *Zulu Dawn*, starring Burt Lancaster, about the Battle of Isandlwana. In it, a supremely overconfident colonial British army with the latest military technology of the day is outmaneuvered and slaughtered by a horde of spear-toting African warriors whom they considered to be primitives. That was the sort of vibe one got from headlines that week such as GAMESTOP MANIA REVEALS POWER SHIFT ON WALL STREET—AND THE PROS ARE REELING and DUMB MONEY IS ON GAMESTOP, AND IT'S BEATING WALL STREET AT ITS OWN GAME.

But by the time the dust had cleared, I had changed my mind. Now I thought it was more like *Attack of the Clones*. The fight is thrilling, even heroic, and everyone cheers for Anakin, hoping he will defeat the greedy Trade Federation, but then you remember that this is just a prequel—you already know how the story will end. There is a larger force afoot, happy to see a fight. Wall Street likes volatility, and it absolutely loves it when millions of new, inexperienced investors rush in with their savings. Who cares if they kill Count Dooku?

In the end, the battle over GameStop and the other "meme stocks" got too exciting. Brokers had to pull the plug to avoid frying the system's circuits, raising all sorts of awkward questions, but not the right ones. Americans were outraged, and so were politicians across the political spectrum. Customers furious at Robinhood, which had more frustrated users than others, resurfaced one of the broker's old marketing lines: "Let the people trade."

Until shortly before our story begins, Wall Street had been worried about the opposite problem. Leading up to the pandemic, the industry was enjoying its longest bull market ever and decent profits, but its customers were wising up. Technology, competition, and financial education were threatening their money machine. Even young savers were catching on to cheap index funds that they would buy and rebalance, or to robo-advisers that would do it for them, depriving Wall Street of tens of billions of dollars that it used to earn by getting people to trade individual stocks or to hire mutual fund managers. One anxious analyst wrote a report calling cheap index funds that don't dangle the promise of beating the market "worse than Marxism."[1]

In fact, it is when individuals believe that they can compete with the so-called smart money that the business has its best years. The degenerates were Wall Street's kind of customer. Nobody expected them to nearly tear the place down when the party got too wild, but brokers like Robinhood and the hedge funds that got bloodied would be better prepared next time. Big investors were clamoring to invest in them.

When I saw what was about to happen that morning, I thought this was something I wanted to write about. When I saw how politicians, the news media, and ordinary people reacted to the following days' roller-coaster ride, I knew I had to. It's a wild and fascinating series of events—a perfect storm of financial innovation, big egos, economic uncertainty, mob psychology, generational strife, and a deadly pandemic. Within a couple of weeks, there were at least four films under development about the "Reddit Revolution." I knew that they would be more like *Trading Places* or *Zulu Dawn*, with maybe a touch of *Animal House* for good measure.

The story I will tell is a different kind of story. No less crazy, but much less black-and-white, full of inconvenient truths that fly in the face of the popular narrative. Sure, the situation got out of hand, and the little guys may have shocked the establishment, but did they really stage a revolution? Far from it. Retail traders have a traditional place in Wall Street's food chain, and that hadn't changed once the dust cleared and the profits and losses were added up. For a short while, though, they were the financial system's apex predator and some of the "smart money" found itself as prey. I'll tell the story in alternating parts, with one following the quixotic adventure of a brilliant young man who really did outsmart Wall Street, eventually inspiring others to try their luck, and the other exploring the mechanisms that led to, and encouraged, this "revolution." In those chapters, I'll detail exactly how Wall Street brought millions of new people to its playing field, hustled them into thinking that they had an edge in the game, and then enjoyed a huge payday.

But I'll share some good news too. There really is a way for the little guy to stick it to the man and, by the end of this book, you'll know how to do it yourself.

First, let me introduce you to the key players of this story—the princes of Wall Street, some of whom nearly became paupers; the Silicon Valley wunderkinds who were too smart to doubt the wisdom of the crowds they enabled; and the reluctant revolutionary with nerves of steel who inspired an army of retail investors to get in the game.

# The Revolution That Wasn't

Chapter 1

# Mr. Kitty Goes to Washington

## Keith Gill

"I am not a cat."

So began the congressional testimony of an until recently middle-class, thirty-four-year-old financial wellness expert from the suburbs of Boston. His quip, a reference to a video of a virtual legal pleading that had gone viral a week earlier, injected a bit of levity into the serious proceedings, being conducted remotely on the afternoon of February 18, 2021, because of the still-raging COVID-19 pandemic. Unlike the hapless, tabby-faced lawyer, Keith Patrick Gill had more than enough tech savvy to disable a Zoom filter.[1]

He had recently come into a bit of money in the stock market—over $50 million at one point—and, indirectly at least, he had modern social media and trading apps, which had radically lowered the bar for novice investors, to thank for it. Even at his peak, that made him easily the poorest of the five men called to testify that day.

Gill, who went by the name Roaring Kitty on a series of YouTube videos and by the screen name DeepFuckingValue on Reddit's WallStreetBets forum, also was the sole man testifying at the virtual hearing who had become rich by risking only his personal capital. It was all earned through a concentrated bet on the stock of a single company that some of the brightest minds in finance were convinced was headed in the opposite direction: GameStop. It takes two to make a market, as they say.

When Gill first made a fortune on paper and then hung on to most of his stake anyway, he became an overnight hero for an online social movement. Millions of people logged on to WallStreetBets each afternoon just to see if he had sold, and members vowed each time:

*If he's still in, I'm still in!*

The revolutionaries couldn't all get rich or even make a profit in the process—though clearly many hadn't thought that part of the plan through—but they could transform themselves from hunted to hunter on Wall Street by collectively weaponizing their modest brokerage accounts. For some, sticking it to the man was just the gravy on top of the profit. For others, it had suddenly become their main goal, and they pledged to hang on even if it cost them money. They were surprised by just how successful they were as millions of people joined them over the course of one crazy week. But, just as the fat cats were in full panic mode, they got bailed out again when the rules of the game were changed. It was "heads we win, tails you lose," just like during the financial crisis. That was the popular narrative at least, and it was the reason Gill had to put on a suit and tie that morning.

# Vladimir Tenev

The other men called as witnesses were wearing nicer suits and were giving their testimony from swanky offices, not the basement of a rented house with a poster of a kitten hanging on the wall. They had accumulated far greater fortunes than Gill, in large part by tapping into the era's gusher of venture capital or by profiting from the longer-standing practice of "helping" Americans invest and grow their savings.

The one who would get the most questions that day from the House Committee on Financial Services, Vladimir Tenev, was the same age as Gill. Slim and pale with shoulder-length brown hair, he bore an uncommon resemblance to Adam Driver, with more than a touch of David Cassidy. Tenev had immigrated to the US from Bulgaria as a child shortly after the fall of its communist regime. As a boy, he was preoccupied with having money so that his family wouldn't get sent back, and he studied hard, majoring in math at Stanford. Tenev had become a billionaire three years earlier by harnessing both Silicon Valley's and Wall Street's money machines to start a company named for Robin Hood, the mythical figure who stole from the rich to give to the poor. But now he was the prime suspect in rigging the game for Wall Street's fat cats by restricting trading just as the squeeze had them on the ropes.

Tenev started out his testimony by reading lines taken straight from his company's marketing materials about how "the financial system should be built to work for everyone," not just people with a lot of money.

Committee chair Maxine Waters was in no mood to hear it, cutting Tenev off as he began and telling him to "use your limited time to talk directly to what happened January 28th and your involvement in it." That was the day three weeks earlier that had outraged everyone from leading politicians on both sides of the spectrum to late-night talk show hosts, making WallStreetBets a cause célèbre.

Although the committee's members had accepted millions of dollars in political donations from the finance industry, sympathies clearly were with the little guy that day. There was just one problem: nobody had broken any rules. Moreover, as we shall explore later in these pages, there was no conspiracy between hedge funds and retail brokers to short-circuit a revolution.

But one pundit's quip that the hearing was a solution in search of a problem overlooked the big picture.[2] It was a missed opportunity to lay bare for the public how a huge and hugely profitable business made its money from the savings of novice investors. For decades, Americans have been forced to navigate a confusing maze of slick marketing messages from companies seeking to help them invest their money, often leading to poor and expensive choices. Compound interest isn't something that people grasp intuitively, but people like the late index-fund pioneer Jack Bogle had by then convinced tens of millions of savers that they were giving up a huge chunk of their potential nest eggs due to what seemed like inconsequential costs.

Now, though, many stock-trading services like Robinhood were "free." So were real-time updates delivered straight to your smartphone and investing recommendations on social media that seemed to have worked out well lately. Index funds, on the other hand, were about as exciting as watching grass grow. A lot of the analysis and news feeds that cost professionals a fortune, and had long given them an edge, had now become available to the little guys, allowing them to compete with and even outsmart elite investors. That was the story, at least. But, if finance was being "democratized," why was Wall Street making more profit than ever?

Had the hearings been called at some other point in time—say, in the aftermath of the dot-com bubble's bursting—people tuning in might have been more interested in how much of the stock market's return was accruing to them and how some of the men testifying that day had become so rich. But February 2021 was a moment in time when most Americans with investment accounts weren't in the mood to check the fine print on their statements. Stocks were booming, and the people affected by the trading restrictions believed that they could do much better than just capturing the market's long-run return. They were Wall Street's ideal customers.

Americans are almost entirely on their own when it comes to financing retirement and their children's education. Those that take the crucial step of setting aside enough money for those goals often get their pockets picked along the way without realizing it. The meme-stock squeeze presented an excellent opportunity to ask some hard questions about how much of our savings wind up enriching Wall Street, and what could be done to change the industry's incentives.

A few of the statements made and questions asked by members of the committee got to that point. For example, Illinois representative Sean Casten had an uncomfortable observation as he addressed Tenev.

"There is an innate tension in your business model, between democratizing finance, which is a noble calling, and being a conduit to feed fish to sharks."

Another member asked Tenev if he should have seen the trading frenzy coming. Tenev called the meme-stock short squeeze a "black swan" event that had a one in 3.5 million chance of occurring. Maybe the former mathematics PhD student's numbers were accurate, but a black swan, a term popularized by bestselling author and risk analyst Nassim Nicholas Taleb, is something one simply didn't anticipate, not just a rarity. Tenev wasn't a passive observer of the increasingly wild and risky behavior by novices over the past year. His firm and its imitators enabled them by making trading with borrowed money and derivatives free, easy, and even fun—a bit too much fun. Robinhood's whole business model prospered when its customers traded a lot, and it did even better because of their recklessness. Plenty of Robinhood's core demographic, young men, already are reckless without any encouragement.[3] They also take their cues from one another—mainly on social media these days. Robinhood's interface and price point put that tendency on steroids. The reason Tenev was testifying that day was that his company had done too good of a job and had to hit the circuit breakers.

Everything we know about the success or failure of individual investors tells us that this was a recipe for poor returns and high risk. So how did Robinhood's customers do? Tenev replied that they had collectively earned $35 billion over and above the money they had deposited. But how much had they deposited and what was their return? Would it be at least as good as just parking the money in an index fund? Tenev tellingly dodged the question, instead noting that his customers had more money than if they had just spent it instead.

## Gabriel Plotkin

One of the sharks in Casten's metaphor was a witness at the hearing. After years in which he chomped more minnows than almost anyone else, though, the revolutionaries nearly beached Gabriel Plotkin, founder and chief investment officer of Melvin Capital Management, erasing billions of dollars from the value of his hedge fund.

Despite being the squeeze's biggest victim, Plotkin wasn't expecting a sympathetic audience that day, and he didn't get it. Part of the reason is that, despite the passage of time, the global financial crisis had made hedge fund managers like him out to be cartoon villains. And the fact that he made part of his money by betting certain stocks would fall made him look even worse in the eyes of the public.

Like Gill, Plotkin had found himself caught up in a securities fraud investigation at the age of thirty-four. He also hadn't done anything wrong, but it was a scare that came close to cutting short a promising career. At the time, Plotkin was a star portfolio manager at SAC, the aggressive hedge fund whose initials stand for the name of its founder, Steven A. Cohen, Wall Street's most feared trader. He had been copied on emails circulated to others at the firm about insider tips on stocks. There is no evidence that Plotkin acted on or even read them. SAC was eventually forced to pay a $1.8 billion criminal and civil penalty, and several employees faced insider trading charges.[4]

His boss's adversity turned into an opportunity for Plotkin, who struck out on his own in 2014, naming his new hedge fund after his late grandfather, a hardworking convenience store owner.[5] With some cash from Cohen and others, he was managing $500 million at the end of his first year in business and immediately began racking up big gains. As Plotkin informed the committee in his written testimony, among his first positions after starting the firm was going short the shares of GameStop—borrowing its shares and selling them in a bet that their price would fall and that he could buy them back more cheaply.

Why GameStop? Plotkin's focus was finding successful companies he thought would rise in value, as most investors might. But instead of just avoiding those that didn't make the cut, he and many other hedge fund managers picked likely losers in the same business, betting against them. If all retailers had a terrible year in the stock market, then his performance might not be so bad because weak companies he had sold short would do even worse, making Plotkin a profit and smoothing out the rough patch. It worked like a charm until it didn't: by the eve of the meme-stock squeeze, Plotkin was managing about $13 billion in his fund. He had personally taken home $846 million in compensation the previous year.[6]

Plotkin was in many ways different from his mentor Cohen, who collected impressionist paintings and modern art and had reportedly paid $12 million for a shark in formaldehyde by Damien Hirst titled *The Physical Impossibility of Death in the Mind of Someone Living.*

Melvin Capital's first office had a single decoration—a framed quote by football legend Vince Lombardi that probably cost about $12: WINNING IS HABIT. In other ways, though, he was similar. Athletic and darkly handsome with a full head of hair, Plotkin might not have looked much like the bald, chubby Cohen, but both had minds made for Wall Street. A sports buff, Plotkin could instantly recall all manner of statistics and had turned that ability toward finance, being able to regurgitate dates and stock prices with ease.[7] Lately both Plotkin and Cohen had invested in the ultimate trophy asset for a master of the universe—a professional sports team. Cohen had become the majority owner of the New York Mets in 2020. Plotkin, along with Daniel Sundheim, a competitor who also lost a fortune in the meme-stock squeeze, had bought a chunk of the Charlotte Hornets basketball team in 2019 from hoops legend Michael Jordan.

The reason hedge fund managers can earn hundreds or even thousands of times as much as the poor schlubs, relatively speaking, who manage mutual funds for mom and pop, is that they are supposed to have an edge. While their average performance hadn't necessarily borne that out in the years since the global financial crisis, they are certainly allowed to do things that someone who works for Fidelity or Vanguard can't with your 401(k). That freedom means that their performance can be different from the market overall—the "hedge" in hedge fund. That is in and of itself a selling point in marketing pitches to the trustees of pensions and endowments who hand over hundreds of billions of dollars to managers like Melvin Capital.

But this certainly wasn't what they thought they were getting when hiring Plotkin. Over the span of several exuberant days for the WallStreetBets crowd, Melvin Capital would bleed a dangerous amount of money as GameStop's share price, and eventually the prices of other heavily shorted companies, surged. Melvin received a quick infusion of $2.75 billion from Cohen and Citadel LLC, the giant financial firm run by Ken Griffin, with Plotkin later insisting it wasn't a "bailout."

## Ken Griffin

Another round of questions was directed at Griffin, the man who decided during the course of a morning phone call on January 25 to hand Plotkin the lion's share of that cash. Griffin is the founder of the hedge fund giant Citadel and the largest shareholder of Citadel Securities, the company that processed more retail stock orders during the meme-stock squeeze than any other firm. When some of the representatives' questions became pointed, Griffin's round, blue eyes looked directly into the camera and seemed never to blink as he gave frustratingly clinical answers. Behind the stare that one finance writer joked "could burn the flesh off people's faces in three seconds flat"[8] was a hyper-competitive, almost robotically efficient manager whose firm was once compared to a gulag, albeit a very well-paid one.[9]

"Even in the context of intense people, Ken would probably be in the top decile of a very rarefied crowd," said former Goldman Sachs boss Lloyd Blankfein of the financier.[10]

Griffin was the oldest and by far the wealthiest man called to testify at the age of fifty-two with an estimated net worth of $16 billion, tied with Plotkin's old boss Steve Cohen on the *Forbes* list of the world's billionaires.[11] Like his fellow hedge fund manager, he was also an avid art collector.

Both men went through incredibly nasty, expensive, and public divorces. In happier times, Griffin's 2003 wedding was held at Versailles, where Donna Summer entertained the guests. He had made headlines just months before the hearing for building up several trophy properties worth an estimated $1 billion, drawing comparisons with the estates built by plutocrats like William Randolph Hearst and John D. Rockefeller more than a century earlier.[12]

He didn't just have the most money and toys—Griffin was also the most influential person to testify. He made more than $60 million in personal political donations in 2020, including to several Republican members of the committee questioning him that day,[13] and his firm paid Treasury Secretary Janet Yellen about $800,000 for a series of speeches after she stepped down as the head of the Federal Reserve. Her predecessor atop the Fed, Ben Bernanke, is a well-compensated senior adviser on Citadel LLC's payroll.

Griffin started his financial ascent very young, trading convertible bonds in his dorm room while a freshman at Harvard after he discovered pricing anomalies. He soon set up his first fund in time to profit from the 1987 stock market crash. In an example of what doesn't kill you makes you stronger, another crash twenty-one years later that nearly put Griffin's hedge fund company out of business opened up new opportunities for his trading venture. Rules enacted after the global financial crisis made it more difficult and expensive for American banks to trade stocks since they had to set aside extra money and reduce their risk to avoid another 2008.

Citadel Securities isn't a bank or a stock exchange, but it acts as a market maker or wholesaler and now trades more shares on behalf of small investors than any competitor by far. It is Robinhood's largest single source of income, paying it for the right to execute its stock and options orders in lieu of their being sent to an exchange where those transactions are visible to everyone. That practice, "payment for order flow," would attract some uncomfortable questions at the hearing.

In much the same way that Robinhood can point to the good it does by "democratizing finance," Citadel can and does tout how much money it saves retail investors by efficiently matching up orders. The numbers are real, but you only save money on something if you decide to buy it in the first place. The practice makes zero-dollar commissions and frenetic trading by investors with small accounts possible.

Before the GameStop squeeze, Griffin was already one of the most prominent people in the financial world, but he was barely known outside it. Resentful about the trading halt and in search of a new villain after Plotkin exited with his wings clipped, Griffin suddenly became the focus of social media–savvy traders' ire. If you can think of a crude or insulting photoshopped image of Griffin, derisively known as "KennyG" online, then it has probably been used on Twitter or Reddit. Griffin kept his mouth shut for months after the squeeze, but his patience reached an end when the details of a federal lawsuit emerged in September 2021 that suggested to some that Citadel asked Robinhood to halt trading in the meme stocks for its own benefit. #KenGriffin Lied became one of the top trending topics on social media.

"It must frustrate the conspiracy theorists to no end that Vlad and I have never texted, called or met each other," wrote Griffin on the long-dormant Twitter account of Citadel Securities.

Griffin's hedge fund business and his trading business can't share notes and there isn't any smoking gun to suggest that he was behind the halt. And why would he be? Without doing anything underhanded, Griffin was one of the main beneficiaries of the innovations that had supposedly leveled the playing field between savvy financiers like him and the little guy. Even the year before the meme-stock squeeze, as retail trading was becoming America's new pastime, Citadel Securities reportedly doubled its revenue to a whopping $6.6 billion.[14]

## Steve Huffman

Steve Huffman, the chief executive officer and cofounder of Reddit, home to WallStreetBets and many other forums, was also called to testify that day. His company was at once a step removed from the financial shenanigans that had led to the hearing being called and also central to the story. Since he wasn't the boss of a financial firm that could see its life complicated by the committee, his answer about the quality of financial advice on Reddit's platform was direct and unapologetic.

"People can say, in fact they do on television all the time, that Reddit

encourages people to make what I would call bad investment decisions," he said. "On Reddit, I think, the investment advice is actually
probably among the best because it has to be accepted by many thousands of people before getting that sort of visibility."[15]

But one doesn't have to spend much time on social media to grasp
that the most prominent and viral posts are rarely the wisest, best-
informed ones. In case there was any doubt as to whether Reddit
wanted to embrace its role in the market tumult, it aired a hugely successful five-second ad during the Super Bowl in the waning days of
the meme-stock squeeze. Starting out as what seemed like another
car commercial, it cut to a statement with Reddit's logo that was so
quick that many later had to look it up online.

"Who knows, maybe you'll be the reason finance textbooks have to
add a chapter on 'tendies,'" it said, referring to chicken-tender lover
Gill's preferred slang for profits. "Powerful things happen when people rally around something they really care about. And there's a place
for that. It's called Reddit."

Alexis Ohanian, who cofounded Reddit with Huffman but is no
longer with the company, compared GameStop mania to the Occupy
Wall Street movement from a decade earlier. He said, "It's a chance for
Joe and Jane America—the retail buyers of stock—to flex back and
push back on these hedge funds."[16] It was a hopelessly romantic view
of the situation. Notwithstanding those few that got whacked by the
meme-stock squeeze, many hedge funds did very well and couldn't
wait to see Joe and Jane's next bright idea—especially now that computer programmers have built algorithms to trade off what they are
chatting about on Reddit more quickly than a human can read it.

And even if that whole class of professional investor had been permanently disadvantaged by the meme-stock squeeze, it wouldn't be to retail investors' benefit. Ironically, as will be explained later, times when
funds that can sell stocks short are running for cover can be the most

dangerous ones for mom and pop. Meanwhile, the people whose job it is to write laws to protect them weren't really helping matters either.

## The Washington Establishment

Committee chair Waters didn't win twenty-three elections in her political career by failing to sense the public's mood. Even days after the facts of the trading halt had become clear, she singled out hedge funds in announcing the hearing's agenda. "Many Americans feel that the system is stacked against them, and no matter what, Wall Street always wins," she said during the hearing itself.

The polling firm Invisibly Realtime Research asked more than thirteen hundred Americans in early February 2021 about their views on GameStop's gyrations and the trading curbs. More than three quarters said that the shutdown of trading was "market manipulation" rather than a step to prevent major losses in other stocks.[17] At a time of extreme polarization in Washington, politicians on both the left and the right echoed those suspicions.

But when it came to actions that would help protect poorly informed retail investors, they had been backsliding for years. In 2012, Congress passed and President Barack Obama signed the JOBS Act, which, despite the acronym, wasn't about employment. It lowered disclosure requirements for many companies and allowed them to advertise offerings to investors. And in 2018, the Trump administration axed the fiduciary rule that would have required brokers to put your interests above theirs for retirement accounts.

In an investor education post on its website weeks after the hearing, Robinhood defined the legal distinction for a lay audience: "A fiduciary is sort of like a babysitter."[18] That certainly doesn't sound cool or desirable to a twenty-one-year-old convinced he is a stock market genius. The following month, Robinhood would file a suit in Massachusetts to overturn a rule that went into effect in September 2020 that required brokers to act as a fiduciary. The suit accused the state of attempting to "bring its residents back in time and reinstate the financial barriers that Robinhood was founded to break down."[19]

The witness who got the least attention in news coverage of the hearings was Jennifer Schulp, the director of financial regulation studies at the libertarian Cato Institute's Center for Monetary and Financial Alternatives. That is a shame, but not because she offered the committee's members any great policy suggestions. The Washington-based think tank promotes "an American public policy based on individual liberty, limited government, free markets," and Schulp made Tenev's and Griffin's cases better than they did themselves. She urged no steps that would make it harder or more expensive for retail investors to trade in order to curb dangerous speculation. But she cited a number of statistics about the unequal distribution of stock ownership by age, education, and race in America and the benefits of being in the market for the long term that could have turned the discussion in a more fruitful direction. That inequality, and a general distrust of experts, played a key role in the meme-stock squeeze.

Gill, the witness who was largely ignored by the committee, would have been more enlightening. He was, after all, the only retail investor testifying. He didn't actively lead the supposed revolution. Instead, he provided the vital spark to the massive wave of stock buying through his steadfastness. More sophisticated than 99 percent of the young people heavily invested in the meme stocks, Gill shared much of their risk appetite and playfulness. Despite facing an investigation at the time, he plugged GameStop, which he continued to hold and would soon buy more of. He even cheekily included a line in his testimony often repeated on the WallStreetBets forum:

*I like the stock.*

Chapter 2

# September 8, 2019

oly shit bro, what made you drop 53K on gamestop?"[1]
Techmonk123 wasn't impressed at all with DeepFucking
Value's sense of risk and reward. The user with the profane
pseudonym had made a $53,566.04 all-or-nothing wager on a single
stock, according to a screenshot of his E*Trade account posted on
WallStreetBets. Even though the subreddit was full of people doing
reckless things in the market with their money, this was a gigantic
and concentrated gamble. What's more, it wasn't even on Tesla, Netflix, or any of the other glamour stocks that had been leading the longest bull market on record. It was on GameStop, a mall-based retailer
of video games that some of the smartest money managers on Wall
Street were convinced was headed the way of defunct Blockbuster
Video as software increasingly became digitized.

Instead of just buying the shares, which would have been foolhardy
enough, DeepFuckingValue had purchased "call options." They are a

derivative contract that pays off only if the stock's price is above a certain level on a certain date. If not, they expire worthless. And on its most recent trading day, GameStop shares would have had to jump by at least 86 percent by January 15, 2021, for this bet to be worth even a penny.

DeepFuckingValue, who would be unmasked sixteen months later as Keith Gill, tagged this initial Reddit post and all the ones that followed as "YOLO," for you only live once. The acronym had become an adjective as well as a verb. For example, someone who made reckless, ill-informed bets was called a "YOLO trader." WallStreetBets was filled with screenshots bearing headings such as

> *Yoloing life savings of 42k into MVIS (I'm 21, need this to moon so I can afford a house down payment in a couple of years).*

Or

> *Yolo'd 230k into $MNMD while on Shrooms*

Or

> *One big YOLO bet and done with this shit?*

Gill had just had what seemed to others on the board like a huge stroke of luck. Interestingly, he didn't see it that way, which tells us a lot about him. News that the value investor Michael Burry, made famous by Michael Lewis's *The Big Short,* had taken a big position in GameStop earlier in the summer had sent the prices of the call options soaring, forcing Gill to pay more than twice as much for some recently purchased contracts as those he had bought less than a month earlier. The screenshot showed that his account was now worth $113,962.61.

The title of his post was "Hey Burry, thanks a lot for jacking up my cost basis."

Value investors like Gill and Burry are from Mars, and day traders are from Venus. DeepFuckingValue was true to his pseudonym and was annoyed that the unexpected arrival of a big name had forced him to pay more for his investment. Deep-value investors trawl through the market's detritus and are willing to wait a long time, if necessary, to see a stock's price rise to the level they think it deserves. If it goes down after they bought it, then many see it as a good thing—a chance to buy more at an even lower price.

Almost anyone else on the board would have been jumping for joy at more than doubling their money. One poster said that DeepFucking-Value should at least cash out his original investment and just gamble with the rest. Another made a similar suggestion. Nobody goes broke taking a profit, after all.

"Perhaps, but that's not how you maximize returns over the long-term," he replied.

The person behind the pseudonym was clearly extremely self-confident. He also showed uncommon sophistication—not to mention politesse—on a board known for crude insults and little regard for spelling and punctuation.

"Pigs get fat. Hogs get slaughtered," wrote another poster about DeepFuckingValue's insistence on hanging on to a small fortune that could shrivel to nothing.

"Again that's not the way to maximize returns over the long-term. That's trading in fear—loss aversion, a common emotional bias," he replied.

"RemindMe! if this stupid fuck lost it all in 1 week," wrote another in response.

As one former skeptic put it in a much later update to an old comment to Gill in the middle of the GameStop squeeze, his original post "aged like a tall glass of milk on a July afternoon in the Mojave Desert."

It is hard to know how much more seriously the handful who engaged with Gill on the message board would have taken him if they had connected his pseudonym to his other alter ego, Roaring Kitty on YouTube, where he would begin making broadcasts from his basement the following summer about GameStop's growth opportunity. Gill, who often wore a red headband to tie back his long brown hair while sipping Belgian beers and gesticulating excitedly, bore an uncanny resemblance to the Mike Myers character in *Wayne's World*. But his thesis was serious and detailed, laid out in bullet points with references to authorities like the valuation guru Aswath Damodaran, who was almost certainly unknown to his audience. Even after his analysis started to bear fruit, Gill testified that he drew only a tiny crowd.

"The reality was people didn't really care about boring, repetitive analysis of GameStop and other stocks, and that was fine."

His goal wasn't to achieve video-investing stardom, but if it had been, then Gill had picked the right moment to start. Young investors were flocking to the market in record numbers and seeking out advice about what to buy on social media from people who were funny and relatable. Around the same time, a young man who made a fraction as much while exclaiming "I don't know what the fuck I'm doing" racked up half a million followers on TikTok.[2] Gill, on the other hand, knew precisely what he was talking about. He had earned a gold-plated investing credential, passing all three of the rigorous exams needed to earn the Chartered Financial Analyst designation. The average candidate spends almost one thousand hours studying for them combined, and most don't pass either the first or the second of the three exams on their initial attempt.

Gill never mentioned his credentials, and it probably wouldn't have mattered. After wallowing in anonymity, he would rise to fame with a group that distrusted experts, and Wall Street expertise in particular. His youth, his love of memes, and his informal style certainly helped to break the ice with contemporaries, but Gill's courteous, cerebral approach was almost a textbook case of how *not* to influence people online. Studies of social media impact show that those who are the surest of themselves tend to attract far more attention.

Two Washington State University economics graduate students, Jadrian Wooten and Ben Smith, wanted to test the hypothesis for the stock market, but they found that financial predictions often don't mention a date and a price in the same sentence—probably a wise move by pundits. So they wrote a program to sort through more than a billion Twitter predictions about the 2012 baseball playoffs and 2013 Super Bowl. They found that expressing confidence but being wrong gained one far more followers than nuanced predictions that were correct.[3]

So how would the thoughtful Gill eventually become central to the GameStop squeeze? Doubling your money, as he had done in the summer of 2019, was nothing special in a crowd of boastful traders on social media in the middle of a raging bull market. But because he had chosen such a speculative financial instrument, when GameStop's price finally began to rise more meaningfully in late 2020 in the weeks leading up to the meme-stock squeeze, Gill's net worth would mushroom and his legend would too. His gains were almost 100,000 percent at their peak. The fact that he mostly held on proved electrifying.

"There was no face to the name—he was just a mythical dude. He became an idolized figure," says Seth Mahoney, a college student and active Robinhood customer who was twenty years old and had been on WallStreetBets for three years and Reddit for nine years at the time of the GameStop squeeze. "He's one of those leaders, like Elon Musk with Dogecoin."[4]

By the time he was at the height of his influence, Gill was only posting memes or updates of his E*Trade account. Yet those screenshots took on a powerful importance as the trade became successful, explains Dr. Jay Van Bavel, a psychologist at New York University attached to its Social Identity and Morality Lab. He notes that social media is all about attention and that the impact of what people see is amplified when a poster can exhibit some past success in getting something right or displaying some perceived knowledge.[5]

"Once enough attention is captured, it can exert influence on real behavior," he says. "In this case, the screenshots provide what is known as social proof, which motivates other people to take the same action in ambiguous situations."

Back in September 2019, though, praise was hard to come by, much less imitators. After deflecting the unsolicited advice to take profits, one user finally congratulated Gill for his gains so far. Gill replied:

*Thanks man! This is just the beginning.*

Chapter 3

# Killer App

I f you had told an enterprising young investor half a century ago that
in the future people would all carry around a device in their pockets
with instant access to the sum of human knowledge, advice from a
community of fellow traders, streaming news headlines and share
prices, and the ability to buy and sell stocks and even options for free
with a few finger swipes, they would have salivated at the potential
for profit. But, instead of educating novices and allowing young people to build up capital, the loudest voices on social media and the slick-
est trading apps are helping Generation Z and millennials give their
elders—victims of the dot-com bust and housing crash—stiff competition when it comes to stupid financial mistakes. Like them, they are
also lining the pockets of already-rich men in the process, just in a less
apparent way.

You need a solid grasp of human psychology, which has hardly
changed in the last fifty thousand years, to dissect a financial mania.
But you can't understand the GameStop squeeze and the way that the

newest generation of investors behaved without also knowing how a handful of smartphone-based apps, developed in the last decade or so, work. They have evolved at record speed and, through a combination of natural selection and intelligent design, have become very good at holding the attention of our hunter-gatherer brains and focusing them on things that make other people money.

Those happy with, and profiting from, the new face of personal finance argue that the likes of Robinhood and Reddit are just more convenient forms of services that have been around forever, warts and all. After all, people have been trading stocks and exchanging often misleading messages about them on the internet for a quarter of a century now. Before that, they traded over the phone or in person and got dubious advice from tipsters. Financial manias and panics are as old as markets. The usual prescription is more and better "investor education," though there is little evidence that it is effective.

The meme-stock squeeze delivered a wake-up call to everyone. Even as it was still going on, furious politicians called hearings, movie studios raced to ink deals for GameStop movies, and hedge funds scrambled to hire data scientists to scour social media so they could get in early on the next mania, or at least stay out of harm's way. There may be nothing new under the sun when it comes to investing or stock tips, but the hyperconnected, algorithmically enhanced version is an order of magnitude more potent. It was strong enough to enrage Washington, inspire Hollywood, and rattle Wall Street.

Knowing how Reddit and Robinhood work is key to understanding this story.

## Born of Silicon Valley

Reddit's WallStreetBets subreddit and Robinhood got started within a year of one another, in 2012 and 2013, respectively. Their growth trajectories have been remarkably aligned, and the overlap in their users is significant. Packy McCormick, a former banker who blogs about popular culture and business strategy, observes that, by the start of the pandemic, being a member of the subreddit and being a Robinhood trader "were practically synonymous. The terms both meant something like 'particularly risk-seeking retail YOLO trader.' WSB fed off of Robinhood, and Robinhood fed off of WSB. Robinhood's growth mirrors WallStreetBets' almost perfectly."[1]

The forum's name tells you a lot about founder Jaime Rogozinski's vision for WallStreetBets. He felt marginalized on some of the older, more staid investing subreddits—especially when he broached the subject of speculative trades or the use of derivatives such as stock options. He wanted a place where people could discuss bets, not just investments.

The technology behind social networks and trading apps might be revolutionary, but were the people on his forum and using Robinhood revolutionaries? Rogozinski shakes his head when asked if the forum's near takedown of major hedge funds was some sort of class war. He says that the ethos of the group was always to find profitable hacks or vulnerabilities. In this case, some members were sophisticated enough to understand the mechanics of short squeezes.

"So this is just a nice setup for them to get into it, and then all of a sudden it starts to gain traction. . . . Everyone's cheering, starting to make a ton of money, and then all of a sudden, you know, boom, headline, these hedge funds are in trouble," he says. "Then it turns into what appears, in retrospect, to be a movement. The intention was always to make money."[2]

Despite being named after the mythical hero who stole from the rich to give to the poor and its stated mission "to democratize finance for all," the same goes for Robinhood. Ironically, the first company started by Vlad Tenev and his cofounder Baiju Bhatt after Tenev dropped out of his math PhD program at UCLA was meant to help hedge funds trade more efficiently. The two learned about the plumbing of the financial system in the process of setting it up and spotted an opportunity. The large firms that were their clients were able to place millions of trades at almost no cost. How hard would it be to create a consumer app that could do the same thing?

"It became clear to us that the smartphone would be your primary tool for accessing the markets and doing financial transactions in general," said Tenev in a 2017 interview.[3]

The idea was a surprisingly hard sell. Tenev said that more than seventy potential investors turned them down. The venture capitalist Howard Lindzon of Social Leverage saw the promise right away, flying to Silicon Valley to meet Tenev and Bhatt. They both showed up to the meeting wearing Google Glass, the height of geek chic. That diminished their gravitas, but Lindzon says they, and especially their idea, impressed him greatly. He had been trying to convince established retail brokers to integrate social media with stock trading, making a buy order as easy as meeting someone special on Tinder.

"In 2007, I was on with E*Trade and later with Schwab, and they were like no, no, no, no, no!"

Lindzon, a former hedge fund manager, had founded Stocktwits, an early social media site for investors, and saw the promise of being able to act on something you just saw or heard about.

"You should be able to swipe right on anything," he says. "I got it right away—the idea that it was only one tap. Because Twitter existed and Stocktwits existed, I knew it would work. You didn't have the trade at the end, but they were talking about stocks."[4]

The venture capitalist Marc Andreessen—who helped design the first commercial web browser and was the cofounder of the early dotcom wonder company Netscape when he was still in his twenties—and the rapper Snoop Dogg also both became early investors. Bhatt, who was in charge of design while Tenev worked on software, got a helping hand from their target audience while the product was being developed. The pair had moved from the East Coast to Palo Alto and would take early versions to a café near Stanford University's campus to let students test it out. Before it had actually finished writing the software, the fledgling company put up a web page inviting people to sign up by leaving their email addresses. Even the list itself became something of a game with people able to see where they were in line to get access to the snazzy new app.[5]

Going viral on social media helped make Robinhood a literal overnight success. The influential computer science forum Hacker News, not Reddit, was where a story about Robinhood's plan to offer smartphone-based, commission-free trading received enough "upvotes" to become number one on the page. The company had fifty thousand potential customers sign up that week. By the time Tenev and Bhatt had an actual app in March 2015, Robinhood already had almost a million customers waiting for it. Rapid growth and more funding rounds followed, and by 2018 their company was valued at $6 billion, making the then thirty-one-year-old Tenev and thirty-three-year-old Bhatt billionaires.[6] The cult of Silicon Valley hero worship of young merchant princes soon followed, and the men were asked about their daily routines (Bhatt wakes early and practices intermittent fasting; Tenev rarely stays up late and enjoys reading classics such as Plato's *Republic* and Sun Tzu's *The Art of War*).[7]

Key to the success of Robinhood is that, unlike Charles Schwab, Fidelity, or TD Ameritrade, it was born in modern Silicon Valley. Even compared with those competitors that got their start during the dotcom era, it had an edge because it grew up after the smartphone had been invented. It is more like an app with a brokerage firm attached to it than a broker that has an app. And Robinhood's app is a thing of beauty, having won the Apple design award the year it was launched. When the company filed for its initial public offering, it stunned experts by revealing that customers who opened the app did so nearly seven times a day.[8] Robinhood had thirteen million customers by the time of the GameStop squeeze, and eighteen million just a couple of months later.

The same digital-first edge can be ascribed to the incredible rise of the e-commerce juggernaut Amazon.com in the face of initially much-larger competitors expected to crush it like a bug, such as Barnes & Noble and Walmart. Like a creature with an evolutionary advantage, Amazon had a slick interface and one-click ordering that allowed it to gobble up more and more loyal customers as incumbents clumsily bolted online stores onto their brick-and-mortar businesses. More recently, companies like DraftKings and FanDuel that got their start in daily fantasy sports with colorful, intuitive smartphone apps catering to Generation Z and millennial users jumped into online sports betting as soon as states began to legalize it following a seminal Supreme Court decision in 2018. They have since grabbed significant market share from Nevada casinos, once the only place in America to bet on a game legally.

Aaron Levie, chief executive officer of the cloud computing company Box and one of Robinhood's earliest investors, laid out the stakes in an article in *Fast Company* published a year before Robinhood was founded. Titled "The Simplicity Thesis," it was accompanied by a photo of a Buddhist monk serenely staring out into the ocean and touted "the radical simplification of everything." Levie warned that making a customer do more work than absolutely necessary placed a target on your back as a business.

"Ultimately, any market that doesn't have a leader in simplicity soon will. And if your company doesn't play that role, another will lead the charge."[9]

But being effective is one thing and being good for the customer is quite another. When it comes to grabbing our attention and profiting from it, unleashing Silicon Valley's "move fast and break things" philosophy on trillions of dollars of personal savings was bound to create some problems. What it mainly did was to make some long-standing ones impossible to ignore.

## "Anyone Can Do It!"

Discount brokers seem to offer an undifferentiated product these days—pay nothing and invest in any of these hundreds of thousands of stocks, bonds, funds, or options contracts. They appeal to different customers and make money in different ways, though. The leader as of 2021, Fidelity Investments, got its start as a mutual fund company and is a big player in workplace retirement plans. Ideally it would like to hold your hand and have a human help you for a fee.

That appeals to many people in a confusing financial world, as it probably should. There are thousands of ethical financial advisers who will help you for about 1 percent of your assets a year and, if you don't have enough to be worth their while or would rather pay a lot less, there's a new crop of algorithm-driven robo-advisers like Wealthfront, Betterment, and SoFi with millennial appeal and pricing to match. There are also, unfortunately, still brokers and insurance agents who sell unsuitable products with hidden fees to those who don't read or understand the fine print.

The reason so many people become self-directed investors through platforms like Robinhood, especially during a bull market, isn't because they are wary of those sharks or don't want to pay for advice. It is because they hear about others getting rich, fear missing out, and then overestimate their ability to guess something that is almost completely random—the performance of individual stocks.

The phenomenon called the "illusion of control" was first described in the 1970s in an experiment by the psychologist Ellen Langer. She gave study participants the ability to buy a lottery ticket for a dollar with half given random numbers and half able to choose their lucky numbers. They were later offered cash for the tickets. The group that chose their own numbers asked for several times as much money and were less willing to sell, despite identical odds.

Because of another bias described by the psychologists David Dunning and Justin Kruger, people who know relatively little about a subject tend to be more confident than those who have an average amount of knowledge. In a bull market like the one in 2020, when almost every stock rose and the ones shunned by investing experts seemed to do best, less experienced investors were more likely to attribute their good fortune to skill rather than luck.

Advertising for self-directed brokers has long targeted those human foibles. A dot-com-boom-era commercial for Discover Brokerage, later absorbed into Morgan Stanley, is a classic of the genre. A scruffy, rotund tow truck driver picks up a whippet-thin stockbroker broken down on the side of the road who notices that the driver has a copy of the investing weekly *Barron's* in his cab. They start to discuss the tow truck driver's trading firm. The broker asks patronizingly, "So, you . . . trade online?" It turns out that the driver just likes to help people and is retired. He shows the astonished broker a picture of his island taped to his truck's sun visor and says, "Technically, it's a country."

One from a more recent bull market shows a young man carelessly sailing an enormous yacht with music blaring and a bevy of dancing models on the deck, its wake causing an older couple to fall off their paddleboards before he himself dives over the railing. "The dumbest guy in high school just got a boat. Don't get mad. Get E*Trade."

Robinhood avoids the promise of extreme wealth in its marketing message. It targets a more cynical generation who came of age during the global financial crisis and saw their parents suffer as a result. But the underlying message is similar—anyone can do it.

Even as it faced heat following the trading curbs it instituted on the meme stocks just days earlier, Robinhood ran a feel-good commercial during the Super Bowl with a cast of mostly young, racially diverse users tapping away at the app as they worked, studied, and had fun. "You don't need to become an investor. You were born one."

The evidence is overwhelming, though, that we aren't born to invest. The psychological biases that allowed our genes to be passed on through 99.9 percent of human history rather than be eaten by a lion also handicap us when it comes to buying and selling stocks. We really should invest, of course, but the more distance we can put between our hunter-gatherer brains and hitting "buy" or "sell," the better. Anything that gets us to make decisions more frequently is likely to cost us and benefit someone else.

## Gamification

Aside from its simplicity, a distinguishing feature of Robinhood's app is that it encourages activity. Winning trades would shower confetti on your screen, for example. The setup led William Galvin, the secretary of the Commonwealth of Massachusetts, to sue Robinhood in December 2020, saying it "encourages customers to use the platform constantly" through "gamification." In particular, he said it is designed to lure young, inexperienced investors through its design.[10]

Robinhood clumsily denied the allegations, saying, for example, that confetti doesn't fall after every trade. "Thus, confetti do not, as a factual matter, have anything to do with frequent trading." It also said that it had enhanced its systems and was offering more educational materials and safeguards.[11] Certainly the app looks different to the seventy-year-old Galvin, who reportedly uses a flip phone and has his staff do his emailing, than to Robinhood's thirty-four-year-old boss or its typical thirty-one-year-old customer. The confetti feature was quietly dropped in the spring of 2021, but other design elements remained.

"This whole area of gamification manifests itself across the marketplace," said Barbara Roper, director of investor protection for the Consumer Federation of America, interviewed weeks after the meme-stock squeeze. Roper had by then spent more than three decades as a Wall Street gadfly, speaking at conferences and to journalists as she tried to bend the ear of powerful people in Washington who were in a position to make Wall Street fairer and safer. The level of concern about Roper's criticism of their business model at Robinhood headquarters surely rose several notches when, six months later, Roper became one of those powerful people herself. She was appointed senior adviser to the chairman of the Securities and Exchange Commission for issues related to retail investor protection.[12]

A month after Roper's appointment was announced, Tenev submitted an op-ed to *The Wall Street Journal* titled "Robinhood Users Come Under Attack" that defended the "fun" aspect of his company's services now under the spotlight because of GameStop mania. "Investing isn't a game, but must it be grim and difficult to understand?" He portrayed a regulatory threat to the business that had made him immensely wealthy as an attack on his customers—the sort of argument that the bosses of tobacco, booze, or gambling companies would love to be able to make with a straight face.[13]

Robinhood wasn't the only brokerage firm involved in the meme-stock maelstrom. It punched well above its weight, though, and rode into the episode brimming with confidence. The company had seen turnover grow by 100 percent in its most recent quarter, and it had just bought its first Super Bowl ad. The millions of mostly young, male users of its intuitive smartphone app can wager as little as a few bucks on a long shot and get the rush of making multiples of their money. They even get a free bet when they first sign up.

Oops, sorry, that actually is a description of the online sports-betting company DraftKings. You get a free share of stock on Robinhood, not a free bet. The demographic profile of its users, its torrid growth, alluringly simple smartphone app, and, frankly, its appeal to those with a gambling problem were all the same, though. It even looks strikingly similar.

"I highly suspect they took a lot of design features from sports-betting apps—even the lottery-style mechanic of getting that first stock," says Keith S. Whyte, executive director of the National Council on Problem Gambling. "There's a similarity in the encouragement to play frequently."[14]

Confetti showers only went so far in drawing in new investors. A big part of the appeal was the choppiness of the market as the pandemic took hold. It coincided with an explosion in trading.

"The volatility—it was the same sort of rush when I play poker," says Seth Mahoney, who was nineteen years old at the time he made his first trade in his new Robinhood account that spring. "You feel giddy."

Like many new traders, Mahoney had some thrilling initial victories punctuated by setbacks. It turns out that winning occasionally, and randomly, like getting the payout of a slot machine, is even more alluring under the right conditions. The renowned behaviorist B. F. Skinner found that rewarding people with a "variable ratio schedule" to get them to do a task gets them to do it most consistently. He also found that the behavior then becomes "hard to extinguish."[15] In other words, it can become addictive.

More addictive than betting on real games featuring top athletes, though? Less than a year before the GameStop squeeze, Robinhood and its peers would have an incredible stroke of luck—some of the most thrilling conditions ever witnessed in the stock market coincided with the exact time the sports world went dark worldwide.

## Nudged into Bad Decisions

Some of the most effective methods used by the new generation of app-first brokers are usually associated with more benign goals than getting young people to trade frequently. For example, research by Nobel Prize–winning economist Richard Thaler about how people can be nudged into healthy choices was adopted during a subtle redesign of workplace retirement rules that was hailed by both employers and consumer advocates.[16] The mutual fund giant Vanguard found that companies that switched from having new employees send in paperwork to sign up for their 401(k) retirement plans to having them do the same to opt out of a modest contribution saw participation rise from 56 percent to 89 percent. And there was a further, ongoing benefit from automatic increases in amounts saved over the years unless a user actively decided otherwise.[17]

But then nobody said that nudges could only be used to help you make good decisions. When signing up for Robinhood, your default setting is a Robinhood Instant account, which allows customers to trade with up to $1,000 of the firm's money before their deposit has had time to clear. You can go from hearing about that hot stock to having a brokerage account and owning it in minutes. In an effect Robinhood surely didn't intend, the widespread use of this borrowing feature by many thousands of brand-new customers during the meme-stock squeeze nearly blew up the firm and the plumbing of the stock market, earning Tenev his audience with Congress.

As a new Robinhood customer around the time of the squeeze, you could instead choose to have a cash account without the ability to borrow the firm's money and trade right away. In addition to the psychological hurdle of actively opting out of the "instant" account, Robinhood described it as a "downgrade," denying yourself immediate gratification. And there was no difference in cost. Alternatively, you could have paid $5 a month for a Robinhood Gold account, which allowed you to borrow up to $1,000 against the value of your stocks for free and then to pay a 2.5 percent interest rate for further margin borrowing.

Tenev said he was surprised by the success of Robinhood Gold, but maybe he shouldn't have been as it targeted a generation accustomed to paying small-dollar monthly subscriptions for services such as the similarly named Xbox Live Gold or streaming services like Spotify and Netflix.[18]

In addition to subscription revenue and the interest earned on margin lending, giving its most eager and impulsive customers added buying power was a shrewd business decision. Robinhood typically sells its orders to trading firms called "wholesalers" rather than sending them to stock exchanges in a system called "payment for order flow." In theory it is a win-win situation because a wholesaler usually is slightly cheaper than an exchange, though it makes a profit too, and Robinhood keeps some of the savings. The company doesn't just benefit from the quantity of trades it can send to wholesalers but their quality—or, rather, lack thereof.

During the first quarter of 2021, for example, leading wholesaler Citadel Securities paid Robinhood thirty-eight cents on average for a one-hundred-share order of large capitalization stocks even as it paid Charles Schwab, with its more sober customers, just nine cents. One industry observer says part of the reason is that Robinhood's customers are less likely than the more experienced, or less hurried, investors at Schwab to specify a price limit they are willing to pay or accept when buying or selling. During the first quarter of 2021, about half of Schwab's orders were "limit" orders that couldn't be filled immediately, but only 11 percent of Robinhood's were. Wholesalers can earn more money on an order that can be executed right away.

Another reason is simply the small size of the orders. Just as wholesalers prefer to deal with retail investors rather than savvy, deep-pocketed pros, they can make more money from very small orders like those typical of Robinhood's customers. But Robinhood also knows how to make the most out of its customers' tendencies. Its unique formula for getting paid relies in part on the spread between the bid and offer price, according to people familiar with the contracts, so when YOLO traders get interested in something like a meme stock rather than a blue chip, it can get paid more.

Finally, market structure expert Larry Tabb has explained that it is ultimately up to each broker how much of the money paid by wholesalers it gives back to customers in the form of price improvement. Tabb guessed that Schwab keeps less of that money for itself than Robinhood does.[19] To be clear, this arrangement is legal and the payments are calculated to two decimal places for anyone who cares to read their broker's compliance forms. The period described came after a stretch in 2018 and 2019 when the Securities and Exchange Commission (SEC) said some Robinhood customers unknowingly got prices "that were inferior to other brokers' prices." The company resolved that case by paying a $65 million fine without admitting or denying any wrongdoing.[20]

## Are You Experienced?

Derivative contracts known as "options" became especially popular with Robinhood's locked-down young users in 2020's wild market, and they were instrumental in the meme-stock squeeze. Some industry professionals were surprised at how easy the approval process was for inexperienced customers to trade options and how many embraced them.

Part of their appeal to young people new to trading is that, unlike a stock that might sit in your account for a long time, options are more literally like a wager. A small amount of money could go "poof" or turn into a much larger sum all by a certain date. Either way, you then have to put up more cash to keep playing. Also unlike typical stock investors, but like sports bettors, most options buyers lose money.

In the summer of 2021, Robinhood agreed to the largest-ever fine imposed by brokers' own regulator, the Financial Industry Regulatory Authority (FINRA). Part of the complaint said that Robinhood used bots to approve people for options trading. FINRA gave the example of a twenty-year-old who said he had low risk tolerance and little experience and was rejected. Three minutes later, he changed his risk tolerance to medium and said he had three years of trading experience—difficult to have at age twenty—and was approved to trade options.[21] Robinhood had good reason to encourage the instruments' use, though.

"They get paid a lot more for options trading," said Roper.

How much more? The brokerage says only 13 percent of its customers make use of options trading. Even so, it earned more money in payments for routing options to wholesalers in the first quarter of 2021 than from stocks.[22] Being on the other side of an options transaction with a retail trader can be very profitable for a dealer, and especially so when that trader isn't experienced. For an options contract controlling a similar number of shares as in the above example, Robinhood was paid sixty-two cents by Citadel compared with thirty-five cents for a Schwab customer. Especially popular were contracts that offered lottery ticket–like returns but usually expired with the buyer losing all the premium paid. Those wild tendencies explain why Citadel pays Robinhood more for options, according to Packy McCormick.

"Saying Robinhood traders are unsophisticated isn't mean, it's facts," he wrote. "The market puts a price on how bad the trading on each platform is, and it pays Robinhood more than anyone else."

## Mob Mentality

It isn't just the potential financial payoff that has made lottery-like bets so popular—internet fame is part of the allure. On algorithmically enhanced sites, only the most appealing messages become highly visible. A core psychological concept known as "reinforcement learning" encourages users to post the sort of things that will turn heads and get clicks. Getting rewarded by your peers for doing something makes you more likely to do it again. On social media, that reward is attention.

The ability to use borrowed money and derivatives makes the one-upmanship more dangerous. If person A with an untraceable pseud-onym says he put a tenth of his money into a stock and person B claims to have made an all-or-nothing bet on a short-term price move that is a long shot, then B will get more upvotes and notice on a forum that embraces "retards" and "degenerates." Even for those who don't feel particularly confident in their investing ability and don't publicly share their misadventures, seeing tales of wild bets displayed promi-nently on a site where they are seeking guidance from peers influ-ences behavior.

More extreme predictions also get more attention, such as the as-sertion in January 2021 that GameStop was headed to $1,000 a share (250 times what it had been worth months earlier). Having on one's phone an app in which people compete to come up with more outland-ish values and another app a few flicks of a finger away that allows the same person to buy a stock seconds later creates a feedback loop. This loop was more powerful in the case of the meme stocks because it be-came untethered from the profits the companies behind them could be expected to earn.

The psychologist and social media scholar Van Bavel notes that the meme-stock squeeze "seemed to create its own form of common sense" on WallStreetBets. "The stock market is constrained by what is known as social reality—the value of stocks is shaped, in large part, by what many people think they are worth, rather than some clear objec-tive value," he says. "If someone can convince enough other people to share their belief about a certain stock, it can change the actual mon-etary value of the stock."[23] For a while at least.

The business models of social media companies and smartphone-first brokers aren't merely similar, then. They have become symbiotic. And in that respect Reddit, a relative midget financially, punched way above its weight during the meme-stock squeeze. Founded as "the front page of the internet," it had about 3 percent as many daily active users as Facebook and a fourth as many as Twitter in late 2020. The video sites TikTok and YouTube were bigger as well and, even when it came to investing, more influential. But Reddit's mechanics and demographics made it the perfect vehicle to send GameStop to the moon.

With a young, mostly male, and much more US-centric membership than other social networks, the site was a logical place for young men able to trade American stocks to gather virtually. Reddit's use of pseudonyms rather than real identities encouraged both brutal honesty and braggadocio. And the more homogenous nature of Reddit groups made dialogue that would be "downvoted" to invisibility on a more conservative forum a winner that gets "upvoted" to prominence on another, and vice versa. For example, there are several large groups devoted to investing, ranging from r/bogleheads, who are devotees of the late index-fund pioneer Jack Bogle, to r/personalfinance, the early retirement forum r/financialindependence, r/FinancialPlanning, and two very different ones devoted to the stock market, r/investing and, of course, r/wallstreetbets.

Of the roughly one hundred thousand active subreddits, Chief Executive Officer Steve Huffman was interested enough in the now-famous forum to personally become an observer, according to company spokeswoman Sandra Chu.[24]

"He does bristle at the suggestion that WallStreetBets users are wild and ignorant."

As a businessman, he has to be pleased with how Reddit has become more valuable since it became the center of the universe for many young investors. Days after the meme-stock squeeze, Reddit ran its first Super Bowl ad featuring WallStreetBets. Days later, the company raised money, doubling its value from a year earlier to a record $6 billion. While unremarkable by Silicon Valley standards, it was a long way from where the company had started.

Reddit was founded by University of Virginia roommates Huffman and Alexis Ohanian barely a year after Mark Zuckerberg started his company in a Harvard college dorm room with his roommates. The fact that it isn't as advertiser-friendly, or as fertile ground for paid "influencers," gave it a different financial trajectory than other social media companies. An iconic scene in *The Social Network* comes to mind as to how the founders' paths diverged—the one where Sean Parker, played by Justin Timberlake, tells Zuckerberg and his former pal Eduardo Saverin that "a million dollars isn't cool. You know what's cool? A billion dollars."[25]

In 2006, Reddit's cofounders sold the company to the magazine publisher Condé Nast, each pocketing a little less than $10 million— chump change. Both would leave the company and then return. There would be highlights and lowlights in between. In 2012 former president Barack Obama did an AMA (ask me anything) session on Reddit, and the surge of traffic overwhelmed the site. Less impressive were offensive subreddits including jailbait, beatingwomen, fatpeoplehate, and some too awful to put in writing here that would be shut down. The venture capitalist Ellen Pao, who lasted less than a year as the company's CEO, would call the site out, claiming it "monetizes white supremacy."[26]

Content that is beyond the pale certainly isn't unique to Reddit. Policing it is tricky and eats into profits, but resistance to doing so also stems from a tech-industry philosophy of openness that sometimes seems almost willfully naïve.

"You have these platforms designed by people who found success at a very young age and had all their precepts verified and there's kind of a casualness and playfulness to it," says Margaret O'Mara, professor of history at the University of Washington and author of *The Code: Silicon Valley and the Remaking of America.*[27]

Uniquely, Reddit tries to control content through human and also sometimes automated moderators. One of the early moderators of Wall-StreetBets was Martin Shkreli, the pharmaceutical executive who infamously raised the price of an AIDS drug more than fiftyfold and was sentenced to prison for an unrelated securities fraud. Though not part of his conviction, Shkreli was the architect of a short squeeze smaller but wilder than those affecting the meme stocks when he led a group that bought up most of the worthless shares of the pharmaceutical company KaloBios in 2015, briefly sending its shares up by 10,000 percent.

The somewhat disturbing, but mostly tongue-in-cheek, motto of WallStreetBets is "Like 4chan found a Bloomberg terminal." The imageboard 4chan is known for attracting anonymous young men, many just teenagers, who often share misogynistic, racist, and even violent content. Relatively little of that can be found on WallStreet-Bets, but it certainly isn't a place for polite dialogue. Founder Rogozinski clashed with members and stopped moderating the subreddit in April 2020 since he objected to the tone and some of the bigoted content on the site that he felt crossed a line.

Andrew Left, a short seller burned by the meme-stock squeeze, appealed to Rogozinski personally after he and his family faced harassment. He says his personal accounts were hacked and that some people texted profane messages to his children. He was so disturbed by the harassment he and his family received that he exited the business of publishing research on short-selling candidates after a long and mostly distinguished career. And when the respected media-industry analyst Rich Greenfield wrote that another meme stock, the movie-theater chain AMC, was worthless, his address was posted on Twitter, and he said his children received death threats by text. He had to involve the police.

It is an unfortunate feature of social media that otherwise decent people say and even do awful things online—particularly when hiding behind a pseudonym. Research by Yale University psychologist Molly Crockett has found that our inability to see a harassment victim's face short-circuits the restraint and empathy we might feel in person. Even though none of the harassers had met Left or Greenfield, the men were viciously targeted.

At its most extreme and obnoxious, then, WallStreetBets not only engineered an epic short squeeze in the meme stocks but also personally intimidated people on the other side of the argument. In the future, investors, analysts, and even financial journalists might consider steering clear of stating their opinion about crowd favorites because of the new power and menace of social media. This ultimately costs the least informed investors money because it can allow manias to grow larger and last longer, pulling in more cash for investments that will likely perform very badly.

## Generals Fighting the Last War

Steve Huffman and Vlad Tenev, whose offices are a short drive from one another in the Bay Area, got hauled in front of a congressional committee because the companies they run had their fingerprints all over the events of January 2021. Plenty of newly rich, thirtysomething tech entrepreneurs had been grilled on Capitol Hill in the past about issues ranging from privacy to foreign election interference, but this was the first time the subject was disruption of the nation's financial markets. Silicon Valley CEOs tend to be a lot less contrite than their older counterparts on Wall Street and far more convinced that they are a force for good.

They also have less reason to worry. When banks and insurance companies are suspected of acting carelessly, it is fairly straightforward to take action because their industries have an alphabet soup of domestic and international regulators and thousands of pages of existing rules to follow. New ones are often written after the fact when actions aren't illegal but just don't smell right.

But tech companies are hard to understand and quick to argue that they are changing the world for the better. Their defense is that technology is just a tool and that sometimes people misuse it. Even if you can demonstrate that "free" trading and social media apps in which the customer is the product have encouraged reckless behavior, what exactly are you going to do about it? Putting curbs on hugely in-demand services would be legally questionable and tremendously unpopular. Trying to stop progress wouldn't only make politicians Luddites—it would probably restrict free speech or, in Robinhood's case, economic opportunity. Either would be practically un-American.

"It's a very effective argument that shuts people down," says O'Mara, the Silicon Valley historian.

Wall Street was just as shocked as Washington by the Reddit Revolution, but it wasn't clamoring for new rules. Even Gabe Plotkin, a prime casualty, seemed cool to the idea at the hearing. And Ken Griffin, one of the people who benefited the most personally from the explosion and who has expressed a strong libertarian streak, was clear in his opposition. Neither of them had expected that free, frictionless trading and algorithmically enhanced social media would shut down parts of the market or spark cascading losses, but you take the bad with the good.

What about Wall Street's customers, though? It wasn't easy to notice in an exuberant era in which sharing screenshots of your financial victories had become commonplace, but many—particularly the newest investors—weren't doing nearly as well as they should have in a bull market. In a country where people are basically on their own when it comes to financing life goals such as college educations, down payments on a home, and retirement, individual savers leave a scandalous amount of money on the table through hidden fees, poor timing, and inappropriate investments. Some technology was helping to remedy that, saving them tens of billions of dollars a year. Other, more alluring technology was making it worse.

It took a historically crazy week of trading to bring the problem to the attention of Congress, and even then politicians seemed more interested in why Robinhood and other brokers had limited trading by the little guy rather than what convinced him to be so reckless with his money in the first place. That might have been different if the Reddit revolutionaries had all lost money. There are always explosive investigations and new rules made or regulatory bodies created after ordinary people suffer a big wipeout in the market. The Great Crash of 1929 spawned the SEC and laws on insider trading; the dot-com crash and frauds perpetrated by companies like Enron and WorldCom, the Sarbanes–Oxley Act on corporate accountability and strict new rules governing Wall Street research; and the housing bust, the Volcker Rule restricting banks' ability to take on risk and the creation of the Consumer Financial Protection Bureau.

The generals are always fighting the last war when it comes to protecting investors, though, and it isn't just a matter of myopia. Stopping the party is always politically unpopular. That might never have been truer than during the episode that was about to light the fuse for meme-stock mania. For a while, it seemed like young YOLO traders were the only people in America interested in buying stocks as a terrifying new virus emerged.

# Chapter 4

# Winter of 2019–2020

Even by the abrasive standards of WallStreetBets, people were being a bit harsh.

The last time we met DeepFuckingValue, aka Keith Gill, he could have easily gloated. He also could have pocketed a handsome profit. Five and a half months later, in February 2020, his all-in bet on the ailing video game retailer GameStop (known on the forum through its ticker symbol GME) wasn't looking nearly as good. Over that time its price had dropped from $4.31 a share to $3.60. That doesn't sound terrible, but because his entire position was in call options that decay in value as time marches on, he had seen his portfolio's value drop precipitously from more than $113,000 to less than $45,000. If the price didn't rise significantly, then he would lose the rest.

"For the amount that you blew on GME calls you could have probably had your very own franchise at this point," wrote a fellow user of the forum.[1]

Gill actually raised the bar for himself by exchanging options that would pay off at $8 for some that aimed even higher, including a batch that only would pay if GameStop shares rose above $12 by April of the following year—a whopping 230 percent gain. His thesis was a risky one. Gill acknowledged that the company's traditional stores were struggling, which was why so many pros had bet its shares would fall, but he argued that video games themselves were a booming business and that the company could "reinvent itself as a premier gaming hub."[2] That wasn't happening yet, though, and September 2019 had been, up to that point, the peak for Gill's account. After GameStop gave a quarterly update in December, the value of his options portfolio had dropped to barely $83,000. The analyst Mike Hickey cut his target price on the stock from $5 to $3 and described the company's announcement as a "Chernobyl experience."[3] Following the earnings release, only one analyst still had a "buy" rating on the stock. That number would soon drop to zero.[4]

"You honestly have a better chance playing roulette," wrote another WallStreetBets user at the time in response to a screenshot of Gill's account statement.

It is fascinating to see the clash of mind-sets. Plenty of people on WallStreetBets were absolutely convinced certain stocks were going higher. Gill wasn't sure at all: his type of investing, deep value, only requires one to be somewhat confident. If your analysis is good then you'll be right more often than you're wrong. Hanging on in the face of disappointment wasn't bravado on Gill's part—it was a rare and profitable way of thinking.

"Well as a longer-term investor I have the benefit of heavily discounting daily moves," he wrote in response to one barb. "Even today, after the typical quarterly sell-off, the longer-term chart still looks decent so there's been nothing to panic over. Let's see what the price does over the next few weeks."

It didn't get any better. By the time the company gave a tepid mid-January update on how its holiday-season sales had gone, Gill's balance had dropped to $56,541.

"You fucking retard everyone told you to sell when you were up 121k. I hope you get out of this in once [*sic*] piece," was one response.

And after Gill's sobering February update, by which time stocks had begun to factor in the possibility that the COVID-19 pandemic could disrupt normal life?

"That 42,377 dollars you lost on a silly gamble would literally change my life. Kind of melancholy to think about on a Saturday morning."

Gill thought the stock price could possibly go as high as $20 or $25, but he wasn't looking for affirmation. In his Roaring Kitty persona, he said he was sharing his insights so others could poke holes in his hypothesis that the once-admired company could have a profitable second act. What he wasn't counting on yet was that the forum could supercharge his gains and send the stock twenty times as high as his target, but he would soon start to have an inkling that he could be onto something much bigger than he originally imagined. Older, but not necessarily wiser, value investors would have made money too but sold far sooner than he did. Gill had the rare advantage of straddling the worlds of value and memes.

WallStreetBets was growing in users and influence and, in a fore-taste of what was to come, certain stocks would pop for seemingly no reason that month. Then it would emerge that they had been touted on the forum. Some professional investors began to pay attention, though not for advice or insights—just to get a jump on what the nov-ices were pumping. It wasn't taken terribly seriously and was far from the mainstream.

The first ever media mention of the subreddit seems to have been in March 2016 by Sally French and Shawn Langlois of *MarketWatch* with the headline MEET THE MILLENNIALS LOOKING TO GET RICH OR DIE TRYIN' WITH ONE OF WALL STREET'S RISKIEST OIL PLAYS. At the time,

WallStreetBets had only 38,000 members compared with 183,000 for Reddit's more sober r/investing subreddit. The article recounted the tale of Florida high schooler Jeffrey Rozanski, aka World Chaos, who had turned a $900 "investment" into more than $55,000 in a few days. He had bet that the stock market would drop sharply, and he guessed correctly.[5]

Others quoted in the article were speculating on an "exchange-traded note" (a stock-like security) with the ticker symbol UWTI that delivered three times the daily gains in the price of crude oil. With energy prices in a deep funk at the time and big exporters trying to shore up its price, the note had several daily double-digit percentage gains or losses that winter and spring. The article introduced Rogozinski, then still a moderator, and F. S. Comeau, a young Canadian trader who said he had lost huge amounts of inherited money in the previous two years and had become physically ill from stress. He said he was stepping away for a while.

The next article mentioning the site revisited Comeau in early 2017. He had decided to get back into the game to try to recover all his previous losses with one gigantic roll of the dice on Apple "put options"—derivatives that rise in value when a stock drops—ahead of the company's quarterly results. He sounded confident that they would be bad, and he had written a five-thousand-word treatise on the site explaining his reasoning. Some found Comeau's argument convincing.

"IT IS SIMPLY NOT POSSIBLE FOR APPLE TO SPIKE UP POST-EARNINGS," he wrote. "It didn't happen to Google, it didn't happen to Western Digital, Qualcomm or even Intel or Microsoft (2%! Yay!), despite excellent earnings (which Apple won't have)."

The bet Comeau described would have returned millions of dollars if Apple's shares fell sharply after the earnings release, but he would lose everything if they didn't. As it turned out, the numbers were good, and the iPhone maker's stock price jumped more than 6 percent. Comeau livestreamed his reaction to the disastrous bet while wear-

ing a wolf mask, shrieking and appearing to have a nervous breakdown.

The bet and subsequent loss was a big attention getter on Wall-
StreetBets as an example of "loss porn." Like dumb physical stunts
that cause broken bones and grudging respect, big swings and misses
are not always viewed by the forum's mostly young, male audience as
a cautionary tale. The episode spawned imitators. As a postscript, Comeau self-published a book, *Wolfie Has Fallen,* claiming that he had
fooled everyone into thinking that he lost a quarter of a million dollars
but hadn't really.

In short, it was hard to know what or whom to believe on the site.
Since Wolfie's fall, WallStreetBets has put more emphasis on "proof of
trade," requiring screenshots to back up big claims, such as the ones
that would make Gill a celebrity. Other sites such as Commonstock
have emerged in the last few years that leave no doubt, linking directly
to users' brokerage accounts. An app called Doji allows traders to follow friends and even invest in a community's stock picks, and the brokerage eToro allows for "copy trading" of successful users' accounts.

Reddit's self-regulating system of upvotes, downvotes, and "karma"—
a measure of an individual user's credibility—served as a crude way
to replicate these high-tech collaboration tools. And of course it had
memes. The forum's entertaining nature had made it vastly more influential than any of the aforementioned services by early 2020. The
COVID-19 pandemic was about to make scrolling through Reddit and
trading stocks a lot more popular for young people, laying more of the
groundwork for the meme-stock explosion. Another vital ingredient
had fallen in October 2019 when every major broker cut its trading
commissions to zero.

Chapter 5

# Race to the Bottom

They called it "Mayday."

Following years of complaints, Washington had had enough of Wall Street's foot-dragging over its longest-standing shibboleth. In 1973 securities regulators told brokers that they had to get rid of fixed stock-trading commissions that dated back to the eighteenth century. Congress promptly wrote a deadline of May 1, 1975, into law. Despite dire predictions of hundreds of bankruptcies, only around twenty firms were forced to merge or go out of business, according to Stephen Mihm, a historian at the University of Georgia.[1]

Imagine a time traveler from the year 2021 arriving on Mayday, halfway through the worst decade for the industry since the Great Depression, and telling young stockbrokers with their wide ties and sideburns that the cataclysm would make them very rich men, that trading would one day be free, and that the whole thing would help a retail trader named Roaring Kitty to briefly terrorize the Wall Street establishment from his basement. It is hard to say what part of that conversation would be the least believable.

Bringing the cost of stock trades and interest rates to zero was an essential ingredient of this story. It would seem like a disaster for Wall Street banks and brokers. It wasn't. For many of their customers, though, it was too much of a good thing.

Ending fixed commissions in 1975 wasn't a boon for long-suffering individual investors at first. Their costs mostly went up while big funds reaped immediate savings. Buying and selling blue chip stocks for mom and pop was a hassle and not particularly profitable. During the surge in retail stock trading of go-go growth companies in the late 1960s when the number of shares being traded doubled in the span of three years, Wall Street was slammed by the "Paperwork Crisis," and the New York Stock Exchange was forced to close every Wednesday for months just to catch up. It wasn't until discount brokers like Charles Schwab really got a foothold in the early 1980s and stock trading became more automated that it started to get cheaper and easier for self-directed investors to buy and sell stocks.

Fast-forward forty years and Robinhood sparked what would be an even more significant change by eliminating commissions altogether, making its money mostly by selling orders to wholesalers such as Citadel Securities and Virtu Financial instead. It wasn't the first broker to do so, but it was the most successful because it married the elimination of commissions with an app that appealed to mostly young users who could now afford to participate. Howard Lindzon, the early investor in the company, told Tenev and Bhatt that the technology was so good that they should charge a dollar or two per trade. He says he is fortunate they ignored the advice from "some old man." The company's valuation went from $8 million at the time to $40 billion in the spring of 2021.

Expressed in dollars and cents, the difference between a modest commission and zero doesn't seem at all significant. By 2013 trading was conducted online, and it cost an individual only around $7 to buy almost any quantity of shares—a far cry from what it had been before Mayday when it was hardly worth buying fewer than one hundred shares, called a "round lot," and stock prices were denominated in eighths of a dollar, not pennies. An investor might need to earn at least 3 percent on a stock just to break even.

Psychologically, though, the difference between paying something and paying nothing was huge, and customers flocked to Robinhood—particularly young ones. Incredibly, half of new retail brokerage accounts opened in the US between 2016 and early 2021 were at the company. The year 2019 was when things really went into overdrive for Robinhood. It went from six million to ten million customers, and Schwab, once the brash upstart, was grudgingly forced to match it that October and offer its clients "free" trading too. Every other discount broker soon did the same. Robinhood gleefully released an ad with the line CHANGE DOESN'T HAPPEN OVERNIGHT UNTIL IT DOES.[2]

It wasn't only commissions that Robinhood's arrival helped to lower but the overall hurdle to getting into the investing game. By the time the rest of the industry followed it and stopped charging, you could open a Robinhood account with pocket change, trade conveniently from a highly intuitive smartphone app, and even buy just a fraction of a share. The median balance of a Robinhood account was just $241—enough to buy barely half a share of retail favorite Tesla or two thirds of a share of Netflix at that time.

"It's that lower barrier to entry," says WallStreetBets founder Rogozinski. "You've got twenty bucks? Cool. It would have been impossible to start a brokerage account with twenty bucks before this."

Some brokers that relied fairly heavily on commissions for their revenue had fretted about the dent that matching Robinhood's price would put into their profits.

"Not everyone is going to survive this," predicted Robert Siegel, a Stanford University lecturer, to *The Wall Street Journal* at the time.[3]

Not only did they survive—they thrived. TD Ameritrade said that by February, daily average trading by its customers had doubled compared with a year earlier. Other brokerage firms reported similar jumps.

Their executives shouldn't have been surprised—at least not if they had kept up with the dismal science. Classical economic theory and common sense teach us that the demand for a good will rise when you reduce its price and decrease when you raise it. Just how much it rises or falls depends on how "elastic" demand is for the product. One that responds less to price, like medicine or a snow shovel, is said to be inelastic. You would have to raise the price of such items by a lot to affect our consumption of them while cutting their price wouldn't convince people to buy much more.

But the newer field of behavioral economics has modified some of those theories because people aren't the rational economic beings economists once assumed. The zero-price effect says that demand for some products rises a lot more if the price goes from a dollar to zero instead of, say, two dollars to one dollar, even though the change is the same. The reaction is seen in how we purchase "hedonic products" that give us enjoyment, like streaming videos for a flat fee per month instead of renting individual DVDs, or in how we keep in touch, using unlimited global communications if we have access to a wi-fi signal instead of making once-expensive long-distance calls.

Buying and selling stocks might seem like it falls into the opposite category of being a "utilitarian product," like a snow shovel, but clearly that wasn't the case for those new to the game and excited to play. And, unlike bingeing the latest series on Netflix, limited by the number of free hours in a day, the sky was the limit when it came to how many trades someone with a bit of spare time on weekdays could make. Young people in particular were about to have a lot more of it.

## The Pandemic Takes Robinhood to the Moon

When Americans finally understood the gravity of the COVID-19 pandemic in late February 2020, stocks plunged. Normally big paper losses are poisonous for retail-investor participation in the market. Uniquely, this episode produced the opposite effect, particularly for the newest, youngest, and most active traders. One reason is that it was the shortest, sharpest bear-market decline from a record high in history. At *The Wall Street Journal*, the newsroom went from planning how to cover the Dow Jones Industrial Average's seemingly imminent break above 30,000 points on February 19 to rushing to put out headlines twenty-six days later when the index dove back below 20,000 points. By then, of course, those discussions were going on in a virtual newsroom over Google Hangouts as journalists were locked down at home like the rest of the country.

A few days later, though, stocks whipsawed higher, and soon they made their quickest-ever ascent into a new bull market. The swift collapse and rebound wasn't so much traumatizing as invigorating to the new crop of investors. Moreover, in addition to the crowd favorites like Tesla Motors, Apple, and Amazon, young traders suddenly became deep-value investors like Keith Gill or Michael Burry—sort of.

For example, an exchange-traded fund with the memorable ticker symbol JETS that held airline stocks had been started with what seemed like perfectly awful timing just weeks before global travel ground to a halt because of the pandemic. But it turned into a huge draw for daring, young bargain hunters. Between its March trough and its early June high, traders could have nearly doubled their money. And, reinforcing the sense that there was a new boss in town, the legendary investor Warren Buffett announced at his company's annual meeting in May that he had sold all of his substantial airline holdings near their nadir.

Surging prices, plunging ones—whatever. Both were good for spurring lots of buying and selling of stocks as long as it meant volatility. WallStreetBets founder Rogozinski points out that traders using apps like Robinhood weren't like traditional savers viewing the market through the prism of their nest eggs shrinking and then recovering—they didn't have a lot of financial or other assets to speak of yet. To acquire some in a hurry, they were largely agnostic about which way the Dow was headed. Betting on bad news used to be costly and complicated, but by 2020 their accounts allowed them to buy notes that traded like stocks but acted like derivatives that would surge in a falling stock market. One popular note that tracked the market's volatility itself rose by more than 3,000 percent in a few weeks, and some who signed up for options reaped even more impressive gains. If they picked the right direction, then they got both money and confetti.

"The idea that the value of the stock itself went down and the market capitalization—they're like, dude, did I guess or not guess it? They could care less if the stock is going down," says Rogozinski.

The numbers bear him out. A site called Robintrack that had access to anonymized data from Robinhood on which stocks were particularly popular on the platform put out a "retail trading barometer" until its access was cut off in the summer of 2020. It looked at the absolute daily change in Robinhood users holding all tradable assets. The barometer doubled between mid-December 2019 and mid-February 2020 when the Dow peaked, hitting 135,000. Between that day and the bottom of the bear market in March, the barometer then quintupled to almost 700,000.[4]

That surge in activity came despite a series of technical snafus by Robinhood as it struggled to deal with the crush of new customers and activity. Trading was halted three times over eight days in March, including some of its most frenetic trading sessions.[5] Customers were furious and criticized the firm on social media—a small foretaste of the lashing it would experience after it throttled the buying of meme stocks during the GameStop frenzy. The company did more than stay put, though. Both March 2020 and January 2021 saw record numbers of account openings.

One reason the broker held on to users is that switching involves hurdles, especially for small fry. As of early 2021, Robinhood charged an unusually high $75 to transfer an account, about three times what some rivals did. At around a third of its median account balance, that is punitive—not to mention the fact that any fractional shareholdings can't be transferred and are instead sold.

"It's the whole roach motel thing—once they get you into a service they make it hard for you to leave," said the small investor advocate Barbara Roper.

The March technical snafus and some later ones didn't slow down the broker's growth. By June 2020, shortly before Robintrack's data series ended, its barometer crossed one million, and even that would pale in comparison with what we know about retail activity seven months later when meme stocks blew up. Zero-dollar commissions played a big role in that extraordinary surge, and brokers actually saw their profits rise rather than fall.

"When something is free, it changes business incentives and consumer psychology," says Dan Egan, a behavioral finance expert who works for low-cost robo-adviser Betterment.[6]

Of course for those customers inclined to buy and hold—and there were many of them—the elimination of commissions saved them a little bit of money and made it possible to get on the investing ladder with a small amount of savings.

"Most of their customers aren't pattern day traders at all," says Wharton School marketing professor Cait Lamberton. "The perception is driven by outliers."

But those outliers were engaging in a degree of speculation that made the WallStreetBets moniker "degenerate" apt. For example, a trader with no experience made 12,700 trades in six months, according to the complaint filed by the state of Massachusetts.[7] The customer profile isn't that different from a casino's. The vast majority of people reading this book have tried their luck at a slot machine or blackjack table at least once. For a small percentage of gamblers, though, it will become an expensive practice and even an obsession, making them disproportionate contributors to a casino's profits.

"If you look at people who are excessively trading and losing both money and time, you see the same patterns," says Keith Whyte, the problem-gambling expert.

Rogozinski admits that there are strong parallels and is more bothered by the hypocrisy of the legal distinction between tightly regulated gambling and stock trading, open to any American above the age of eighteen. Speculative trading is efficiently taxed, and it benefits established, respectable companies, enriching their shareholders. The subtitle of a book he published about WallStreetBets in 2020 is *How Boomers Made the World's Biggest Casino for Millennials.*

To the extent that Wall Street had become like a much larger Vegas for millions of young Americans, different parts of the financial services industry played their own roles as trading exploded when the pandemic set in. Brokers like Robinhood and E*Trade and wholesalers such as Citadel and Virtu were like taxis, hotels, and restaurants that were loving the rush of drunk tourists leaving fat tips. The role of "the House," which involves outsize risk and reward, was played by the part of the business that embraces "good volatility."

A glance at the results put up by the two largest investment banks amid a sharp recession and a global pandemic tells the story: Goldman Sachs and Morgan Stanley made nearly $23 billion in combined revenue in their markets divisions for the first six months of 2020 alone, which was 54 percent more than a very healthy first half of 2019. The hedge fund manager William Ackman's Pershing Square Holdings made a multibillion-dollar bet on the plunge and had its best year ever, gaining 70 percent.[8] Melvin Capital Management's Gabe Plotkin, who would later become the main victim of the GameStop Revolution, practically printed money in 2020, personally taking home $846 million in compensation. Hedge funds overall had their best returns in a decade.[9]

## Locked Down and Loaded

Another reason that retail trading activity rose is that, while millions lost their jobs, they also suddenly had very little on which to spend their money. Add to that the $1,200 stimulus checks sent by the federal government to even employed people and an extra $600 in weekly jobless benefits, and young people, some unexpectedly living rent-free with their parents again, suddenly had a lot of spare cash. The US savings rate went from 7.2 percent at the end of 2019 to more than 12 percent in March and then an all-time record of 33.7 percent in April, far eclipsing what had been seen during any postwar economic downturn.

When researchers at Bank of America pointed out that the arrival of stimulus checks coincided perfectly with a surge in new account openings at Robinhood, critics were quick to accuse them of stereotyping millennials and Generation Z. The evidence is strong, though, that there was a connection. A June survey by SoFi, a financial firm that caters largely to those age cohorts, found that, of those people who had received stimulus checks, around half put those funds into brokerage accounts. More than one in five respondents said that they had begun trading for the first time during the pandemic. The second-most-common reason they cited for diving in? "I have extra money."[10]

Boredom has been mentioned as an explanation for the retail surge, but it was more than that. The temptation to put that money to work in the stock market was especially strong for those inclined to gamble. Online sports betting had recently been legalized in several states and had been embraced by the same twentysomething, largely male demographic that was flocking to Robinhood and WallStreetBets. A study done by the National Council on Problem Gambling found that sports betting was the only game of chance for which activity was negatively correlated with age.

The most wagered-on event of the year, the "March Madness" NCAA Men's Basketball Tournament, was canceled on March 12 because of the pandemic, at the height of the stock market's volatility. Almost the only thing other than replays of already-decided games on ESPN was Korean baseball. Over one third of respondents to SoFi's survey said that they opened trading accounts "to replace activities that Covid restrictions have eliminated." The people transitioning from sports gambling to trading were overwhelmingly young and male, as is the crowd on WallStreetBets. A survey of the forum's membership in 2016 showed 92 percent were younger than thirty-five, and nearly 98 percent were men or boys.[11]

The pandemic spurred other crossover activity. During the spring it was hard to go onto social media and avoid hearing something, good or bad, about Dave Portnoy. The brash founder of the digital media company Barstool Sports, who said he had only bought "one, maybe two" stocks in his life before the pandemic, began livestreaming "Davey Day Trader Global" to his 2.5 million (as of mid-2021) Twitter followers, making bold bets and crude jokes.[12] The sports gambling firm Penn National had just taken a major stake in Barstool two months earlier. A tweet by Portnoy in June took a poke at the world's most successful investor:

> I'm sure Warren Buffett is a great guy but when it comes to stocks he's washed up. I'm the captain now.[13]

And, last but not least as a factor in the retail trading boom, the Federal Reserve cut overnight interest rates to zero on March 15 while upping and widening its monthly purchases of bonds. By design this caused other interest rates for both savers and borrowers to collapse, making the idea of just sticking the money in a risk-free savings account or government bond unappealing. Rates had been suppressed to a greater or lesser extent by the Federal Reserve and other major central banks ever since the global financial crisis eleven years earlier, but now they plumbed new lows. If you were to have bought a benchmark ten-year Treasury note for $1,000 at its nadir in March 2020, then a decade later you would have gotten your money back and have made a measly thirty-two bucks.

The flip side of zero-interest rates is that it didn't just make stocks or even more speculative cryptocurrencies the only game in town but also allowed brave investors to juice their returns more cheaply with margin debt—loans that use your account's holdings as collateral so that you can increase your buying power. Some brokers catering to more seasoned traders with large accounts were offering margin borrowing for as low as 0.75 percent, but even Robinhood made the terms tempting—with its own "zero price effect" twist, allowing Robinhood Gold users to rack up margin debt of up to $1,000 free of charge.

"Margin can help investors take advantage of investing opportunities, and maximize their potential gains if the stock price goes up," the company helpfully told anyone interested in applying when it cut its borrowing rate by half for sums above the first $1,000 in December 2020. Many would use the facility to buy shares of GameStop and other meme stocks just a month later with alarming consequences for the broker.

Lending rose across the board, which is always a warning sign for those working to protect investors, but it posed more problems for Robinhood's customers, because of either their lack of experience or their lower standards or possibly both. An examination of regulatory filings by CBS's *MoneyWatch* showed that Robinhood's users were almost fourteen times more likely to default on a margin loan—that is, to be forced to sell collateral or put up more cash—than those at other retail brokerage firms.[14]

Margin debt outstanding naturally plunged with the brief bear market, but then it rebounded at a furious pace. By the anniversary of the February 2020 market peak, margin debt as a share of the US economy was comfortably in excess of what was seen at the top of the tech stock bubble in 2000. The increase was even more dramatic at Robinhood: between the beginning of 2020 and March 2021, margin borrowing by its customers grew by more than 700 percent.

## The Halloween Candy Effect

And with that, all the stars were aligned for a further surge in retail trading activity.

"Free money, zero commissions—you have the Halloween candy effect. Everybody will take more," says Peter Atwater, an expert on social mood and a professor at William and Mary.[15]

In June 2020 Robinhood said that it had processed 4.3 million "daily average revenue trades," or DARTs, that month. As frenetic as March had been, June was three times as busy. Its users were trading far more frequently than those at other discount brokers that had more recently moved to zero commissions. Larger Charles Schwab, which caters to an older and much wealthier crowd, reported only 1.8 million DARTs.

Looking at all retail traders combined, Bank of America said that its activity in June 2020 was more than three fourths higher than in the same month a year earlier.[16] Naturally, the pros were pretty active too in a wild bull market, but the rise in retail trading was of a different order of magnitude. Various estimates put individual investors' buying and selling of stocks at about 10 percent of the market's total in 2019. Credit Suisse said that it had risen to between 15 percent and 18 percent in early 2020 and an astonishing 30 percent by early 2021 when the GameStop squeeze happened.

The race to the bottom in costs coincided with the quality of some of the companies that novices embraced. Over-the-counter or penny stocks, a hotbed of shady companies called that because they are often quoted at a few cents or even less, saw an astounding trillion shares traded in December 2020—about fifty times the turnover of the regulated Nasdaq.

"Free is sort of a Rubicon that, once you cross it, people are less thoughtful about how to consume it," explains Egan, the behavioral finance expert.

Sometimes this was a case of mistaken identity by new investors unfamiliar with the sketchy penny stock world. A tiny medical company called Signal Advance, initially valued at $7 million, briefly was worth more than $1 billion after Elon Musk tweeted to his followers that they should use the encrypted-messaging app Signal. And sometimes the confusion seemed deliberate. A firm named Tongji Medical changed its name to Clubhouse Media Group and surged by over 1,000 percent when Musk mentioned the unrelated and unlisted audio app. Incredibly, its value even eclipsed the real app's private market valuation.

There are too many examples of fools rushing in to recount, but an episode that sticks out, because securities regulators intervened to keep novices from losing a staggering amount of money, is the rental-car company Hertz. Crushed by the collapse in travel, Hertz filed for bankruptcy in May 2020, and it seemed likely to everyone on Wall Street that its shareholders would get nothing when the process was done. Yet since airlines and cruise companies had surged back from the brink on heavy retail buying, and Hertz's stock could still be bought and sold, bold investors dove in, helping to send its worthless shares up by 900 percent. *The Wall Street Journal* interviewed a twenty-three-year-old salesman from San Francisco who sank his "entire life savings" into Hertz and then sold his shares the next day after doubling his money.

"I decided, you know, if I'm gonna do it, I should do it big, and I'll make a play and see what comes out of it," he said.[17]

Then Hertz's management tried something that even solvent going-concern GameStop hesitated to do seven months later when its value briefly swelled, likely on the sound advice of its lawyers. Hertz had the nerve to propose issuing up to a billion dollars of new stock. Instead of plunging, the stock spiked by a further 70 percent on the news as even more Robinhood users bought shares, according to Robintrack, with an estimated 170,000 accounts owning it at the peak. The company explicitly said in the offering prospectus that all the money it raised would probably go to its lenders. The SEC, an organization generally known for bolting the barn door well after the shareholder-abuse horse has bolted, stepped in this time, though only after some of the stock had been sold to the public.[18]

Financial pros thought this was funny, but in 2020 it was novices who were laughing all the way to the bank. Aggregating the one hundred most popular stocks bought by Robinhood users in 2020, the fintech blogger Noah Weidner constructed an index called the RH Top 100 Fund that rose by almost 102 percent for the year compared with less than 6 percent for the stodgy Dow Jones Industrial Average.[19]

## Lottery-Ticket Mentality

While it is always better to be lucky than smart, many of the investments favored by Robinhood traders are the sort that do well in times of speculative froth but the worst when the party ends. Risky investments are more volatile and exciting and can develop exaggerated and self-fulfilling momentum in a sustained bull market. Add to that the magnifying effect of borrowed money, whether through margin debt or the ability to buy long-shot options contracts.

Stimulus checks, meanwhile, gave young investors more than just starting capital. Behavioral economics tells us that people are more pained by losing money than they are pleased by making it. When people are playing with "house money," though, in the form of government cash in this case, then they tend to roll the dice more readily. The world also looks different for a twenty-five-year-old with negative net worth because of student loans and poor prospects for homeownership than it does for middle-aged or retired, upper-middle-class people who have more stock market wealth. The differences in the way that the economic shock of the pandemic was felt and the likelihood of different cohorts remaining employed enhanced that divide.

"When people feel immediate scarcity, they're willing to gamble a little," says Lamberton.

The same effect can be seen in sales of lottery tickets. Americans with incomes below $30,000, who tend to have practically no savings, spend a vastly higher share of their income on them. People who call the lottery a tax on innumeracy aren't just being insensitive, though—they lack perspective. Poorer people might be less educated on average, but the reason they plunk down their money every week is that thrift is unlikely to do much to improve their situation anytime soon whereas a Mega Millions jackpot, however unlikely, would make a massive difference. And at least they can dream.

"It's financially irrational but psychologically rational," says Larry Swedroe, the author of nineteen books on personal finance and the current director of research for Buckingham Strategic Wealth.[20]

The other type of free money, zero-interest rates, supercharges the appeal of the most speculative, lottery ticket–like stocks—the same ones that spark young investors' imagination. A company that doesn't have much in the way of profits today but can tell a good story about why it will dominate an exciting growth field like electric cars or online food delivery at some point in the future is more appealing if interest rates are unusually low, as they were in 2020. A basket of companies tracked by Goldman Sachs that lost money surged by close to 300 percent between the beginning of 2020 and the week of 2021's meme-stock bubble. Part of the rationale for making money so cheap after the financial crisis was to get investors to take risks and jump-start the economy because hanging on to cash was so unappealing by comparison.

## FOMO

The companies about which it is easiest to spin enticing tales are those that are the newest to the stock market. Though it didn't quite rise to the manic levels of the dot-com bubble, 2020 had the lowest percentage of companies new to the market that were profitable other than that period. Similarly, many initial public offerings, or IPOs, surged on their first day. Reading about those pops not only creates buzz for the company but also excites investors about future opportunities, stoking FOMO—fear of missing out.

Back during the dot-com era, retail investors almost never got access to a hot deal and were instead forced to buy stocks as soon as they began trading at a much higher price. The results were not good. Following the period that still holds the record for biggest first-day IPO pops, 1999 and 2000, the three-year buy-and-hold return of IPOs was negative 53 percent, according to Jay Ritter, a professor at the University of Florida.

Being able to buy shares at their offering price and quickly sell them in an IPO was like being handed an almost-surefire winner, but the privilege was reserved for favored clients, including executives of companies with whom big banks sought future business. Even two decades later, this very lucrative corner of the financial world hasn't been democratized at all. Instead, retail investors continue to play a crucial but subordinate role in Wall Street's food chain by refreshing their screens again and again as the crush of "buy" orders is processed on the day the stock starts trading and they try to catch part of the action.

But in 2020, and especially early 2021, there were a record number of offerings that were sort of like IPOs that retail investors snapped up with abandon: SPACs. Special purpose acquisition companies, also known as "blank check firms," were so popular with retail investors that two of the stocks that faced trading restrictions by Robinhood in January 2021 were of that category. They sold themselves to the public with the proposition that the sponsors of the company would take a pile of cash they raised from the public and buy something good or give back the money in a couple of years. The sponsors had a strong ulterior motive to find something that at least looks good. This proved an ideal way to bring companies to market that often weren't even up to the standard of a profitless IPO wonder. To stand out from the crowd, many relied on endorsements from celebrities and athletes, including Jay-Z, Shaquille O'Neal, Serena Williams, Ciara, Peyton Manning, and Alex Rodriguez. In just the first four months of 2021, SPACs, largely sold to retail investors, raised more than $100 billion.

One lowlight that briefly proved to be a retail favorite was Nikola (as in Nikola Tesla, whose surname graced the era's biggest wonder stock), a company that demonstrated a hydrogen-powered truck, garnering a valuation of about $35 billion, which is several times what some actual, profit-making truck companies were fetching. Then a short seller released a video showing that the demonstration model had simply been rolled downhill rather than moving on its own power. The wheels quickly fell off the story.

In February 2021, two consumer protection bodies sent a letter to Congresswoman Maxine Waters, who had presided over the Game-

Stop hearing, noting that the SPAC boom was "fueled by conflicts of interest and compensation to corporate insiders at the expense of retail investors" and that they sought to "end-run longstanding rules designed to promote fair and efficient markets."[21] The issue of small investors' handing tens of billions of dollars of their savings to financiers with ulterior motives elicited less outrage from Waters than hedge funds' using sophisticated investors' money to bet that some share prices would fall.

SPACs are too new for a comprehensive history, but IPOs aren't. Buying into one at its market price makes for a pretty lousy lottery ticket. A database on the performance of nearly eight thousand IPOs maintained by Dr. Ritter shows that only 1 percent of stocks bought at their first-day closing price would have made you at least ten times your money over five years while four in ten would have lost you at least half of your money.

## Feel the Bern

If the returns on speculative stocks turn out to be anything as awful as they were in the dot-com bubble and participation was encouraged by zero-dollar commissions, as Dan Egan, the behavioral finance expert, and others say, then "free" will have turned out to be very expensive for investors. He suggests that adding some costs would limit the damage.

"I don't want it to be onerous where you block low-income people, but I don't want them to buy too many lottery tickets."

Robinhood's Vlad Tenev and Citadel's Ken Griffin both were asked at the February 18 congressional hearing whether free trading would be jeopardized if a 0.1 percent financial-transactions tax were instituted. Both demurred but said they didn't support such a measure.

Politicians such as Bernie Sanders who have proposed such a tax seem more interested in wielding it as a way to redistribute wealth rather than to discourage excessive speculation or rein in a stock bubble. Critics have pointed out that it would be a drag on the likes of pension funds.[22] But costs could be capped, and an individual would have to buy about $7,000 worth of stock to pay the $7 commission that was typical before Robinhood appeared.[23] That hardly seems egregious compared with what individual investors paid before Mayday. It would make rapid-fire trading prohibitively expensive, though.

It would also disadvantage professional high-frequency traders who are often on the other side of active retail investors, picking their pockets little by little. These are investment funds—though *investment* might be a misnomer—that exist to exploit small inefficiencies in markets. They use computer algorithms and extremely fast connections to the data centers where stocks are actually traded, jumping ahead of longer-term buyers by nanoseconds and often fractions of a penny.

"It wouldn't hurt anything, but it would stop a lot of this crap," says Swedroe. "And then give that money to the Securities and Exchange Commission to step up enforcement."

Most taxes are progressive—paid more by the wealthy. If all investors were sober and prudent, then that would be the case with taxing financial transactions too. Stocks are overwhelmingly owned by the top 10 percent by wealth and income. But Robinhood acknowledged among the risk factors in its own securities filing that it "could be impacted to a greater degree than other market participants" by a financial-transactions tax, meaning that its customers' activity would slow down more than others. That is because, much like low-income people who play Powerball, its users trade far more relative to the amount of money in their accounts—an incredible forty times as much as a Schwab customer, according to one study. At that level, "free" trading is anything but. As activity exploded, so did Robinhood's average revenue per user, from $37 a year in 2017 to $137 in the first quarter of 2021 when the GameStop squeeze happened. Most of that comes from selling orders, collecting fees, or charging margin interest.

If politicians are concerned about alienating voters by instituting a transactions tax, then unelected bureaucrats could take the heat and instead target margin lending. Since the 1970s the Federal Reserve has mandated that such loans be capped at 50 percent. What it means is that investors with $1,000 in qualified stock can borrow up to another $1,000 by using their portfolio as collateral. If those stocks fall sharply, then they would need to find more cash or be forced to sell some of that stock—a margin call.

Whatever might be done to put speed bumps on retail trading, whether it is instituting a tax or taking some other measure, it would likely be anathema to Tenev, Griffin, and many others in the finance industry. WallStreetBets users might think of it as a move to placate hedge funds, but—Plotkin's experience notwithstanding—those funds would probably be sorry to see less turnover in the market too. Wall Street was having a great time at the meme-stock party until it got out of hand because free money and free trading were very profitable for them—a reverse Robin Hood effect if there ever was one.

Chapter 6

# April 2020

An awful lot can happen in two months.

When we last met Gill at the end of February, it looked like disaster was about to strike. What had once been a healthy profit on his portfolio of call-option contracts on GameStop had turned into a loss as stocks began to sell off in anticipation of disruption caused to everyday life by the COVID-19 pandemic. That disruption turned out to be far more severe and long-lasting than almost anyone expected, making a trip to the mall to pick up the latest *Halo* or *Madden* disc unthinkable.

By early April, GameStop's share price had dropped to an all-time low of $2.57. Hedge funds were now even more confident that the chain would soon go out of business, and they boosted their financial bets on that outcome accordingly—not that it had to even get that bad for the value of all of Gill's options contracts to expire worthless with the stock so far below their exercise prices. But, incredibly, Gill's portfolio would hit its highest value yet by the end of the month at $215,589, and he was starting to gain more respect on the forum.

"This person deserves a wikipedia article about how big his balls are," wrote cd258519.[1]

It wasn't just GameStop that bounced back. The share prices of other companies such as restaurant chains, cruise lines, and airlines that were harmed the most by the pandemic had begun a furious rebound that surprised everyone except the people who didn't know any better—the least experienced investors in the market. To hedge fund managers who had paid for their Hamptons homes exploiting dumb money over the years, this bout of irrational exuberance looked like another great opportunity. But to some on WallStreetBets, the funds' hubris had all the makings of a trap that could cost them a fortune.

Why were novices so sanguine about the market in the middle of a crisis and older investors so cautious? And why was the idea of sticking it to the Park Avenue crowd so delicious? Consider their perspective.

The way you react to stock market calamities depends in large part on what you've experienced in your life and how much you have to lose. Middle-aged, upper-middle-class savers had endured two vicious bear markets and had substantial savings at risk with retirement looming. By contrast, people in their twenties had little or sometimes negative net worth and hadn't even graduated from high school during the white-knuckle weeks in 2008 when the world's banks were teetering. Moreover, the only lesson they had learned during their short investment careers had been to buy the dips because the Federal Reserve had always stepped in to save the day. The sentiment had long ago spawned its own acronym on message boards: BTFD. WallStreetBets has an online store where you can get a BUY THE FKN DIP T-shirt. "Any real trader knows the Dips are the best sales you can get out there!" it says next to the $24.99 price tag, tax and shipping not included.

This was a big dip, to be sure, but the lesson that the young investors had learned so well was reinforced with record speed. The Dow Jones Industrial Average erased all its gains since the election of Donald Trump almost three and a half years earlier in barely a month. The bear market's brevity was historic too, though. According to Howard Silverblatt, a walking stock market encyclopedia at S&P Dow Jones Indices, it was the fastest-ever return to a bull market by far at 4.9 months. The same recovery following the global financial crisis had taken 131.4 months, and the one after the dot-com crash took 60 months. Even the rebound from the 1987 stock market crash, in which most of the damage to stock prices was done in a single day, took 31.4 months, according to Silverblatt.

Up until early 2020, mainly older, whiter, richer people viewed the general level of stocks as important. The rise of Robinhood and the shift to commission-free trading by all its competitors in late 2019 had led millions of young people to open new brokerage accounts before the pandemic. The onset of lockdowns would turbocharge that trend as young people looking for something to do had, unexpectedly, some extra cash in their pockets and time on their hands. These new traders might have had smaller bankrolls on average than their parents, but they made up for it by being far more engaged. Between November 2018 and the end of 2020, for example, data collected by JMP Securities shows that average daily website visits to Schwab, the original discount broker with an older clientele, rose by just over 20 percent. Visits to Robinhood over that span surged by more than 550 percent.

But where had the appeal—not just of making money but of doing it at the expense of people much older and richer—come from? Wall-StreetBets founder Rogozinski points out that a typical twenty-five- or thirty-year-old member of the group might not have been in the stock market in 2008 during the financial crisis but was old enough to form a jaded opinion of high finance.

"I believe that this story for these people started backwards," he says. "Their mind-set starts before they invest in the stock market and they see the negative aspects of the stock market. They see themselves graduating from college, no jobs, parents losing their house, having to move into their basement—you know, a lot of great sob stories. And they weren't invested in stocks at the time—they were students, or they were young. They're not in the stock market and they get hurt by it. Imagine that?"

The trillions in paper wealth created in the longest-ever economic expansion in the country's history were unevenly distributed. Even counting indirect holdings through pension funds, some 84 percent of stocks were owned by the wealthiest 10 percent of US households, according to a study of Federal Reserve data.[2] And it wasn't just more money in absolute terms but a more meaningful amount. The share of household wealth made up by stocks was about two and a half times as high for those above age fifty-five or with incomes above $100,000 compared with those younger than thirty-five or with incomes less than $53,000, according to Pew Research.[3]

In 2020 the median net worth of Americans aged twenty-five to twenty-nine, including any home equity, was barely $7,500. When the government pumped cash into the economy, this was the group most likely to receive stimulus checks on the basis of income limits, but it also was far less likely than older, upper-middle-class Americans to have jobs that could be done remotely as the pandemic forced the country into lockdown. And even if they were fortunate in that way, they probably weren't working from the comfort of a home they owned. A study by the Stanford Center on Longevity showed that barely a third of millennials owned their own home at age thirty whereas nearly half of baby boomers were homeowners back when they were the same age. The unemployment rate jumped from 6.4 percent in February to a whopping 25.7 percent in April for Americans between the ages of twenty and twenty-five—almost double the unemployment rate for those aged forty-five to fifty-four.

Adding insult to injury, much of the federal government's response to the crisis, such as zero-interest rates and forgivable business loans, had a far bigger benefit for people who already had money. Americans for Tax Fairness calculated that between March 18, 2020, and February 19, 2021—from the trough of the bear market through the end of the meme-stock squeeze—the collective wealth of the 664 American billionaires had grown from $3 trillion to $4.3 trillion. That increase alone works out to $3,900 for every American man, woman, and child, which puts the $1,200 stimulus checks mailed out at the start of the pandemic in perspective.

While not minimizing the very real hardship many faced in the pandemic's opening months, tens of millions of young people found that stimulus cash, plus enforced saving and, for some, historically generous unemployment benefits, were nice but not life-changing infusions. It came in handy for stock speculation, though, and there were some interesting ideas percolating in early April 2020 about how to weaponize those portfolios.

One of those ideas caused a serious stir in the shares of GameStop. On April 13, a user on WallStreetBets with the pseudonym Senior _Hedgehog wrote a post with the headline GAMESTOP (GME)—THE BIGGEST SHORT SQUEEZE OF YOUR ENTIRE LIFE.[4] It pointed out a few fundamental attractions of the stock, discussing the console cycle, the fact that demand for video games was surging during the pandemic, and that the increased memory size of digitized games meant that discs were still in demand. But the main point was that, of GameStop's 65.5 million shares outstanding, 55 million (or 84 percent) were sold short—that is, borrowed from owners and sold to profit from their price dropping before being bought back more cheaply. In a preview of tactics seen during the great meme-stock squeeze, Senior_Hedgehog advised anyone who owned the stock to contact their broker to make sure they weren't being lent out.

The main way that a hedge fund like Melvin Capital bets against a stock is to "locate a borrow." The hedge fund's broker finds someone who owns shares and borrows it from their broker, usually without the owner noticing anything. The fund that borrows the stock then sells it to someone else who also has no idea that they just bought a borrowed share. It usually makes no difference to anyone but the short seller and the brokers involved, who make some money in the process.

Lending out shares is a source of income for retail brokers too, including Robinhood. It had $1.9 billion in shares owned by its clients lent out at the end of 2020. During the year, it made more than 10 percent of its revenue from securities lending. It earns more on those that are heavily in demand, such as the meme stocks when they faced a squeeze. Ironically, then, the fact that many of its customers owned GameStop allowed Robinhood to earn a meaningful amount of money lending those shares out to the people its customers were seeking to bankrupt.[5] It is possible to instruct your broker not to lend out your shares and thus create artificial scarcity to make a stock harder to sell short, which is what Senior_Hedgehog was suggesting.

GameStop shares surged by 22 percent on April 13. Then they jumped by nearly 26 percent the following day to close at $5.95. This was a short squeeze, but it wasn't the big one yet. The brief surge certainly didn't spook Gabe Plotkin or many other deep-pocketed funds betting against the retailer. In fact, the rally would soon lead them to increase their wager.

At the end of the month, the always-astute Gill weighed in: "Plus there's now an opportunity for a short squeeze of some sort, though that was never a part of my original thesis. I still think it's unlikely but when the shorts exceed the float the possibility needs to be factored in."

Cockiness on the part of some big hedge funds and the swelling confidence of a group of investors who seemingly couldn't lose would create the fuel for a brutal collision. As Senior_Hedgehog wrote:

*THE THRUSTERS ARE LOADING.*

Chapter 7

# Get Shorty

The most memorable line about selling stocks short has been attributed to the nineteenth-century speculator Daniel Drew: "He who sells what isn't his'n must buy it back or go to pris'n." Just being in the stock market with all its gyrations is scary enough for most people. Unless you use borrowed money, though, the very worst thing that can happen is losing every penny, and that would take some truly poor decision-making. Even then, nobody would show up to foreclose on your home or repossess your car. Just keeping your nerve and staying invested have almost always worked out nicely in the long run.

Now imagine being an investor for whom all that is upside down. You are constantly swimming against a long-term historical current. The best short sale ever will make you a 100 percent return, but your losses are theoretically unlimited. Instead of at least collecting a nice, steady dividend on your stocks, you have to pay a fee to borrow them, and the people who lent them to you can jack up the borrowing rate unexpectedly. Prison is no longer on the table for short sellers who get caught in a squeeze, but governments around the world routinely ban your livelihood at some of the few really lucrative times to be doing it. Malaysia's prime minister proposed caning as a punishment for the practice in the 1990s. Short sellers are called hyenas, jackals, and vultures, and a Google search for "short sellers are" helpfully offers to autocomplete your query with "scum."

What a fun business!

The Reddit revolutionaries despised short sellers more than the general investor population did, which is saying something. One reason might be that some of their generation's heroes like Elon Musk had an ax to grind with the profession. Or it might be that shorting is mainly the preserve of hedge fund managers who are richer, flashier, and more famous than other Wall Streeters and therefore more worthy of contempt. And since hedge funds must play their cards close to their vest because of securities regulations, sometimes outlandish theories were cooked up about how the secretive business was manipulating prices or buying off reporters. Whatever the reasons, hurting short sellers became something of a sport on WallStreetBets, and its members were about to learn how to aim for the kill shot.

Any fund manager might throw in the towel on an investment. Maybe it has done so badly that hanging on is getting hard to justify. But if enough people buy a stock that many short sellers have targeted, pushing its price higher, the short sellers might be forced to exit the position by buying it back, in the process exacerbating the rise in the stock and their own losses. That is a short squeeze. A "corner"—which is extremely rare and is very difficult to execute legally since securities laws were changed in the 1930s—is an extreme type of short squeeze when there simply aren't enough shares to purchase because some person or group has sewn up the supply. Then you can practically name your price, and the short seller has to pay it or "go to pris'n."

You could be forgiven for thinking that the environment in which Senior_Hedgehog and other WallStreetBets users hatched the idea of putting the squeeze on hedge funds that had borrowed nearly all the available shares of GameStop was some sort of boom time for short sellers. The truth is precisely the opposite. It was an awful year to bet against flaky companies. During 2020, short sellers in the US market alone lost a staggering $245 billion according to Ihor Dusaniwsky, managing director at short-selling specialist S3 Partners.[1]

In just the three months leading up to the meme-stock rally of January 2021, a basket of fifty of the most heavily shorted US stocks with market values of at least $1 billion nearly doubled, according to Goldman Sachs.[2] That had short sellers running for cover. On January 15, 2021, just before the big squeeze began in earnest, short interest as a share of market value for the benchmark S&P 500 stock index was near its lowest level ever, just barely higher than at the peak of the tech stock bubble almost twenty-one years earlier. Pessimism was going out of style.

Incredibly, the vitriol against hedge funds showed no signs of abating after the ruinous episode that was about to follow. House Committee on Financial Services chair Maxine Waters opened with the following statement as she called for hearings about the GameStop squeeze:

> Hedge funds have a long history of predatory conduct and that conduct is entirely indefensible. Private funds preying on the pension funds of hard working Americans must be stopped. Private funds engaging in predatory short selling to the detriment of other investors must be stopped. Private funds engaging in vulture strategies that hurt workers must be stopped.[3]

This not only revived unhelpful tropes about short sellers, an important part of Wall Street's ecosystem, but also misunderstood who was losing money in the episode and also whose money was at risk. The largest investors in hedge funds these days are people entrusted with the savings of retirees or university endowments. The winners in the squeeze, at least temporarily, were individual speculators.

"After being beaten up and left for dead on the side of the road, suddenly short sellers are the villains," says an exasperated Jim Chanos, founder of Kynikos Associates and dean of the short-selling community.[4]

But did the WallStreetBets crowd really engineer the "biggest short squeeze of your entire life"? Not unless they were very young.

## A (Short) History of Squeezes

Volkswagen would briefly become the world's most valuable company as the result of a short squeeze. In the spring of 2008, Porsche, which had long held a 31 percent stake in its fellow German automaker, indicated its desire to gain more influence over the larger company but stated explicitly that it had no intention of going as high as 75 percent since the state of Lower Saxony held a block of 20 percent of the shares, giving it considerable sway. Germany's corporate world is very clubby, and there are some unwritten rules. As Porsche bought and the price rose, hedge funds felt that Volkswagen shares had become artificially inflated in the process, and they amassed a short position of nearly 13 percent of its stock so they could reap the benefit when it reverted to normal—nothing approaching GameStop levels. It was more than enough for what came next, though. Porsche surprised everyone that October by announcing that it had control of 74 percent of the shares through stock and derivatives. This meant that the short position was about twice the remaining number of shares not controlled by Porsche or Lower Saxony. On paper, the ingredients were there for a corner, had that been Porsche's intention.

Fahrvergnügen instantly turned to schadenfreude as hedge funds found themselves in an impossible position and with little sympathy in the middle of the global financial crisis. Volkswagen's shares surged in what was called "the mother of all squeezes." Hedge funds lost an estimated $30 billion—the equivalent of six GameStops' worth.

But that was all ancient history to the Reddit army, right? Not according to user-traffic data from the *Financial Times*, the venerable British newspaper. The investigation editor Paul Murphy, who founded the paper's *Alphaville* blog, points out that there was a surge in readership for a post on the site about the Volkswagen squeeze with 81 percent of the traffic from Reddit and much of the rest from other social media sites. The clicks overlapped perfectly with the rise in GameStop shares in January 2021. The degenerates were taking notes.

Volkswagen was an unusual case, though—more a miscalculation than a deliberate act. To find episodes of a failed corner similar to GameStop's, one has to go back to the time when backroom share-price manipulation was more or less legal. The "Piggly Crisis" of 1923 was a classic example. Memphis businessman Clarence Saunders, who started Piggly Wiggly, the first real supermarket chain, was enjoying success but found that short sellers in New York were targeting his firm's shares in the mistaken belief that it was facing financial difficulties. It wasn't—some affiliated stores not owned by the firm but bearing its name had gone into receivership in the Northeast. Saunders could have shrugged it off, as so many other executives should have, but didn't when subject to short bets. Instead, he waged war and nearly won, but lost everything.

Saunders hired the famed speculator Jesse Livermore, known in his youth as "the boy plunger" and the real character behind Larry Livingston in the semiautobiographical Wall Street classic *Reminiscences of a Stock Operator*, to engineer a corner. Livermore bought about half of the two hundred thousand available shares for Saunders at around $40 apiece, and the campaign soon pushed Piggly Wiggly's price to around $70, inflicting some paper losses on the short sellers.

But Livermore then dropped out of the fight, not seeing a way that the corner would work. Saunders had borrowed heavily to buy the shares. How would he get out without eventually selling and playing into the shorts' hands? He came up with a brilliant plan, deciding to sell fifty thousand of his shares at a below-market price of $55, but on installment using supermarket circulars to advertise the "once in a lifetime opportunity" to ordinary people. (This sort of thing was allowed in the 1920s.) That meant he could sell the shares without short sellers being able to borrow them yet.

Then came the trap: Saunders called in his shares—the same move urged by Senior_Hedgehog to prevent them from being borrowed by short sellers. Delivery was due the next day, and their price shot up to well over $100 as short sellers panicked. The plan would have enriched Saunders and ruined his enemies had the exchange not stepped in and suspended trading. Shades of Wall Street "rigging the market" against outsiders ninety-eight years later, but for real!

The delay allowed the short sellers to scour the country and find enough shares at $100 or so to take their lumps but avoid default. Saunders had made some money on paper. Now, though, he owned almost the entire company and couldn't sell the stock to repay the loans he had taken out to buy it because trading was suspended. He launched a local campaign to sell more shares through subscription but failed and began selling off properties. It wasn't enough, and he was forced to sell his beloved company. Beating financiers at their own game is hard.

The whole exercise was unnecessary because, unless a company is set to raise money by selling new shares, a temporarily lower price has no practical effect. Since borrowing a stock costs money and involves a theoretically unlimited risk, short sellers don't have the luxury of sticking around too long. This is why they are often so vocal about their case, infuriating management. But saying a stock's price is too high is no different from saying it should be higher when you own some of it, which is done all the time.

## Naked Ambition

Executives who complain that short sellers are trying to ruin their companies either don't understand this or more often do understand it but are appealing to the general public and politicians who might not. The reasons vary from vanity to self-preservation to greed—their bonus awards become less valuable if weaknesses are exposed and the share price reacts accordingly. A 2004 study by Harvard University economics professor Owen Lamont showed that those companies whose managers took aggressive action against short sellers tended to perform much more poorly and to frequently go bankrupt.[5] A copy of the paper was handed by a staffer to Dick Fuld, chief executive of the investment bank Lehman Brothers, shortly before it became the largest corporate bankruptcy in history. He angrily dismissed it.

Another major misunderstanding about short selling, and this came up at the congressional hearing into GameStop, was the notion that short sellers illegally sell shares out of thin air. Gabe Plotkin may have sold "what isn't his'n," but he assured the committee that "any time we short a stock, we locate a borrow." So-called naked shorting, once common, is almost always the result of innocent clerical errors these days. The fact that more than 100 percent of the available shares of GameStop were sold short by early 2021 looked suspicious but happened because people who bought shares from short sellers lent them out again—a legitimate process called "rehypothecation."

Another thing that critics of short selling don't consider is that only willing lenders of shares make the process possible. While short sellers don't cause a permanent loss of value in a pension fund or insurance company's long-term shareholding of a stock if their case has no merit, they might provide a tidy source of extra income for them. Even Robinhood makes money by lending out its clients' shares, helping to finance that free trading. One rare objection to the practice came from Japan, "the land where capital goes to die," when its government pension fund decided in December 2019 to stop lending out its foreign shares to short sellers.

"I never met a short seller who has a long-term perspective," said the head of the fund to the *Financial Times*. The move is costing his pensioners about $100 million a year.[6]

Despite the image of short sellers as pessimists, most short selling actually is part of long-term investing strategies. Moreover, short squeezes aren't exactly rare, and they are rarely spectacular. What generally happens is that there are a lot of bets against a company that is expected to do poorly or report bad news, but the news is slightly less bad—say, a decent earnings report—and some short sellers decide to cut bait and rush to buy back the stock. Sometimes inexperienced investors will see a stock rise rapidly on a short squeeze and mistake it for some fundamentally good news about a troubled company, buying some shares themselves. It is a classic rookie error.

## You S3XY Thing

The rookies were having a field day following the explosion of retail trading in 2020, though. Measured in total dollars lost, a squeeze in a single stock eclipsed the amounts lost even in Volkswagen. According to Dusaniwsky of S3 Partners, short sellers lost more than $40 billion on the electric-car pioneer Tesla just during that year, making it "far and away the most unprofitable trade in 2020 and . . . the largest yearly loss we have seen historically."[7]

According to the valuation guru Aswath Damodaran, who teaches finance at New York University's Stern School of Business, there have been "at least three and perhaps as many as five short squeezes on Tesla" with 2020 just being the most recent.[8]

"With Tesla, individual investors who adore the company have been at the front lines in squeezing short sellers, but they have had help from institutional investors who are also either true believers in the company, or are too greedy not to jump on the bandwagon," he wrote.[9]

Tesla chief executive Elon Musk has made a sport out of taunting short sellers. His most infamous poke was in August 2018 when, with bets against the electric-car maker's shares mounting, he tweeted out: "Am considering taking Tesla private at $420. Funding secured."

However odd it seemed that an executive would make such an announcement during market hours on social media rather than through a press release and an official corporate filing, many failed to dismiss it because pranks like that aren't legal for the head of a publicly traded company. The stock surged as much as 14 percent that day on heavy buying. There was of course no funding lined up to buy the company. An immediate clue was the supposed $420 share price—a marijuana reference. Musk and the company paid fines and took other steps, such as having a compliance officer monitor Musk's tweets, that were soon forgotten. When you're famous, they let you do it.

Rather than being contrite, Musk embraced the moment and put a pair of red satin short shorts on sale on Tesla's website for a price of $69.420—the extra decimal very much intended. "Run like the wind or entertain like Liberace with our red satin and gold trim design. Enjoy exceptional comfort from the closing bell." The 69 reflected the adolescent sense of humor of a man whose car models spelled out S3XY (Musk says Ford Motor sued to block the trademark on a Model E, so he had to compromise with the Model 3).

Musk made no secret of his glee at the difficulty in which short sellers found themselves during the GameStop squeeze. One tweet questioned the whole practice: "u can't sell houses u don't own, u can't sell cars u don't own, but u *can* sell stock u don't own!? this is bs—shorting is a scam legal only for vestigial reasons." A few days later, he modified a quote by Robert Oppenheimer, creator of the hydrogen bomb (who was himself quoting the Bhagavad Gita): "I am become meme, Destroyer of shorts."

Betting that a stock will decline isn't a scam or in any way unethical unless it is accompanied by something underhanded. The imagery used when discussing short sellers, usually animals that survive on carrion, is pejorative, but why not go with it. A world filled with rotting, bloated corpses would be decidedly less pleasant. Likewise, a world in which you can only bet on a stock rising would be unbalanced. Financial theory says so, and real-world evidence does too.

We know because there have been numerous short-selling bans in history, either on individual stocks or on entire stock markets that were dropping. At the height of the financial crisis, the SEC banned short selling on hundreds of financial firms to, in the words of Chairman Christopher Cox, "protect the integrity and quality of the securities market and strengthen investor confidence."

A study by the Federal Reserve Bank of New York found that the ban did the opposite. Prices fell sharply while it was in place and stabilized when it was over. Affected stocks actually did worse than those for which short selling was allowed. The same effect was seen following a short-selling ban in 2011 after the US had its credit rating cut by Standard & Poor's, and stocks fell sharply. More recently, some European countries decided to ban short selling when markets initially plunged in the wake of the COVID-19 pandemic's arrival. A study by a group of fund management bodies and exchanges showed that stocks in countries without short-selling bans performed better.[10]

## Short People Have Reason to Live

Short sellers make it cheaper and easier for everyone to trade. They also aid in price discovery, stopping bubbles from forming as easily. At times when it is too hard or too expensive to bet against a stock, prices can be wrong, harming the least informed investors.

The most famous case was in March 2000 when, just weeks before the tech bubble burst, the networking company 3Com sold 5 percent of its stake in Palm, maker of PalmPilot personal digital assistants—the iPhones of their day. The company planned to spin off the rest to shareholders in a tax-free transaction later that year. Given the number of Palm shares they were to receive and the market price of Palm after it started to trade, a share of 3Com should have been worth at least $145 but instead was $82. The upshot was that either the rest of 3Com's business was somehow worth less than nothing or Palm was grossly overvalued.

*The Wall Street Journal* pointed this out the next day. Selling Palm short and buying 3Com shares would have created an instant profit known as an "arbitrage" and fixed the mistake in the process. There was more than $20 billion there for the taking, in theory at least. But the cost to borrow the small number of Palm shares was just too high, so the gap persisted. Thousands of retail investors got stuck overpaying instead.

Another reason to be thankful for short sellers is that they have an incentive to uncover bad behavior. While the big corporate scandals on Wall Street ultimately get prosecuted by the SEC, the agency isn't very good at finding them.

"Short sellers are real-time financial detectives, regulators are financial archaeologists," quips Chanos, who is most famous for uncovering the massive fraud at Enron.

The modus operandi for short sellers is to do the research, take their position, and then let the world know about it. In the case of Enron, *Fortune* reporter Bethany McLean spoke with Chanos, started digging, and prepared a cover story with the in-retrospect under-stated headline IS ENRON OVERPRICED? Enron boss Jeffrey Skilling, who would later go to prison, called her unethical. Enron executives flew from Houston to New York to try to convince her editors to drop the story, and Kenneth Lay, Enron's chairman, told her editor that McLean was relying on a source with a profit motive in seeing Enron's shares fall. Of course she was—in much the way that dozens of busi-ness articles every day quote executives with stock options or seek out the opinions of fund managers who happen to own a stock.

A more alarming episode came more recently when two journalists at the *Financial Times* were not only pressured by the German finan-cial technology company Wirecard and reportedly spied on but also became the target of a criminal complaint for stock manipulation for allegedly colluding with short sellers. Like Enron, Wirecard eventu-ally collapsed, but not before gyrations in its share price inflicted big losses on short sellers who were correct but early. At the time of writ-ing, its former CEO is in prison and its former chief operating officer is an international fugitive.

Most targets of short sellers aren't run by unsavory characters, and most short sellers don't shout their opinion from the rooftops. Plotkin, the chief victim of the short squeeze in GameStop, quietly established his position in 2014 because he thought it wasn't a very good business. Most of his holdings were of stocks he thought would rise in price.

Picking those that will drop is hard. Even Chanos, considered the best short seller in the business, has reportedly lost money much of the time in his main short fund, Ursus, established in 1985. So why do it? Funds that invest with Chanos gain a degree of protection from choppy markets. It is when the tide goes out that you see who has been swimming naked, so low-quality companies tend to fall sharply, or sometimes go to zero, during a downturn. Having that as part of an investment portfolio can make for better and smoother overall returns.

"The act of being short allows you to be long," explains Chanos.

That isn't just a marketing pitch—it is borne out by the excellent overall performance of his main fund, which benefits when the market rises like an ordinary fund while holding short positions in what Chanos's team sees as weaker companies. As the GameStop debacle shows, though, taking an infinite risk with even a small part of your portfolio the way that Plotkin did requires a very cautious and steady hand to avoid the possibility of a devastating loss.

With so much on the line, short sellers do their homework and pick their spots carefully. The stocks they have targeted the most have lagged the ones they targeted the least over the years by a substantial amount on average. The problem with this winning formula is that it occasionally goes very, very badly. Like picking up nickels in front of a bulldozer, some short sellers were about to get their fingers crushed.

Chapter 8

# Summer-Fall 2020

Thinking of day trading?

"Teens and retirees are especially susceptible to this potentially risky idea that could greatly affect their financial health," said a timely blog post published on September 1, 2020. It went on to spell out the dangers of using a "free trading app" or dabbling in options.

The advice from MassMutual's In Good Company was as ironic as it was sound since it came from Keith Gill's financial wellness team. Unbeknownst to his employer, the licensed broker was about to step out of the shadows and inspire a speculative frenzy.

First Gill had to endure a trying summer, though, financially but especially personally. His sister Sara died suddenly in June. Gill, still lightly followed, would vanish almost completely from social media, except for occasionally posting his E*Trade account balance. The congratulatory messages from the degenerates had turned back to snarky ones as excitement over the short squeeze faded and GameStop shares again began to languish.

"What a way to blow 100k," wrote one WallStreetBets user at the end of June, by which time Gill's E*Trade account balance was down to $121,271.

"A true contrarian play, but covid 19 is going to wipe the floor with this trade," wrote another. "It was already difficult to execute the turn around in good times, but to try doing this with the rona spread everywhere? Also, has anyone been to their local gamestop? They are ghost towns."

In July, the stock would dip back below $4. By the end of that month, Gill's account was worth $112,238—still more than twice where he had started a year earlier, but well off his peak. It was the previous September, in 2019, when he first came to the subreddit's attention. His portfolio's value had shot up following the arrival of a financial celebrity—the iconoclastic, one-eyed doctor turned value investor Michael Burry, made famous by *The Big Short*. As the doubters were returning, an even more influential person—at least as far as the most active participants in the mid-2020 stock market were concerned—was quietly building a stake that would soon make Gill a millionaire.

Burry is a gifted investor, but the only reason he had any name recognition with the WallStreetBets crowd was that Christian Bale had played him in the film adaptation of the Michael Lewis book. Unlike the Batman actor, Burry came across as almost as much of a wet blanket to Generation Z and millennials as Warren Buffett, who turned ninety that August. On his Twitter feed, where he goes by the name Cassandra, the Trojan priestess cursed for always being right but never believed, he was wary of the most popular investing themes. As he wrote shortly after the meme-stock squeeze:

> Speculative stock #bubbles ultimately see the gamblers take on too much debt. #MarginDebt popularity accelerates at peaks.

*At this point the market is dancing on a knife's edge. Passive investing's IQ drain, and #stonksgoup hype, add to the danger.*

Ryan Cohen was a lot more fun. The founder of the pet e-commerce site Chewy, he had sold his still-unprofitable company to PetSmart for $3.35 billion three years earlier in what was then the largest e-commerce deal ever. Though he was by then no longer with the company, Chewy's initial public offering in 2019 was hot stuff, nearly doubling in value on its first day of trading. Adding further shine to his halo, Chewy was a pandemic winner as both pet adoption and online shopping surged. Its stock tripled between the March stock market low and the end of August, and it would rise fivefold by the time of the meme-stock squeeze.

A millennial the same age as Gill and Vlad Tenev, Cohen had gotten his start at the tender age of thirteen by building websites for businesses. His late father, Ted, a hardworking private business owner, was his role model and instilled a love of the stock market in his son. The elder Cohen, who bought and held conservative blue chip stocks, never with borrowed money, showed young Ryan a chart of long-run stock returns. Deciding he would follow in his father's footsteps as a businessman, Cohen skipped college and, after running some other internet ventures, at age twenty-five thought he had found a business to disrupt by selling jewelry online. Just as he was preparing to launch the venture with his partner, Cohen went to a pet store to find some healthful food for his poodle and had an epiphany—he was passionate about animals and the industry was huge.

"So although we were only a week away from launching the jewelry business, we pivoted. We sold all the rings, necklaces, and bracelets—and the safe—and started learning everything we could about the pet industry," wrote Cohen.[1]

His inspirations were Jeff Bezos, the Amazon founder, and the late Tony Hsieh, who started the customer-obsessed online shoe retailer

Zappos. Chewy matched prices found elsewhere, but it spent far more on support for "pet parents" than competitors, employing a whole team to send out cards expressing condolences when a pet died. Despite rapid early sales growth, Cohen had even more trouble raising money than Tenev and Bhatt did at Robinhood, in no small part because online pet goods were considered something of a cursed category. He claims he struck out on over one hundred pitches to venture capitalists. Cohen finally found a Boston-based investor who liked the story.

It took a leap of faith. Even twenty years later, Pets.com was still the poster child for e-commerce excess in Silicon Valley. Taking advantage of a hot market for anything dot-com, it went public with hardly any revenue in 1999, but it spent heavily on advertising, including a float in the Macy's Thanksgiving Day Parade and an infamous sock puppet ad in the 2000 Super Bowl. Star analyst Henry Blodget, who would be permanently banned from the securities industry for making stock recommendations that he disavowed in private, had a "buy" rating on Pets.com for much of its time as a public company.[2] That wasn't very long—the e-tailer ran out of cash and declared bankruptcy in 2000, just nine months after its initial public offering.

If you could defy the skeptics and make a bundle selling pet food and flea medicine online, then maybe you could figure out video games. Cohen had quietly amassed a 9.9 percent stake in GameStop by August 18, 2020, and filed the required 13D form with the SEC that made his position public on August 28. The share price surged by 42 percent in the next two trading sessions, and Gill promptly posted a screenshot of his E*Trade account showing a balance of $823,391. Not surprisingly, the tone on the subreddit became favorable to him once again:

*Well deserved, you believed when others did not.*[3]

But Gill still was being second-guessed by some. One user pointed out how much more he would have made had he invested in Tesla. Another, who claimed to have owned GameStop but sold too soon, told Gill that in his position he "would use this spike as an opportunity to sell" as the business was awful, and the only good news was "whales"—deep-pocketed speculators—dabbling in the stock.

> *I bet this stock tanks after earnings next week on the usual poor sales and awful guidance.*

It didn't and, like Burry a year earlier, Cohen had ideas about how management could boost the share price. He would make an even bigger splash on September 21 when he disclosed that he was holding talks with GameStop's executives and board members in order "to produce the best results for all shareholders."

With the prospect of a cyber-savvy activist shaking things up, the next day the stock jumped back above $10 for the first time since March 2019 and suddenly Gill was a millionaire. A screenshot of his account statement showed a value of $1,501,166. It would never go below seven figures again. A couple of posters wondered whether DeepFucking-Value was a pseudonym for Michael Burry, but most congratulated him and, as usual, wondered when he would finally take profits:

> *This was an intelligent thought out gamble and everything worked out in his favor for an absolute massive payout due to his patience and procedural precision. Let's see what kind of payout he walks away with. Who knows what is to come, and when this diamond hand genius will sell.*

Gill had made a small fortune on paper, and GameStop's share price was now close to the upper end of his estimates of its value a year earlier. At this point, if Gill had been a by-the-book value investor, he might have cashed out, and this story could have been very different. But suddenly he had reason to aim even higher with Cohen on the scene and seeking to shake things up.

As Roaring Kitty, Gill was hosting YouTube live streams about GameStop that began to attract more than just a handful of viewers. Some lasted more than four hours as he answered questions submitted in the comment stream. The WallStreetBets subreddit was gaining momentum too, crossing the 1.5-million-user mark the same week in September that Cohen put out his statement, up from 1 million early in 2020.

But GameStop and Gill were far from the main attraction at this point. Technology stocks hit their highest level ever on September 3 with the Nasdaq Composite breaking the 12,000-point mark for the first time. The index would then plunge by a sickening 5 percent the following session, its worst day since the March pandemic panic, as investors got cold feet about how quickly glamour stocks had risen. Over a little more than three weeks the index would move into correction territory, dropping by nearly 13 percent. Even retail favorite Tesla had temporarily run out of juice. Elon Musk's presentation on the electric-car maker's "Battery Day," which took place the same day that Cohen's statement about his discussion with GameStop was released, was a fiasco. The stock shed more than 15 percent of its value over two sessions.

GameStop's share-price surge following Cohen's arrival only emboldened professional skeptics. When Senior_Hedgehog first mentioned the idea of a short squeeze in April, shares sold short were an extremely high 80 percent or so of those available to trade. By the eve of Cohen's arrival in late August, that had gone above 100 percent—a number possible because of the process of rehypothecation (shares being lent, sold, and then lent again). Following his September 21 statement about having been in touch with management and the ensuing share-price surge that made Gill a millionaire, short interest edged above 140 percent. That is practically unheard of.

Short sellers' confidence was setting them up for a disaster because the bet was now dangerously crowded. Had they been monitoring the chatter on WallStreetBets rather than just focusing on Cohen's intentions and the chain's still-shaky business, they might have reduced their wagers instead.

The company still looked like it would descend into Blockbuster Video–like oblivion, but a debt restructuring had bought it time. The longer a business can hang on, the more unexpected things that can happen to challenge investors' assumptions. As Gill had predicted, GameStop defied expectations and stayed alive for the next console cycle, with Sony and Microsoft unable to satisfy demand for their latest hardware during the pandemic.

In theory, there were far easier pickings for short sellers than GameStop, with so many unprofitable companies commanding stratospheric valuations. In practice, though, many of them were no longer tethered to reality—more like Beanie Babies or cryptocurrencies than corporations that were supposed to have some intrinsic value. Relentless buying of many stocks popular with retail investors had made selling their shares short a good way to lose money in a hurry. It seemed safer to keep betting against a name from yesteryear like GameStop that everyone knew was headed for the scrap heap, a theater chain like AMC bleeding cash as its venues sat empty because of the pandemic, or an anachronism like BlackBerry, even if it was going to take a while. Who on earth would get excited about them?

The short sellers were making a dangerous miscalculation. More and more WallStreetBets users were becoming aware of the extreme level of short interest in such stocks. On September 19, two days before Cohen's communication with the company became public, a poster with the username Player896 made a detailed case for why GameStop could at the very least last a few more years and the importance of the fact that Burry and Cohen now owned 15 percent of the shares combined. The last part of the post, titled "Bankrupting Institutional

Investors for Dummies, ft GameStop," should have been a wake-up call to Melvin and others.

> *120% has never been seen before. The short theory was that GameStop would not make it to the new console cycle and the short-ers would collect their tendies. But GameStop made it. Current short fees are like 60% and from some figures we can draw on, we estimate that around 70% of the shorts got in under $7, GameStop is currently nearing $10. 70% of the shorts are underwater. Even if you don't believe that any of their initiatives will work you have to admit that the company will be able to continue operating for another two years off the new console hype alone. When the stock hits roughly $15, we can expect to see several margin calls trigger a fucking massive short squeeze.*

There were relatively few mentions of GameStop on the forum the following month, but they began to rise in early November. For example, the stock was mentioned 84 times on November 13 and 180 times on November 15, according to TopStonks.com. The next day, Cohen released a public letter urging a road map to control costs, a focus on profitable stores, and a better e-commerce business. He even highlighted the heavy Wall Street betting against the company.

> *GameStop is also one of the most shorted stocks in the entire mar-ket, which speaks volumes about investors' lack of confidence in the current leadership team's approach.[4]*

The stock surged again, and so did the attention paid to the retailer on the subreddit. On November 25 there were 683 posts mentioning GameStop, and by November 28 that had risen to 1,343 posts. By the end of November, Gill's net worth had topped $3 million.

The stock had now nearly quadrupled since July, and it seemed like the easy money had been made. The story was in the process of changing dramatically, though. Instead of buying low to sell high, some WallStreetBets users were showing an interest in buying high to make others buy even higher. Melvin Capital was shaping up as their main target.

Plotkin had goofed. Shares sold short must be reported, but the individual funds behind those positions don't have to be. Melvin, though, made the error of identifying itself as having bet against GameStop through a routine securities filing that summer showing that it held 3.4 million put options on the retailer—a contract that had a similar effect by giving it the right to sell GameStop shares at a fixed price in the future. It had also sold shares short. Now, in the minds of many on the subreddit, there were good guys, Cohen and Gill, and an identifiable bad guy who, of all things, had given his fund a name that was just asking to get sand kicked in its face.

A post on October 27 by Stonksflyingup was titled "GME Squeeze and the Demise of Melvin Capital." It used a clip from the television series *Chernobyl* portraying the scientist testifying to the uncomfortable Soviet tribunal interspersed with flashbacks to the accident.

*The 70 million shorted shares all rush to cover. Melvin Capital got too greedy.*[5]

Confused technicians in the doomed reactor push buttons with Cyrillic letters on the instrument panel with no effect.

*GME share price is now a nuclear bomb.*

A shot of the reactor exploding.
Sparking a financial chain reaction isn't easy, even with all the

fissile material Plotkin and other hedge fund managers had created. Despite the degenerates' large and growing ranks, simply buying up the company's shares at ever higher prices was an expensive way to stick it to Melvin and probably wouldn't have worked. There was an easier way to make a stock go nuclear, though: harnessing other people's money with what Buffett once called "financial weapons of mass destruction."

Chapter 9

# Cheat Code

ight-A-Right-Left-Left-Right-RB-Right-Left-A-Y

If that sequence means anything to you, then you're probably part of the mostly young, male demographic of WallStreetBets. The cheat code will make you invulnerable for half an hour on what is still the most profitable video game of all time, *Grand Theft Auto V,* released during GameStop's heyday in 2013. With it, you could cause all sorts of mayhem on the mean streets of the fictional San Andreas.[1]

WallStreetBets founder Jaime Rogozinski says looking for hacks is very much part of the subreddit's ethos too. In November 2020, a member of the community who goes by the username MoonYachts was one of a handful to take that to heart through what he called a "free money cheat" on Robinhood. He discovered that, as a Robinhood Gold customer, if he sold call options—a type of derivative that opens sellers up to theoretically unlimited losses—the firm mistakenly credited him with the cash for their value.[2] By seemingly increasing his cash position without requiring him to actually put up more money, he had enough collateral in his account to do it again and again, giving himself theoretically infinite borrowing power. MoonYachts eventually parlayed his $4,000 account into a bet worth well over $1 million.

"You automatically become chair of the Fed Reserve because you've figured out how to print money," quipped an impressed user of the subreddit.

One of its moderators chimed in that MoonYachts probably wouldn't be allowed to profit from Robinhood's lapse.

> That being said—we are on path for the 4th time Robinhood has to release a patch/implement new rules to their platform due to one of y'all. I'd be lying if I said I wasn't proud.[3]

Once it was reported by CNBC, the broker quickly moved to restrict the practice. Customers employing the trick could have been wiped out by even a small move in prices, and Robinhood might have been left on the hook for huge sums in the very likely event that its mischievous customers didn't have enough actual cash in the bank to cover their losses.

Retail investors swapping notes on WallStreetBets and trading on their smartphones using Robinhood weren't the only ones having a bit of fun with options. During the summer of 2020, traders noticed a huge new presence on the market aggressively buying contracts on the biggest technology firms such as Facebook, Apple, Tesla Motors, Amazon, Nvidia, and Netflix—major components of the Nasdaq Composite Index. The bets were so large that traders dubbed the buyer "the Nasdaq Whale." His estimated $4 billion options position was the equivalent of gaining exposure to tens of billions of dollars' worth of those stocks.

"Someone is playing with house money and they're rolling large," observed the risk expert Larry McDonald in his weekly *Bear Traps Report* in late August.[4]

The derivatives veteran Scott Nations, president of Nations Indexes, recalls thinking at the time that the options market for individual stocks just wasn't equipped to handle the sort of buying his company was seeing that summer. It turns out that was actually the point, and some on WallStreetBets were taking notes.

## Earthquake Insurance

A quick primer on what the whale was buying: a "call" or "put option" is basically a financial contract. If you buy one, then it confers the right, but not the obligation, to buy or to sell, respectively, a stock or other financial instrument at a certain price at a specific future date. The most a buyer can lose is the price, or "premium," paid for this right. But the person who sells it to you takes on a huge risk for that up-front payment—sort of like an insurance company selling you a policy, except with no limit to what it might have to pay.

Insurance companies aren't stupid—they go out and buy their own insurance in case of a disaster like an earthquake that could bankrupt them. Options dealers do too but, unlike Allstate, they are able to buy even more coverage as soon as they start to feel some tremors. Normally that is just a technical detail, but it was central to the Nasdaq Whale's strategy and to the Reddit revolutionaries who would shake Wall Street's foundations months later.

Options that seem to have a low chance of ever being worth something because the "exercise price" is far from today's stock price can appear very cheap. If the unexpected happens and the stock surges (or plunges in the case of a put option), then a buyer can earn multiples of the premium—a payoff akin to a lottery ticket. Say, for example, that you pay a dollar for a call option on ABC Corporation expiring in a month at an exercise price of $110, and the price of the stock is now $100. The contract you bought is "out of the money"—the stock's price needs to rise by more than $10 for the option to be worth exercising. Then it needs to rise by one more dollar for you to earn back what you paid—your premium. If it rises by another $10, though, then the buyer of the option will have earned ten times his investment.

It will probably expire worthless, but the dealer who sold it knows that a lot can happen between now and the expiration date and has to watch the price carefully. The more ABC Corporation's stock tends to jump around, the more the dealer will charge you for the option initially—an important wrinkle to remember later in our story. You can sell the option to someone else before it expires, but if ABC Corporation's stock is at or below $110 on the expiration date, then your premium gets you nothing—your money is gone.

The cheapest options you can buy are those that are well out of the money and also don't have a lot of time left before they expire. An options dealer might sell them to you for pennies, and you will almost always lose all of the premium you paid. But every once in a while a buyer's profits are huge.

They were for Keith Gill. The one thousand GameStop call options with a $12 exercise price expiring on April 16, 2021, that he owned at the end of July 2020 were then worth just eighteen cents apiece. Each options contract actually represents the right to buy one hundred shares, so eighteen cents times one hundred times his one thousand contracts made them worth $18,000 at the time in Gill's E*Trade account. The stock price was just $4 at the time, so Gill's options were deeply out of the money, but not worthless—a lot could still happen.

A lot did. On January 25 and 26, 2021, as meme-stock mania took off, Gill sold half of his options for about $11 million. The five hundred contracts he still owned on January 27, 2021, were worth a whopping

$16.8 million that afternoon. Even though there was by then a lot less time remaining until the call options expired, the incredible volatility of the stock in the preceding weeks and GameStop's much higher share price at the time made them far more valuable.

Options, or similar instruments known as "warrants," have been a feature of financial markets for a long time, but the formula for pricing them accurately, jointly discovered by Fischer Black, Myron Scholes, and Robert Merton, was only unveiled in a 1973 academic paper that won the latter two men the Nobel Prize in Economics in 1997 (Black had died two years earlier, and Nobel Prizes aren't awarded posthumously). The formula, along with advances in computing power to constantly spit out the correct price, led to an explosion in options trading.

## Read the Fine Print

Derivatives can be very useful for professionals but also dangerous when misused. The proliferation of trading software and the disappearance of commissions mean that individuals have increasingly gotten in on the fun, and the occasional blowups, in the past couple of decades. The social mood expert Peter Atwater observed that a lot of individuals getting into call options typically is a sign that bad things are about to happen to the market. He likens it to excited people who are last to a party and looking for the quickest way to get drunk.

"Call options provide the perfect tequila shot."[5]

Wall Street's bartenders had never been busier than in 2020 and early 2021. Even now that trading them was "free," options were a profitable product, but also one for which brokers cover themselves extra carefully in case of lawsuits. Their self-regulatory organization, FINRA, requires that anyone wanting to trade options download a 183-page, 44,000-word form. It is unlikely that many have actually read the document. Far more riveting are dozens of books on the subject written for a lay audience. A sampling on Amazon includes *Get Rich with Options, 7 Trades to a Million*, and an inadvertently honestly named one: *Options Trading Crash Course*. Stockbrokers regularly hold free "options education" seminars online or in suburban hotel conference rooms to interest customers in the lucrative—for the broker—product.

Not every retail options trader is an inveterate gambler. A popular and conservative strategy, for example, is "covered calls"—selling call options on stocks you already own. In exchange for limiting your potential profit on the stock, you get a little bit of money up front in the form of the premium—sort of like a bird in the hand instead of two in the bush. Less advisable are complicated strategies with names like "Iron Condor," "Bull Spread," and "Butterfly" that can involve both buying and selling options.

For the most part, options have been a sucker bet, but their complication and regulatory speed bumps have limited the sums lost by individuals. The recent wave of smartphone-based trading has led to record amounts spent and lost, though. Between December 2019, the month that many retail brokers transitioned to commission-free trading, and February 2021, the heady aftermath of the GameStop squeeze that saw millions of new accounts opened, options volume nearly tripled according to the Options Clearing Corporation.[6]

While you don't need to have the Black-Scholes-Merton equation tattooed on your arm to buy an options contract—few people on Wall Street can do the math unaided—the iPhone interface on Robinhood makes buying these complex financial instruments easier than ordering a burger on Grubhub. A video tutorial on its website in the spring of 2021 showed a user clicking a magnifying glass to search for a stock, in this case the fictional Meow Industries (Roaring Kitty would approve). He clicks "trade" and then "trade options." There are four icons: an up arrow, a down arrow, a squiggly line, and a wavy line. It defaults to the up arrow, meaning "I think it's going up." Clicking that arrow gives him a menu of expiration dates, defaulting to one. He clicks on a strike price. Robinhood helpfully tells him how much Meow's shares will have to rise for the customer to break even. Click, type in the number of contracts and your limit price, and, voilà, the newbie is about to own an option.

Veterans have expressed alarm at the hefty losses and quick approval process for options trading. Robinhood paid the largest fine in FINRA's history without admitting fault for using easily gamed bots to approve customers. Even before that, one trend that belied Robinhood's claims that it had carefully screened customers was a rash of users buying and immediately exercising out-of-the-money options—a move that anyone with a rudimentary understanding of what they had just bought wouldn't make. It guarantees you will lose all your money.[7]

"If you're at one of the biggest brokerage houses then you have to fill out a form more than two lines long to trade options," scoffs Peter Cecchini, a derivatives authority who is director of research at Axonic Capital. "The sample of people using them (through Robinhood) are not options sophisticates."[8]

A trader who posted screenshots of his Robinhood account on WallStreetBets in February 2020, while not at all typical in terms of his results, offered the sort of social proof that got more novices to jump in. Going by the username Kronos_415, he told *Markets Insider* that he had six months' trading experience but had turned $5,000 into $131,000 in a month on Tesla call options.

"I think a fair market price is $800," he said of the electric-vehicle maker's stock at the time, noting that $900 was too speculative. But he followed this by telling the reporter that he expected the stock to reach $2,000 a share within a couple of years, in which case $900 was a bargain—stocks don't usually more than double in two years.[9]

The most infamous and tragic example of one of the new wave of active traders getting in over his head was that of Alex Kearns, a twenty-year-old Robinhood customer who took his own life in June 2020 after receiving a message that his account was restricted and that he had a negative balance of $730,000 as a result of an options trade.

"He shouldn't have been allowed to trade these complicated options in the first place. He had no training, no income, no qualifications, to make those sophisticated trades," said Alex's father in an interview with CNN.[10]

"We were devastated by Alex Kearns' death," said Robinhood in a statement. "We remain committed to making Robinhood a place to learn and invest responsibly."

The company said it made enhancements to customer support in the wake of the suicide. It certainly didn't discourage options buyers, though. In the months following the incident, its users would drastically increase their activity, particularly in those contracts with the most jackpot-like returns—contracts with little time left to expire that are out of the money. Most didn't open users up to unlimited losses, but they frequently weren't smart bets either. Recall that Citadel and other wholesalers' payments to Robinhood for options order flow were higher than they were for other brokers. The former banker Packy McCormick asserts that they prefer customers who leave money on the table.

## Method to the Whale's Madness

The trade by the mysterious Nasdaq Whale, while executed by professionals, had some similar elements to what was in favor with retail traders that year. He was buying call-option contracts that had the most bang for their buck—relatively short-dated, out-of-the-money ones—and he got the direction of the market right. From June through August, the Nasdaq Composite had a strong rally, rising by 24 percent, and the big tech stocks that led the charge did even better than that.

That wasn't mere good luck, though, because the whale's gamble was even bigger than believed. By early September it emerged that the buyer was Japan's SoftBank Corp., led by the risk-loving billionaire Masayoshi Son. Reporters also learned that his $100 billion Vision Fund had simultaneously purchased billions of dollars of many of the underlying tech stocks. At face value that just sounds like two gigantic bets instead of one.

There was a method to Son's madness, though. As with short selling, options dealers are taking on a theoretically unlimited risk by transacting with you, and they aren't in the risk-taking business. That usually means that they will buy a little bit of the stock after selling you a call option, and, if it rises in price, they will keep buying more and more of it before the option expires according to complicated formulas—like the aforementioned insurance company that can buy more coverage when it feels tremors.

Of course, that insurance it buys gets more expensive as a quake seems imminent. SoftBank was buying so many options that it started to affect the price of the shares, forcing the people who had sold the options to protect themselves by buying more as prices rose. At the same time, short sellers like Jim Chanos, who were watching stocks like Tesla rally on what looked like pure hype, had borrowed shares to sell them short. The sudden surge forced some of them to buy shares as well, to limit their own losses, exacerbating the upward pressure on stock prices.

SoftBank needed a big score at the time because it had just lost $9 billion in the fiscal year that had ended in March. Its stake in the office company WeWork, which had been headed for an initial public offering in 2019 worth an estimated $47 billion, had crumbled by around 90 percent as of September 2020 after its eccentric founder, Adam Neumann, departed under a cloud. And the value of SoftBank's stake in the ride-hailing app Uber, which already was on the market, sank as a result of the pandemic.

If the Nasdaq Whale's maneuver seems more like a roll of the dice by a gambler down on his luck than the moves of a canny investor, well, that's because it was. Throughout his career, Son has taken enormous risks that at the peak of the dot-com bubble in 2000 made him the world's richest man—for three days. He also holds the record for the most money ever lost by an individual as his net worth shriveled from $70 billion to $600 million. One overlooked clue about the identity of the whale came over the summer when SoftBank said it had raised a $555 million fund partially owned by Son to invest in stocks. It turns out that it was just the tip of the iceberg in his massive bet—555 is pronounced "go-go-go" in Japanese.[11]

## Retail Investors and Options Mania

"Go-go-go" was the mantra of retail investors dabbling in options for the first time as well. The "notional value"—the amount of stock controlled by their contracts—was many times higher than the whale's bet. Robinhood's revenue in the first quarter of 2021 from selling its order flow to wholesalers such as Citadel was $331 million—some 263 percent more than the same period a year earlier—with most of it from options trading.[12] The popularity of call options as opposed to put options, for which options buyers benefit from falling stock prices, was enough to change the entire shape, or "skew," of the market, causing a stir among derivatives experts.

There was so much buying of call options by individual investors that the tail began wagging the dog. Recall that short sellers lost $245 billion in 2020 in what was their worst year in history, largely by betting against crowd favorites that seemed to rise to irrational levels. Though most retail options buyers didn't realize it at first, heavy buying of options on stocks like Tesla that happened to have high short interest was creating a feedback loop in which dealers were forced to buy the stock to protect themselves from losing money, putting pressure on short sellers to also buy back the shares they had borrowed as their losses spiraled, and so on.

Sometimes many people targeted the same stock at once as social media sites like Reddit or TikTok amplified certain voices, making them seem prescient as opposed to briefly influential. This often led to quick scores on the options, like the bonanza reported by Kronos_415, boosting the instruments' popularity. Copycats who were a bit late to the party often just lost their money, but they helped those who were early to make even more. The most sought-after contracts were those that cost the least and that often meant ones expiring in just days that were out of the money and so had little hope of being worth anything. As SoftBank grasped, it was precisely the type of contract that could have the most bang for the buck on the price of the stock.

When a member of WallStreetBets got the idea in September to "trigger a fucking massive short squeeze," as detailed in the post "Bankrupting Institutional Investors for Dummies," another chimed in with a more sophisticated strategy than just buying the shares. It was the same thing SoftBank had done, but this would be aimed at a company that was by then primed like a powder keg: GameStop.

Options could act as a force multiplier in exacerbating a squeeze, just as they had with Tesla, but in a far more concentrated and effective way in GameStop's case. It was a much smaller company, and the short bet much greater relative to the number of available shares. Buying the stock to force it up was expensive. Buying the cheapest options contracts wasn't—not at first. The trick was getting options dealers to be unwitting accomplices in a short squeeze because their risk managers told them they had to.

"Sup gamblers. Feel bad about missing the gain train on TSLA? Fear not—something much greater and stupider is here," wrote Jeffamazon. "In order to capture the biggest upside, the highest strike call option is best. The weeklies have the highest delta, so Citadel will be forced to hedge the most by buying shares. In other words, we'll get the biggest bang for our buck in squeezing these."[13]

## The Gamma Squeeze

What Jeffamazon described was a "gamma squeeze," which is what the whale had been up to. Gamma and delta are two of the "Greeks," as options traders call them—letters in the Black-Scholes-Merton formula that determine the price of the option. Delta, mentioned in the post, denotes the sensitivity of the option to a dollar move in the stock. Its delta determines how many shares a dealer who sold you an option will purchase of the stock as insurance for each dollar it subsequently rises.

As a stock gets closer to a call option's exercise price, its delta gets higher too, so a dealer will have to pick up the pace of buying. A contract that is out of the money with little time left until it expires—the sort that costs pennies but has lottery-like returns—can see its delta rise quickly if there is an unexpected rally in the stock. Gamma describes the pace at which delta increases. It is roughly the same relationship that acceleration has to speed.

A gamma squeeze can occur when there is a lot of buying of call options that then forces options dealers to buy more and more of the stock in a sort of stampede. In the case of GameStop and the other meme stocks—which also had heavy short interest, the result of many individuals buying call options simultaneously that were out of the money in a relatively small company and had just days left until they expired—it created a self-fulfilling prophecy. Short sellers and options dealers had to buy no matter what because their risk was literally infinite.

Just in time for meme-stock mania, Robinhood sent a note to customers in December 2020. This is how a message to one user read:

Hi [Name Redacted],

As part of our ongoing effort to improve your trading experience—you can now open new options positions up to 3PM ET on the day they expire. This has been one of our most requested features and your feedback is very important to us.

Keep in mind, opening new options positions close to or on their expiration date comes with substantial risk of losses for reasons that include potential volatility of the underlying security and limited time to expiration.

Sincerely,

The Robinhood Team

The money that could be made or lost was real, but buying a derivative that had an hour left in its existence was more like a game than investing. And if your game was blowing up hedge funds, then it was like being given a nifty cheat code.

Player896, Stonksflyingup, and Jeffamazon had come up with a brilliant strategy for costing other people a lot of money. Unfortunately, they never quite spelled out how the WallStreetBets crowd would make any of their own once the squeeze was over—at least not all of them. To get an idea of what might happen, they could have read SoftBank's quarterly results, posted in early November 2020. While at one point the company had a big paper profit on its audacious bet, it actually lost $1.3 billion when all was said and done as tech stocks plunged in September. Gamma squeezes are fun but can result in a nasty hangover. SoftBank also lost $12 billion in market value the week after the Nasdaq Whale story broke as its shareholders became uneasy about the transformation of what they thought was a venture capital fund into a high-stakes gambler—and a losing one at that.

For now that detail didn't concern the members of WallStreetBets. This was going to be fun.

Chapter 10

# Holiday Season
# 2020-2021

There were an estimated 26,730 hedge funds in 2020 with about a third of them thought to be active.[1] Even the deepest dive into Greek mythology—once a rich source of fund names—will no longer find a good classical one that hasn't yet been taken. The last twenty-five years have seen firms shift to using the founder's initials, a fierce animal, a significant street, an impregnable bastion, or the combination of a color with a geographic feature. There is even an online hedge fund name generator that will spit one out according to that tried-and-true formula.

Gravitas and understated sophistication are key—Blue Ridge, Tiger, Pershing Square, Citadel, Drawbridge, Eton Park, and of course SAC Capital Advisors, Gabe Plotkin's old employer, founded by the eponymous Steven A. Cohen. Then there was Melvin Capital Management. It attracted a bit of snark in the trade press when Plotkin hung out his own shingle in 2014.

Nobody in the investor community was laughing at the dweeby name six years later, though, as Plotkin racked up consistently impressive returns and became one of the highest-paid people in the world, managing a hefty $13 billion. Many of the other men on the hedge fund "rich list"—and they were all men—were well known to those who followed society headlines for their lavish parties, high-profile philanthropy, and expensive divorces. Some had written books or had been the subject of them. Several would make appearances on CNBC to opine on the direction of markets or would write open letters to companies they were trying to shake up.

Plotkin was by comparison practically invisible, but his numbers spoke for themselves. Cash poured into red-hot Melvin Capital in 2019, and he was invited to speak at the prestigious Sohn Investment Conference in New York that year, a gathering for which attendees pay thousands of dollars to charity to hear fund managers' best investing ideas. Plotkin was so obscure outside his industry that the one photo that ran alongside every article about Melvin's near collapse at the hands of retail traders was one snapped of him speaking at the event.

By the time he came to the attention of the crowd on WallStreetBets in the fall of 2020, though, a Google search brought up a few examples of Plotkin's master-of-the-universe lifestyle for those inclined to resent extreme stock market wealth. In addition to his purchase of part of the Charlotte Hornets the year before, making the sports-loving fund manager a partner of retired superstar Michael Jordan, in November he closed on the $44 million purchase of two adjacent Miami homes where his new neighbors would be Cindy Crawford and much higher-profile hedge fund manager Dan Loeb. Plotkin applied to tear down one of the houses to build tennis courts and a playground for his children. That same month, Melvin Capital's name cropped up in a securities filing that would cost him many times the home's purchase price. The firm had raised its put-option position in GameStop to 5.4 million contracts from 3.4 million a quarter earlier, according to a 13F filing on November 16. Its routine disclosure was made exactly three weeks after the apocalyptic video titled "GME Squeeze and the Demise of Melvin Capital."

Plotkin's analysts aren't paid to spend time on retail message boards full of memes and crude humor—or at least they weren't until one started costing them billions of dollars. They also didn't look for mentions of the firm's name or those of their boss. But the firm's employees did become aware as soon as early November that GameStop was getting a lot more mentions online. What they saw, though, were things such as "I like the stock" rather than any serious analysis or a sign that more people were shopping at its stores. So the pros remained focused on the business itself, which they were convinced had serious problems. Sales and profits—the sorts of things they were trained to study when getting their MBAs and CFAs—didn't look at all good, yet the retailer's price was higher than it had been in years. From the traditional Wall Street way of thinking, they were even more justified than before in selling it short.

For a short while, it seemed like the market was starting to snap out of its temporary insanity. GameStop's share price dropped by 19 percent on December 9 after the company reported tepid third-quarter operating results. Sales had declined by nearly a third compared with a year earlier, the company had shut 11 percent of its stores in the past year, and it had lost $18.8 million. Keith Gill was still a millionaire, but the value of his E*Trade account dropped to $2,251,938 by the end of that day's trading session.

Then Gill got an early Christmas present courtesy of Ryan Cohen. The e-commerce entrepreneur announced on December 21 that he had raised his stake in GameStop from 9.9 percent to 12.9 percent, and he issued a statement in legalese indicating that his patience with the company's management was wearing thin.

"While the Reporting Persons desire to come to an amicable resolution with the Issuer, the Reporting Persons will not hesitate to take any actions that they believe are necessary to protect the best interests of all stockholders," read the official securities filing.

In the preceding ten days or so, Gill had gone from entertaining the possibility of a surge in GameStop shares as a result of extreme short interest to sounding convinced of it, pointing out that the big one still lay ahead. His cerebral arguments about GameStop's business that had attracted a couple of dozen people fell by the wayside, and he began actively pumping out mostly movie-based memes. One on December 10 had a still of the scene where Inigo Montoya speaks with Vizzini in *The Princess Bride*: "Short Squeeze. You keep using that phrase. I do not think it means what you think it means." In other words, the real action was still to come.

On December 21, after Cohen had made his move, there was a still from the scene in *Scarface* where a coked-up Tony Montana, labeled "Ryan Cohen," takes on his opponents with an AR-15 assault rifle and grenade launcher in the final battle. "Say hello to my little friend," he says.

By the end of the next day, Gill's account surged in value, hitting $3.4 million. His legend was growing on the forum. Mentions of GameStop on WallStreetBets jumped, topping eight thousand between December 21 and December 23. At this point, it would have been prudent for Plotkin to at least take some money off the table even without reading what the degenerates were planning. Yes, GameStop was troubled, and not a single analyst had a buy recommendation on it, but some brick-and-mortar retailers had defied the skeptics and turned themselves around. With a proven e-commerce executive agitating for influence and more shares sold short than were available to repurchase, he was taking a huge risk.

For Gill, meanwhile, less was suddenly more as he let his numbers do the talking. He was quickly becoming a legend for the simple fact that he continued to hold on to his shares and play it cool after making seventy times his money. He was asked by another user on December 22, "Seriously, what is your exit strategy?" Gill responded, "What's an exit strategy?"

By mid-January, it was almost too late for Melvin and other firms that had sold the stock short to make their own exit. On January 11, GameStop announced underwhelming holiday sales, which fell by 3.1 percent compared with a year earlier. But that was just noise by this point. The more significant news that day was that the company had reached an agreement with RC Ventures LLC, Ryan Cohen's holding company. The board of directors would expand its rolls from ten to thirteen members and then reduce that to nine when four current members' terms ended later in the year. Then one third of the board would be made up of Cohen and two of his former Chewy colleagues, Jim Grube and Alan Attal, the pet-goods retailer's former chief financial officer and chief marketing officer, respectively.

"Their substantial e-commerce and technology expertise will help us accelerate our transformation plans and fully capture the significant growth opportunities ahead for GameStop," said Kathy Vrabeck, the board chair and one of the members who had agreed to step down.[2]

"We are excited to bring our customer-obsessed mindset and technology experience to GameStop and its strategic assets," said Cohen. "We believe the Company can enhance stockholder value by expanding the ways in which it delights customers and by becoming the ultimate destination for gamers. Alan, Jim and I are committed to working alongside our fellow directors and the management team to continue to transform GameStop. In addition, we intend to bring additional ownership perspectives to the boardroom."

By January 13 the fuse was lit. Keith Gill's net worth surged to $5.79 million that day and $7.37 million the next. This is when Plotkin became aware that he, his firm, and his other holdings were being mentioned on social media. It was also when his fund started to bleed red ink: GameStop shares jumped from $19.95 on January 12 to $31.40 on January 14, their highest price in four and a half years.

It is hard to attribute all of what happened next to the degenerates. Many of the stocks sold short by hedge funds exposed to GameStop, such as Bed Bath & Beyond and BlackBerry, began to act strangely while those stocks that they owned as "longs" did too. When pros smell blood and expect some other fund to be a forced buyer or seller, they don't hesitate to pile on and make a quick profit at the bleeding funds' expense. Unlike the members of WallStreetBets, the people who make the big bucks on actual Wall Street care only about their own net worth. As the fictional Gordon Gekko put it: "If you need a friend, get a dog."

Plotkin at least had the good sense to play his cards close to his vest. When funds that have borrowed stock try to wriggle out of a trade that is going badly, their buying can send a signal to the market and pour gasoline on the fire. Then a short seller appeared on the scene who had made his career by being as loud as possible. His challenge to the WallStreetBets crowd was like trying to smother the fire with dynamite.

Chapter 11

# Poking the Bear

The sporty, handsome New York fund manager was confident in his bet, and the biggest names on Wall Street agreed with him. Many had committed serious money to the same trade. But a brash outsider was convinced he could make a fortune by proving them wrong and used the internet to broadcast his thesis to anyone who would listen. He was patient and eventually proven right, forcing the hedge fund manager into a crushing loss.

This isn't the story of Gabe Plotkin versus Keith Gill—it was Bill Ackman and Andrew Left who duked it out in public over Valeant Pharmaceuticals four years earlier. A professional short seller, Left had identified what he correctly believed were improperly inflated sales at the Canadian company, once a hedge fund darling, made through a related mail-order pharmacy. In March 2017, Ackman finally threw in the towel, by which time Valeant had lost more than 90 percent of its value.

Ackman was the richest opponent Left had taken on, but far from the nastiest. After a report alleging fraud at a Chinese construction company, a Hong Kong tribunal fined Left and banned him from trading local stocks for five years. Another company set up a website solely to deride him and his firm. Executives thrown under Left's harsh spotlight have sued him unsuccessfully for libel and defamation. Left ended one report about a company called MedBox that sold marijuana vending machines with a note to its chief executive officer: "Your first reaction will be to want to sue me. I hope you do!"

The snappily dressed CEO didn't sue, but he went on CNBC to refute the claims. "The people who did this report really didn't do their due diligence. . . . It really has no relevance and no basis in fact." In a separate segment that day, an unshaven Left, his shirt rumpled and partially unbuttoned, came on to support his findings. His slovenly appearance, and just the fact that he was a short seller, sowed some doubts about his research. They shouldn't have. Three years later, MedBox was accused by the SEC of fabricating almost 90 percent of its revenue.[1]

Left, who works out of a home office in his Beverly Hills mansion decorated with memorabilia from infamous failures like Madoff Securities, Lehman Brothers, and Enron, has regularly had his integrity attacked in the media. He says his mother had feared for his physical safety during the Valeant battle. But his targets have largely fared far worse. Left claims that fifty companies he has identified have been targets of regulatory intervention since 2001 when he set up his first research firm. Some executives have faced criminal fraud charges.

Growing up in modest circumstances in Coral Springs, Florida, Left was a serious young man—a debater in high school who at one point wanted to be a rabbi. The argumentative part is easy to see in the fifty-year-old version, as well as the yearning for justice, but it is hard to imagine his leading a congregation given the stream of profanity to which one is subjected in even a casual conversation with him.

Finance wasn't part of his original plans—Left says he never even knew anyone who owned a stock growing up. After attending college in Boston, he needed a job and found one by answering a newspaper ad that said he could earn $100,000 a year. It didn't turn into a career, and he didn't even make much money, but the decision both pointed him to his true calling and gave his future opponents fodder to criticize him. The job turned out to be at a high-pressure boiler room selling retail investors inappropriate commodity investments. Left resigned after just ten months, but when the firm was punished four years later by the National Futures Association, he and every other current and former employee were formally sanctioned.

The charge that Left "made false and misleading statements" to swindle customers has been brought up by his targets ever since. The experience inspired him to seek out stocks being pumped to naïve retail investors and then dumped by boiler rooms in the 1990s, including by Stratton Oakmont, "Wolf of Wall Street" Jordan Belfort's company, and to make profitable bets that the stocks would drop.

After penny stock promotion went into hibernation following the dot-com crash, Left set up his own research firm called Stocklemon, which would later become Citron Research, and he started looking for companies he thought were up to no good. When Left found one, he would bet against it and then let the world know about it through online reports and his contacts with investigative journalists. As his reputation grew, just the fact that he was sniffing around would be enough for an initial drop in a company's share price. He wasn't always right about them in the long run, but he often was. A *Wall Street Journal* analysis of 111 companies on which he wrote reports showed that their share prices fell by an average of 42 percent in the following year.[2]

## Doctor Evil or the Village Idiot?

If short sellers have a bad name, then activist short sellers have an awful one. The criticism is largely undeserved. Investors who have no problem with a parade of fund managers and corporate executives coming on financial news channels such as CNBC to "talk their book," touting stocks they own in their portfolios, are quick to criticize those making a bet in the opposite direction. But most stocks don't make shareholders money, and there are many executives who take short-cuts, legal and occasionally illegal. Moreover, the need to speak up is more urgent for a short seller because sitting back and waiting is expensive, and regulators are slow to move. When a short seller is wrong, the losses can be painful and the mockery harsh.

"I've always joked that short sellers are either Doctor Evil or the village idiot," quips Jim Chanos, the man who exposed Enron.

People like Chanos and Left are something of a dying breed on Wall Street. Hedge funds with a dedicated short-selling approach had seen their assets under management drop from more than $22 billion in 2018 to less than half as much by 2020, according to Eurekahedge. To put that into perspective, hedge funds overall had about $3.8 trillion in assets by the end of that year.

Of course, tallying up funds that do nothing else but bet against stocks vastly understates the general level of short selling. Melvin Capital alone had more than $13 billion under management at the start of the year and, like many hedge funds, was long overall while engaging in the practice. Since stock markets generally rise over time but take occasional sharp tumbles, betting on high-quality stocks and against low-quality ones can simultaneously smooth and enhance a fund's returns. Being short makes it easier to be long—something that individual investors who are glad to see stock prices rise should feel fairly good about. It also helps to expose frauds well before regulators catch on and to hasten the popping of bubbles.

Naturally, investors don't feel good when the stock in question happens to be one in their portfolio. The members of WallStreetBets were already aware of Left and Citron. In late November, he called the perennially loss-making data analysis firm Palantir Technologies "No Longer a Stock but a Full Casino" in a research report.[3] The retail-investor darling lost more than a fifth of its value in just a few days, and the episode enraged many on the subreddit. Around the same time, Left published a skeptical report about the electric-vehicle maker NIO, dubbed "the Chinese Tesla," which by that point was worth as much as larger, more established, and far more profitable automakers.

"Anyone buying NIO stock now is not buying a company or its prospects, rather you are buying 3 letters that move on a screen," he wrote.[4]

Its shares fell by about 8 percent.

Some members of the group started a positively slanderous Change .org petition to have Left investigated by FINRA and the SEC that had more than thirty-seven thousand signatories as of March 2021.

> *Throughout the previous years Citron Research, a dedicated 're-search' company, founded by Andrew Left, a questionable short seller, who has been sued and convicted by regulators as well as governments, has been publishing deliberate yet legal falsehoods made to pass as facts in order manipulate stock prices for own gains.[5]*

Unlike Valeant or the penny stocks he targeted earlier in his career, Left wasn't alleging fraud in the case of Palantir or NIO—just extreme overvaluation. But after scoring two quick wins against retail favorites, Left miscalculated badly by targeting GameStop.

## Suckers at This Poker Game

On January 19, when GameStop's price went as high as $45 a share, Left tweeted from his company's account:

> Tomorrow am at 11:30 EST Citron will livestream the 5 reasons GameStop $GME buyers at these levels are the suckers at this poker game. Stock back to $20 fast. We understand short interest better than you and will explain.[6]

It was one thing to have a bunch of anonymous hedge funds other than Melvin, which had been silent, on the other side of the trade. It was another to have a brash, dedicated short seller, who had already raised the hackles of some on the subreddit, challenge them so brazenly. The response was electric.

"WSB vs Citron, the battle we've been waiting for. Lets [*sic*] turn that lemon into lemonade," wrote one poster in response to Left's announcement. Another said that WallStreetBets could remain irrational longer than "Citron et al" could remain solvent.

> Shitron thought they could spook boomers into panic selling, not realizing that the majority of $GME shares are owned by people who despise them. They're literally fueling the fire burning their money with tweets like this.[7]

> Yup. I really don't care about melvin. Shitron got me with NIO and its payback time.[8]

> Melvin is small fodder. Citron is the one we want to fuck badly.[9]

And there were less polite responses—hundreds of them. Left had kicked over a hornet's nest.

A poker game was an apt analogy—just not in the way Left assumed. The WallStreetBets crowd didn't seem to him like it held a great hand given GameStop's already-stretched value, but the adaptation of the old line about markets staying irrational longer than you can remain solvent rang true. GameStop's boosters on WallStreetBets were playing like a drunk, fearless tourist in Vegas with a huge stack of chips. Left, Plotkin, and anyone else with a short position was bullied into folding.

## Call Off the Mob

Those are the breaks. Disturbingly, though, Left was bullied in other ways too. Wall Street isn't a warm and cuddly place, but he and his family suddenly faced a wave of virtual and real harassment unlike any he had seen from his targets over the years, some of whom had been actual criminals. He says that he and his children received menacing texts, his social media accounts were hacked, he was bombarded with phone calls, he was signed up for a fake Tinder profile, and strangers showed up at his home. He says he had faced pressure before in his career but nothing of this sort. And he had never resorted to such tactics either.

"Maybe because I don't use Reddit and I have respect for people," he says.

Left had always thought of himself as an outsider on Wall Street and was shocked to be portrayed as "the man" to the online crowd. He was forced to delay his planned video on GameStop owing to hacking of his account. He called Jaime Rogozinski, the founder of WallStreetBets, to ask for his help in calling off the mob and said that he also contacted the FBI about anonymous threats. A few days later, he posted a video on YouTube that sought to extend an olive branch to the Wall-StreetBets crowd and to point out that he had been in the game since many of them were children.

> *Before there was Reddit, before there was memes, before there was Instagram, and, yes, before there was Facebook, there was Citron Research.*[10]

The vitriol seemed to intensify after GameStop's share price soared, and Left had made clear that he exited the trade "at a 100 percent loss." To Peter Atwater, the expert on social mood, the group's desire to rub it in wasn't surprising.

"At major peaks in sentiment, we become vengeful—it's that sense of invincibility we get," he says. "Making money isn't enough. We need our opponents' heads on a stick. There's a *Lord of the Flies* quality when you think you're invincible."

Plenty of mockery was aimed at Plotkin too—particularly the fact that he had named his fund Melvin. One poster imagined an office intern giving him a report about WallStreetBets:

> *Sir, it appears that they are buying whenever the price falls, and when the price rises they buy as well. They are making fun of us and do not care if they lose money. They are collectively encouraging each other to "never sell" and "diamond hands", a term used for people who hold onto positions strongly.*[11]

Melvin's losses on GameStop and other short positions would be the largest of any fund in dollar terms during January's meme-stock squeeze. Left, whose fund was far smaller but more concentrated, was coy when asked how much he had wagered on GameStop.

"You know, it's never enough when you were right and always too much when you were wrong."

## "We've Actually Become the Establishment"

He had lost big before and at least one of his previous losing short bets felt personal. Left sold short shares of Tesla and even sued the company and its founder Elon Musk in 2018, accusing him of violating securities laws. His suit cited Musk's tweet in which he falsely claimed that he had secured funding to take the carmaker public.

Left's first wife moved in soon after with a man who had made more than $2 billion through an early investment in Tesla. Left was paying over $30,000 a month in support to his ex-wife even after the new couple had a lavish Palm Springs wedding. He attempted to stop the payments now that she had remarried, but she successfully argued in court that it was only a commitment ceremony.

"Tesla investors find more than one way to stick it to short-sellers," quipped Left to the *New York Post*.[12]

In the case of GameStop, Left cut bait quickly. He was surprised by the number of traders who piled into the meme-stock squeeze.

"Bring a five-year-old to my office and I can beat them. Bring a thousand five-year-olds to my office and I'm in trouble," he says.

It seemed it was more due to the shock of the pressure tactics than a financial loss when, days later, Left announced in another YouTube video that he would cease the business of publishing short reports permanently.

"Twenty years ago I started Citron with the intention of protecting the individual against Wall Street, against the frauds and the stock promotions . . . [but] we've actually become the establishment."[13]

## Muzzling Critics

However one feels about Left personally, the development should be unnerving to anyone interested in market transparency. Some observers like Alexis Ohanian, Reddit's cofounder, compared the group of traders who sent meme stocks surging and fund managers scurrying to the Occupy Wall Street movement. For anyone cast as a villain, it seemed to have more in common with the board's own description: "Like 4chan found a Bloomberg terminal." The imageboard 4chan is known for what might be the most infamous episode of senseless online harassment, Gamergate, in which many figures, starting with female video game developers, received an endless stream of menacing, misogynistic messages.

Seeing a thick-skinned, veteran trader who had faced so many threats chased out of the business at what was already an ebb tide for his profession was unnerving. It is one thing for short sellers to find themselves on the wrong side of the market for an extended period—that had happened before. The additional element of feeling unsafe was new and had the potential to distort the market.

Short selling is a tough, often unpleasant business, but a useful one for the rest of us who, even if we are just passive index-fund investors, lose some money when the Enrons and Valeants of the world grow large and respectable enough to make it indirectly into our retirement portfolios. Companies don't even have to be frauds to cost passive investors money: GameStop and its fellow meme stock AMC became the most valuable companies in the widely held Russell 2000 Value Index fund for a number of days. Investors who bought the conservative fund for their portfolios unwittingly overpaid for it.

Potentially subjecting yourself to the vitriol of an online mob might prove too much for the next Andrew Left or Jim Chanos. And proposed rule changes seeking greater transparency could make short selling even tougher. For example, WeLikeTheStock, a political Super PAC headed by the retail investor Chad Minnis to support the agenda of WallStreetBets, would support proposals to make hedge funds reveal their specific shorts, which would make targeting them for squeezes easier in the future. Funds that own a lot of shares in a company are required to show their hand, but that is because they can exert voting influence—something a short seller can't do.

"It is like watching the police doing a bank raid," said the hedge fund manager Crispin Odey in an interview with *Bloomberg.* "There were already fewer short positions in the market before the Reddit mob began their attack than we have seen for 15 years."[14]

Left, meanwhile, unwisely put a target on his own back and challenged WallStreetBets because that had been his formula for success in the past. For someone who followed Left's career and had spoken with him personally, his conciliatory tone on the video in which he announced he was leaving the business seemed unnaturally even-tempered. He was clearly still spooked by the experience. In a phone conversation days later, when asked what he thought about Keith Gill and the following he had inspired, Left sounded more like his old self.

"Boo-boo Kitty or whoever—fuck him, I don't give a shit."

# Chapter 12

# January 22, 2021

When did the meme-stock squeeze happen? Most people would say during the week of January 25, when GameStop went from being a place they might have walked past in the mall or taken their kids to buy the latest edition of *Madden* to a symbol of a shocking uprising against the financial elite and front-page news. The press search service Factiva shows an incredible 12,700 mentions of the company that week and 10,800 the week after in English-language publications. Similarly, Google search trends show that GameStop, WallStreetBets, and the movie-theater chain AMC, another meme stock, came out of nowhere to become three of the most searched terms in the United States that week.

The pieces, as we have seen, fell into place well before then, and the process was probably unstoppable by the second week of January. Yet a perusal of the weeks before indicates virtually no media coverage even as the squeeze was building. Up until the January 11 board appointment of Ryan Cohen and his two old associates from Chewy, there was a single mention of the company that wasn't about how to find a sought-after PlayStation 5 console or some video game—an item in *Barron's* titled GAMESTOP STOCK HAS SOARED DESPITE FALLING SALES: REALITY COULD EVENTUALLY CATCH UP. It quoted Benchmark Company analyst Mike Hickey.

"We're not seeing anything to get excited about," he said. "They're missing numbers, not beating numbers."[1]

Hickey had a $5.00 a share price target on GameStop shares at the time, and an analyst at Credit Suisse had a target of just $3.50 a share.

Anthony Chukumba, who had followed GameStop for years, spending hundreds of hours poring over its finances, visiting stores, and listening to conference calls, went one step further—he dropped coverage of the stock entirely. The Loop Capital analyst was convinced the company was headed for bankruptcy, even with Ryan Cohen shaking things up. Chukumba based his decision on the health of its business, though, while the revolutionaries were paying attention to short-term supply and demand for the retailer's shares. For a while that would be the only thing that mattered.

In the two trading sessions following Cohen's appointment to the board, the stock doubled. The trap had been sprung. On January 13, the first media mention of a squeeze that could overwhelm short sellers was by the CNBC host and former hedge fund manager Jim Cramer in an interview on *TheStreet*, the investing site he founded. Cramer read a note sent to him from a fan that laid out the planned squeeze and mentioned Melvin Capital by name. His takeaway: "It's game over for the shorts, theoretically." Cramer went on to say that "non-analysts" were behind the rise of stocks like GameStop and that Wall Street analysts had to catch up.[2]

The next day saw the first article tying the gains to the subreddit, written by the *Wall Street Journal* markets reporter Caitlin McCabe, who had been following the forum.

"For weeks, members of Reddit's popular WallStreetBets forum have been touting GameStop, encouraging others to scoop up shares of the videogame retailer and begin making bullish wagers," she wrote. "Several posts on the forum had noted that short sellers' bearish GameStop bets had been at elevated levels."[3]

The article didn't even make it into the list of the top-ten most read Money and Investing section stories for the week, much less those most read paper-wide. By contrast, during the height of news coverage about the meme-stock squeeze, nearly every top article had to do with GameStop, Keith Gill, or Gabe Plotkin. The *Journal*'s exclusive interview with Gill was the most read article overall.

But GameStop was already becoming the only thing that mattered for those on WallStreetBets or in certain corners of the hedge fund world. On January 13, the turnover in its shares was double the number outstanding, and the next day there were 16,517 mentions of GameStop on the subreddit. By that day, the stock was worth more than ten times what it had been the previous spring. All the ingredients for the epic short squeeze had fallen into place bar one: Andrew Left would make his ill-advised taunt five days later, on January 19.

Left wasn't just lighting his own money on fire by making that public challenge—he was pouring kerosene on a far larger stack owned by others like Plotkin. Up to that point, funds such as Melvin Capital that had built up those huge short positions in GameStop and the other meme stocks didn't advertise the fact because they weren't the type of fund that was looking to find the next Enron. They did it as a bet on the best and worst of a breed, seeing GameStop as a clear example of the latter. According to finance textbooks, there are some ways to have your cake and eat it too by getting more return for the same amount of market risk. Retail and consumer stocks, Plotkin's specialty, have something in common with one another, and so they rise and fall on some of the same economic trends. A recession or a delayed launch of the next version of the Xbox would mean trouble for, say,

Best Buy, a recently successful electronics retailer where you could buy video games, but even more trouble for GameStop. Owning one and shorting the other would smooth out the bad times and enhance the good ones for Melvin.

That was the theory at least. Sometimes hedge funds are wrong, and floundering companies turn things around or attract bargain hunters. But the funds certainly don't expect those stocks to jump by 3,500 percent in a month after posting lousy results. Those sorts of gains might be expected by a company that had just cured cancer.

Plotkin and other hedge fund managers who were short the stock certainly were aware by January 19 that something was seriously amiss. They were like holidaymakers at a fancy chalet in the Alps—still enjoying a lavish meal in exclusive surroundings. They could hear the distant rumble of an avalanche, but there wasn't enough room for everyone to fit into the Range Rover parked outside and escape.

"These guys are sitting there thinking 'I've got to get out, but in a stealthy way that's not going to cause a run,'" says Ihor Dusaniwsky, managing director of the short-selling analysis firm S3 Partners.

Left's challenge to the degenerates was the equivalent of shooting off a cannon to hasten the disaster and bring down a few more tons of rock and ice from the massif. The masters of the universe were already going to take a big hit. Now some were about to get buried.

Gill, in his Roaring Kitty persona, was sitting in the basement of his rented three-bedroom home toasting his new benefactor with one of his favorite Belgian beers, Delirium Tremens, named for the shaking and confusion heavy drinkers experience when trying to sober up.

*Cheers to Ryan Cohen. This is sick—this is hilarious.*[4]

Even as WallStreetBets members were planning on inflicting pain on Left and Plotkin in the thousands of replies to Gill's latest screenshot of his E*Trade balance that afternoon, the man himself didn't offer any forecast of how long or how far the short squeeze that was making him rich would go:

> *This is above my pay grade, as I hope most people know by now.*[5]

The aw-shucks attitude and his new practice of only posting account screenshots without commentary probably enhanced Gill's influence, but there was likely another, more practical reason: he was still registered as a broker by his employer, MassMutual, and technically subject to fines and sanctions by FINRA for recommending risky or inappropriate investments. He didn't actually have clients as a financial wellness specialist, but now millions of small investors were starting to make bets, many using borrowed money or derivatives, to push up a stock that would enrich him. Between January 11 and January 14, Gill's net worth jumped from $3.16 million to $7.37 million. Then it leapt again at the end of the following week. January 19 brought the first media mention of DeepFuckingValue in *Motherboard*—one of the few outlets not too prudish to display the Reddit username without an asterisk or two to avoid printing profanity. It would still be more than a week before the pseudonym was connected to Gill.

> *So, essentially, people on WallStreetBets along with several You-Tube and TikTok investors guessed as long as a year ago that if they bought shares of GameStop at a low price, the short sellers would eventually be forced to cover their short en masse, which would drive the price up. Most notable among these is a user named DeepFuckingValue, who posted screenshots of them buying more than $50,000 worth of GameStop stock when it was valued at less than a dollar in 2019.*[6]

The article got many details wrong, confusing the timeline and mixing up options with shares, but it kicked off a wave of fascination with the mystery investor.

On January 22, the Friday before the meme-stock squeeze went from an obscure concern of market junkies to front-page news, WallStreetBets members could smell blood, and they were employing their potent new weapon, the gamma squeeze, to full effect. A call option expiring that very day with an exercise price of $60.00 was the most actively traded contract of the trading session. The insanely speculative bet paid off as GameStop shares went as low as $42.32 and as high as $76.76 during the day, closing at $65.01.

Volatility is part of an option's price, so those gyrations made any unexpired options contracts like those held by Gill more valuable, but it also made it more expensive to enter into or maintain a short position. By January 19, the day Left issued his challenge, the borrowing rate for GameStop shares was a steep 24 percent per year, according to Dusaniwsky. For the vast majority of American stocks, it was 0.3 percent. That reflected how dangerously crowded the ill-fated short trade had become.

This was no longer just a plaything of small-money speculators: one of the most read stories that Friday in *The Wall Street Journal* was about sharp losses at Melvin Capital, which an anonymous source said was by then down by 15 percent for the year. A group of fifty stocks monitored by Goldman Sachs with the heaviest short interest was up by a whopping 25 percent for the year—ten times as much as the stock market overall.

The effect was now spreading into the group of corporate hasbeens that would collectively be known as the "meme stocks." The value of the nearly bankrupt movie-theater chain AMC would rise tenfold. The stock price of the once-hot intimate apparel company Naked Brand rose by 750 percent and the stereo headphone maker Koss by 2,100 percent, seemingly out of nowhere.

Another blast from the past was BlackBerry, the Canadian smart-phone pioneer that was to Apple with its iPhone what Blockbuster had been to Netflix and, as many believed, what GameStop was becoming to increasingly digitized video game publishers—headed for irrelevance.

BlackBerry's shares had doubled since the fourteenth and had more gains ahead of it on no company-specific news. The troubled retailer Bed Bath & Beyond, a victim of Amazon's success and also heavily shorted by hedge funds, would see its price triple at its peak. Bizarrely, the Blockbuster analogy even spilled over into the penny stock that represented the company disposing of the assets of the once-ubiquitous and now bankrupt video-store chain, BB Liquidating Inc. It doubled on June 22 and, on a gigantic wave of buying and selling, would rally by more than 3,000 percent by the following Tuesday . . . to two tenths of a cent.

Clearly there had already been a good deal of angst in the hedge fund world in the week since GameStop shares had doubled in value on Ryan Cohen's board announcement. Short interest is only officially reported with a lag, but it is possible to estimate how much activity there is on any given day. Figures from S3 Partners show that short interest in GameStop went from 135 percent of the stock's available shares before the announcement to 120 percent when Left made his challenge a week later to just 87 percent at the end of the trading day on January 22. There had been a rush for the exit, but that was still way too high—the avalanche was about to hit.

The bad news for Plotkin and the other short sellers was a huge boost to Gill. His net worth jumped to eight figures. He was now a member of the 1 percent and about to become a hero of the other 99 percent. Enjoying his last few days of anonymity as DeepFucking-Value and Roaring Kitty, Gill had cemented his status as a hero on WallStreetBets.

"I've never been this glad about someone else making money," wrote one poster.

Another lamented not taking advantage of the opportunity. Game-Stop's shares ended the day above $65. They had closed below $4 a share just a year earlier.

"There are PLENTY of these opportunities to come in the future, just pay attention, be patient and be even more retarded," wrote another.

"Exactly! Like next week's big opportunity: GME," responded another poster, using GameStop's ticker symbol.

He had no idea how right he was.

Chapter 13

# Rise of the Apes

Who said trickle-down economics is dead? Two months after the meme-stock squeeze, the Dian Fossey Gorilla Fund received news that a member of the WallStreet-Bets subreddit had symbolically adopted a baby gorilla, Urungano. In the next six days, there was a torrent of thirty-five hundred further adoptions from the group raising $377,000.

"It's safe to say that the investor community on Reddit is not traditionally who we think of as our supporter base. But they definitely surprised and overwhelmed us over the weekend," wrote the organization on Twitter.

Clearly the herdlike behavior of a social network can be a force for good. Some of the donations that made their way to the rain forests of central Africa probably represented the flip side of the losses suffered in January by the investors in Melvin Capital and other hedge funds. An emerging call to arms, "apes together strong," from the 2011 film

*Rise of the Planet of the Apes*, was a play on one of the subreddit's nick-
names for fellow members that started around the time of the meme-
stock squeeze—a reference to powerful but not very bright animals
that could do great things if united. But it wasn't to everyone's liking.

"If you're new here, 'apes together strong' was never a thing until
the last couple weeks," read a post titled "Stop with the ape crap"
from That_Guy_KC. "It showed up with all the new people (bots?).
Before then, we called people retards, not as a sign of strength in numbers, but to make fun of people that think they understand the market
and get burned."[1]

Another user, BinotheBullish, agreed, saying the nonsense started
when the group hit three million members.

According to their profiles, the two old-timers had joined Reddit in
August 2019 and November 2020, respectively.

WallStreetBets had 650,000 members when Keith Gill posted the
first screenshot of his E*Trade account statement in September 2019,
1.6 million members in October 2020 when the video about "the demise of Melvin Capital" was posted, and about 1.9 million when Andrew Left taunted members of the subreddit. And then it really took
off: by the end of the following week, when *The Wall Street Journal*
published the first interview with Gill, there were more than 6 million members. The group's rolls would top 9 million by the end of February.

WallStreetBets might be the only subreddit you've heard of, but it
was very much in Reddit's minor leagues when DeepFuckingValue
first appeared, ranked the 373rd most popular forum by number of
subscribers. It was fairly active for its size, though. In terms of average number of daily comments, it was in seventy-third place that year,
jumping to tenth in 2020 as retail trading exploded in popularity, and
first place every day between January 24 and February 4, 2021, the
heart of meme-stock mania.[2]

Popularity is a double-edged sword, though, and not just for those who yearned for the good old days when everyone on the board was just a retard or degenerate. The rush of new members coincided with an almost single-minded focus on the meme stocks and efforts to harness the power of millions of people throwing their cash around. As soon as the GameStop rally began to fizzle, users—some suspected that they were "bots," accounts made to look genuine and used to engineer an outcome—latched on to new objects of speculation such as silver, briefly overwhelming the market for the precious metal.

The attention and the distractions would prove too much for WallStreetBets. Open conflict would break out between the moderators amid talk of movie deals, and Reddit was forced to step in and ban some who attempted to stage a takeover and lock others out. A few months later, there were a number of splinter forums more directly focused on continuing the cause of the meme-stock squeeze such as r/GME, r/AMC, and r/superstonk, each with between three hundred thousand and four hundred thousand members.[3]

But that would come later. For a brief while, the subreddit's ranks were swelling by up to a million people a day, some joining out of curiosity but many others because they wanted to be part of history, participating in the "revolution" in a small way by opening a brokerage account and buying a few shares or call options. A crowd can make a political candidate successful, a song or movie a hit, or a video or tweet viral. A lot of people who each have just a little bit of money can make a stock rise too—especially at a time when so many traders take their cues from social media and check their account frequently on a device that never leaves their side.

## Goliath versus Goliath

Until the meme-stock squeeze, though, their fellow investors had never pinpointed the precise way to push up the most sensitive stocks at the exact right time. They had also never done it to make a state-ment by sticking it to the man.

That is why the GameStop saga amazed people who had spent their careers working on or writing about Wall Street. In a business where you are constantly reminded that "this time is never different," here was something completely different—brokerage accounts as a tool of class warfare. Jaime Rogozinski, the founder of WallStreetBets, who split with the forum's other moderators in the spring of 2020, insists this was never part of the board's ethos. Yet the group's ranks were growing so quickly that its character, not to mention the wider social mood amid all the excitement over what was being billed as a revolu-tion, was bound to evolve.

At least according to what they said and wrote, making a profit seemed to be a secondary concern of many of the millions of new mem-bers who opened brokerage accounts and bought a handful of shares after hearing about GameStop, stoking the craziness when the squeeze hit the headlines. A meme appropriated by members of the forum was a clip from the late Heath Ledger's portrayal of the Joker in *The Dark Knight* lighting a huge pile of cash on fire in front of astonished fellow criminals. "It's not about the money—it's about sending a message."

The message was that the playing field had been leveled. It both had and hadn't. For Wall Street writ large, the meme-stock squeeze was a profit bonanza. And while some amateur speculators would earn fortunes, some always do when markets are tumultuous. As a group, though, small retail traders' hyperactivity was costing them. But for those professionals who found themselves on the other side of the trade from a crowd of loosely organized, highly motivated individ-uals, the meme-stock squeeze was a wake-up call that would force them to change how they did business.

A million people with $1,000 of buying power each, either in cash or through margin borrowing or call options, have as much heft as a hedge fund with $1 billion. And by acting in a coordinated manner, the apes weren't just strong—they literally could play by different rules. Since the passage of modern securities laws in the 1930s, it has been illegal to collude and buy up a stock to manipulate its price—for example, to engineer a short squeeze. If it became known that three hedge fund managers had agreed behind closed doors to target a fourth fund with a big short position, then they would soon be getting a visit from the SEC. But a million traders doing so out in the open wasn't necessarily illegal, and in any case was something the SEC couldn't possibly go after. WallStreetBets, dubbed "the world's first decentralized hedge fund," enjoyed unique freedom of action.

Individuals in general also were now a much larger force on the market than just a year or two earlier. An analysis of nine thousand US stocks and exchange-traded funds by VandaTrack shows that average net retail purchases of stocks were around $135 million a day in the six months before Schwab, TD Ameritrade, and other brokers matched Robinhood in charging zero commissions in October 2019. During 2020 that jumped to $942 million. And at the height of the meme-stock squeeze, retail investors' net purchases were nearly $1.6 billion a day—about as much as those by all mutual funds and hedge funds combined. This was Goliath versus Goliath.

## The Trap Wasn't Airtight

The apes' view was dangerously naïve in two important ways, though. They really did intimidate hedge funds by trading like big, dumb, enraged animals who had learned social cohesion, but they imagined that a cabal on Wall Street was actively trying to thwart them. Hedge funds don't care about who else makes or loses money. On the other hand, they care very much about limiting their own losses and jumping on anomalies.

The apes didn't appreciate that new funds were filling the vacuum left by those forced to bow out. The first group of funds took their lumps and escaped because the trap wasn't nearly as airtight as people on the forum imagined. The reason that short interest remained somewhat high is that a new batch of professional opportunists couldn't resist taking their chances betting against the meme stocks for an entirely different reason than Gabe Plotkin had—they were expecting the air to come out of the bubble.

As we will see, the new group of short sellers also underestimated the power of the movement and was blindsided by some unexpected developments. But they were early, not wrong—apes could get greedy too. Many retail investors sold the meme stocks during their rise rather than *HODL-ing*, a verb drawn from the cryptocurrency world that originated from a typo. It means to hold on for dear life. And some who did hold on past the peak expressed regret at fortunes that got away rather than satisfaction at having stayed true to a cause. A separate subreddit was started at the tail end of the meme-stock squeeze, r/GMEbagholders, where Redditors commiserated about their losses on the meme stocks.

It was unrealistic to expect so many apes to "hold the line" that short sellers would be forced to pay any price and incur infinite losses. As prices of the meme stocks climbed higher, the refusal on principle of many retail traders to sell weakened. That wasn't part of the romantic narrative, but it is the natural thing to do when you have made the equivalent of several years of your salary in less time than it takes the milk in your fridge to expire.

"If I'm having a hard time meeting rent and all of a sudden there's 400 grand in my account, it's hard not to sell," says a Wall Street veteran who saw plenty of retail investors head for the exits during the height of the squeeze.

The exodus was happening even as media coverage marveled at the group's solidarity. Citadel Securities, which processed by far the largest number of retail trades during the squeeze, later said that the only day of the week that it saw retail investors buy more shares of GameStop than they sold was Monday, January 25, when they purchased a net $2.06 billion. On Tuesday they sold $1.91 billion and on Wednesday $776 million. Retail investors were net sellers of smaller sums on Thursday and Friday too, though that was after the trading restrictions were enacted by Robinhood and others.[4]

There is a buyer for every seller, so who bought? One group included hedge funds covering their short sales, repurchasing stock they had sold without owning. Another was options dealers mechanically buying shares as a gamma squeeze unfolded that they would soon dump as the contracts expired.

And, of course, despite diamond hands turning to paper hands, a great many apes did buy and happily hold on to shares of GameStop in order to be part of something. It might have been the first stock many of them ever owned. As one often sees in religious groups, the most recent converts are especially enthusiastic. The chorus on the subreddit every time Gill posted another screenshot of his E*Trade account:

*IF HE'S STILL IN, I'M STILL IN!*

## Social Proof

Reddit is different from social networks centered on personalities and followers. It is possible for a relatively new user to post something that captures the attention of a forum and gets enough upvotes to move to the top. Nevertheless, there are things about your identity, which is a pseudonym with an avatar rather than your real name and a photo, as one might see on Twitter or Facebook, that give you a head start. One is "karma."

DeepFuckingValue hadn't been on Reddit long enough to be a member of the social network's aristocracy in terms of conventional karma gained through years of post engagement, but he was showered with gifts by other members of the forum. These gifts—donations to Reddit to pay for server time—can be given to admired members. As of April 2021, DeepFuckingValue had an impressive three million karma and a collection of badges that made the space above his posts resemble the chest of a North Korean general. Among them were the Blow Award, depicting a pile of cocaine, which gives both the recipient and the board one thousand coins, and the Ternion All Powerful Award, the most expensive gift one can give on Reddit at $125.

He gained influence through the sheer fact that he held on through many ups and downs and made a tremendous amount of money but also because his online behavior, such as clever use of memes, made him relatable to fellow millennials. The more Gill made, the less he wrote, yet the more influential he became.

"He stopped commenting after a while and just used GIFs," says Quinn Mulligan, half of the filmmaking duo behind a planned documentary about the Reddit traders, *Apes Together Strong.* "He was funny. But he was just so bullheaded and seems like such a genuine person, which is rare."[5]

The resulting enthusiasm was complemented by many other users' posting about their gains on GameStop as it climbed. The parade of gaudy numbers had the same effect as late-night infomercials about get-rich-quick schemes that show testimonials by ordinary people in the same demographic as the gullible insomniacs. The people are relatable, yet they claim to have finally paid off all their bills and quit their jobs after ordering the DVDs and following the easy instructions. The concept is called "social proof."

Rachael Cihlar, an influencer marketing expert at Mavrck, which specializes in the field, wrote that, despite a lack of trust in institutions such as governments, the news media, and, in the case of our investments, financial experts, faith in our peers remains high.

*As our trust in institutions like Wall Street and hedge funds (that have gotten us into trouble before) continues to decline, the power of the people has taken over on social media, or in this case on a specific subreddit. One person perhaps didn't have the power to change the market, but when thousands and even millions came together to purchase GameStop stock, they influenced the masses and that trust and influence moved markets. Consumers saw retail investors making meaningful returns on their investments, so they joined the throngs.[6]*

An annual survey by the public relations firm Edelman showed that the country's "Trust Index" was near the lowest in the survey's history in 2020. For example, only 36 percent of respondents called a journalist very or extremely credible while 53 percent said the same about "a person like yourself." A viral *New Yorker* cartoon captured and mocked the zeitgeist in early 2017. A passenger stands up in his seat on an airplane, asking for and receiving a show of hands: "These smug pilots have lost touch with regular passengers like us. Who thinks I should fly the plane?"

Especially for a generation whose formative years included the global financial crisis, Wall Street's advice had a credibility problem. These were the people who had told them or their parents that "subprime is contained," that bitcoin was too speculative, and that they should be happy making 8 percent a year in mutual funds.

Peers and wealthy influencers from outside the traditional financial sphere, such as Silicon Valley executives Elon Musk and Chamath Palihapitiya, are seen as far more reliable than the man with a nice suit in a brokerage commercial. Millennials and members of Generation Z, who tend to shun stuffy experts, are often more likely to trust strangers who use a pseudonym online—even if it is DeepFuckingValue. After all, he had made a truly epic return by just hanging on. It was a textbook case of social proof in action. To WallStreetBets founder Rogozinski, though, it was corrosive.

"The fact that this Roaring Kitty, Keith Gill, made so much money, is something that makes me uneasy, because his success is much more dangerous than a tweet from Elon Musk," he says. "People will see that success and see the dollar signs and follow him and they're much more likely to coattail him and are more likely to buy at the top following him than by listening to Chamath's podcast."

Rogozinski sees a bright side to the specific culture of the forum he founded: losing a lot of money and sharing it—what is called "loss porn" in the community—is embraced too.

"They're able to vicariously pass this experience on," he says. "That's one thing that makes WallStreetBets really a great place, is that honesty. That's why they share losses—not that they celebrate them, but just to embrace the reality of what it is."

The members of the forum were forty-eight hours away from some ultra-graphic loss porn, but first came the most exuberant trading days ever.

# Chapter 14

# January 26, 2021

f a stock you own has gone up by 18 percent in a year, then you've done very well, earning about twice the market's long-run annual return. If it has risen that much in a month or a week, you should be ecstatic. But GameStop shareholders were suddenly full of doubt after the retailer's value was that much higher after a single session on Monday, January 25. The reason: the stock surged out of the gate in morning trading, more than doubling, but it gave up all those gains by lunchtime. Then it clawed back what seemed like a modest victory.

WallStreetBets was full of braggadocio and regret about paper fortunes made and lost that evening. One user who saw $50,000 come and go claimed he needed the money for knee and back surgery but that he couldn't live with himself for selling and letting Wall Street off the hook. He wanted to wait until he made $1 million so he could buy his mother a house "after these fuckers stole ours in 2008."

Another claimed to have hit $80,000 in profit that morning. Others threw out even higher numbers like $600,000 or $800,000. The sums were certainly plausible for those who had purchased the sorts of options contracts recommended on the board that would exert maximum pressure on hedge funds. Sprinkled among these messages were exhortations to hold until GameStop shares hit $1,000 or more—otherwise Andrew Left and Gabe Plotkin would slip out of the trap.

*NOW. Is the time where we can hit them where it hurts. We need more buys after hours today, pre market tomorrow and every single fucking dip that comes up tomorrow. We have the power right now and we will not lose it. Participate and be rich, or watch us patiently.[1]*

As he raced to exit his disastrous short bets from his home office in Florida—his Midtown Manhattan one still closed because of the pandemic—Gabe Plotkin got on the phone with his old boss Steven Cohen and with Citadel's Ken Griffin on the morning of the twenty-fifth. Within hours he had personally negotiated the terms of a big infusion of cash from the two billionaires' hedge funds. Instead of an ordinary investment, their firms got what are called "nonvoting revenue" shares that would give them even more of a benefit if Plotkin regained his magic touch. Cohen, already a big investor in Melvin, was having a rotten week too. Griffin, who also owned most of the company that was processing billions of trades a day powering the meme-stock squeeze, was having a much better one.

Like two businessmen reaching for the check after a business lunch, Griffin was feeling flush and ponied up most of the money, some $2 billion, while Cohen chipped in $750 million.

Although Plotkin later insisted that it wasn't a bailout, the money would help stabilize what was a ruinous fire sale at Melvin Capital. The fund would lose more than half of its value, in excess of $6 billion, with most of that loss coming by Tuesday.

One person who took some money off the table with almost perfect timing on January 25 was Keith Gill, the still-anonymous inspiration for the degenerates pushing the meme stocks higher. According to the screenshot of his E*Trade statement posted at the end of the day, he sold two hundred of his one thousand April call options near the peak, banking $2.2 million in cash. He had paid just forty cents a contract, or a total of $8,000 for them. The following day he sold three hundred more contracts for a cool $9 million. The other members of the forum may have insisted that they would hang on until GameStop went "TO THE MOON," but Gill was prudently guaranteeing that, in the worst-case scenario, he would walk away a very wealthy man. Nobody on the board who had made the short squeeze a mission rather than a moneymaking opportunity seemed to fault him—nor should they have. Even after Tuesday's session, Gill still had $18 million at risk.

By the afternoon of the twenty-fifth, the GameStop story began to show up in mainstream news publications. Mentions of the retailer on WallStreetBets surged again from sixteen thousand on Friday, the twenty-second, to twenty-eight thousand that Monday, and more than fifty thousand on Tuesday, the twenty-sixth of January. The subreddit was now number one in terms of traffic on the social media site—a status it wouldn't relinquish until the following week.

On January 26, an even bigger wave of buying took GameStop shares to $150, and this time the momentum didn't falter. The stock ended the session $147.98—more than twice its highest-ever close prior to the meme-stock squeeze. It had fetched less than $3.00 at one point the previous spring. A peeved Anthony Chukumba, the analyst who had dropped coverage of GameStop weeks earlier, says he was bombarded with calls from clients asking about the company he thought was worthless.

"I didn't go to Harvard Business School for this shit."[2]

GameStop had two other distinctions that day—it was the most traded stock on the planet, and it had created its first billionaire. No, not Gill—though he was doing just fine with a net worth of nearly $23 million at the close of trading. Ryan Cohen, who had bet big on the retailer the previous summer and played a pivotal role in bringing the stock, and by extension Gill, to WallStreetBets' attention, was a member of the ten-figure club.

Millennials who wanted to be part of history weren't the only ones watching the site and starting to put money to work. Plenty of people on Wall Street who had never given much thought to the retailer were taking an interest, and they were overwhelmingly skeptical. More than one market veteran admitted that they joined the forum during the week as observers. What they saw gave them reason to suspect the top was very close. The rebels had identified some weak hands and ambushed them.

"But after $100, that's when it became a morality play," says the veteran short seller Jim Chanos.

Even as Plotkin, Left, and other short sellers were covering their positions—both would be out of the trade by Tuesday—others were entering the fray by selling the stock short or buying put contracts. They had the right idea, because when breathless rallies in smaller companies lose momentum, they do so violently. Monday's 50 percent drop in the retailer's shares in a couple of hours looked like a preview of an even larger collapse. Jordan Belfort, the "Wolf of Wall Street," who took part in many stock manipulations in the bad old days, says he was expecting the same thing.

"I didn't think it was possible that individual investors could get enough buying power together and stay in something long enough without deserting it as it went up . . . because it's very difficult, and I know that market really well."[3]

But sometimes funny things happen in markets. While GameStop was finally in danger of losing momentum, with even its biggest "diamond hands" booster DeepFuckingValue dumping half of his stake, perhaps the most influential person in the world as far as young investors were concerned was about to weigh in on the situation and breathe new life into the squeeze. Eight minutes after the stock market closed on Tuesday, Tesla boss Elon Musk tweeted out a link to WallStreetBets along with a single phrase:

*Gamestonk!!*[4]

Chapter 15

# The Influencers

Being rich is, of course, a comparative status," said one of the wealthiest men in America in a widely circulated magazine article. "A man with a million dollars used to be considered rich, but so many people have at least that much in these days, or are earning incomes in excess of a normal return from a million dollars, that a millionaire does not cause any comment."

The slightly archaic turn of phrase, though not the view of a million dollars being chump change, might have tipped you off to this quote's vintage. It was from an interview with the auto executive and stock market speculator John J. Raskob in *Ladies' Home Journal*, titled "Everybody Ought to Be Rich," that hit newsstands one week before the peak of the Roaring Twenties bull market and two months before the Great Crash of 1929.[1]

The American public was already deeply, fatefully in love with the stock market by then, but Raskob, who had started several investment trusts over the years, was suggesting a way for people to supercharge their participation and do some catching up with the leisure class. He told readers about a trust that had been set up for executives at General Motors in 1923 called the Managers Securities Company with $5 million in cash contributions and $28 million in borrowed money—a very aggressive approach that no mutual fund would allow today. He pointed out that the minimum investment in the fund of $25,000 was by then worth "more than one million dollars." Raskob suggested setting up somewhat less aggressive trusts in which an ordinary saver—he called him "Tom" in the example—would put up $200 of his own cash and borrow $300 on an installment plan, just like he did when purchasing his "motorcar" on credit.

The medium might have been different—print and radio instead of television and social media—but Raskob's grasp of psychology would resonate today. When our peers are getting rich, we fear missing out. An influential, already-wealthy person who can point us in the direction of a shortcut will capture a lot of attention and get us to ignore what are, with the benefit of hindsight, obvious red flags.

By suggesting that there were oodles of millionaires in America—which, even at the peak of the epic twenties stock market bubble, there weren't—the opening paragraph of the interview gave readers the sense that they were late to the party. At the time, disposable income per person in the United States was a little over $6,000, and $1 million dollars was the equivalent of more than $15 million in today's money. In any case, this was the most reckless advice possible given at the worst possible time. "Tom" would have been wiped out early in the crash and still would have wound up making installment payments, likely with no job and no spare cash. The Dow Jones Industrial Average plunged almost 90 percent by the summer of 1932, banks failed in droves at a time before federal deposit insurance existed, and the unemployment rate reached a devastating 25 percent.

## Elon, Chamath, and Dave

Raskob was the Elon Musk of his day with a dash of Silicon Valley financier Chamath Palihapitiya thrown in for good measure. Like Musk, Raskob had become fabulously wealthy with the latest wonder technology, which also happened to be a car. Though Musk had gotten into hot water with securities regulators in 2018 for falsely suggesting on Twitter that he had lined up money for a buyout of Tesla Motors, sending its stock price and his net worth surging, his "GameStonk!!" tweet, which included a link to WallStreetBets in case you failed to get it, didn't violate any laws. Except perhaps indirectly, he wasn't seeking to personally enrich himself by egging on the Reddit revolutionaries—just to endear himself to them. Some later tweets helping to drum up interest in Dogecoin, which he owned, might have been a different story, legally speaking, if the cryptocurrency were an actual registered security.

A former Facebook executive and chief executive officer of the investment firm Social Capital, which had launched several blank check companies snapped up by retail investors, Palihapitiya benefited more directly from a bit of Twitter mischief on the same day. He tweeted that he personally had bought $125,000 of GameStop call options expiring in February with a $115 strike price: "Let's gooooooo!!!!!!!!"[2]

The stock rose almost 10 percent instantly, and the volume of small share lots typical of retail traders surged in the tweet's immediate aftermath, according to an analysis provided to *The Wall Street Journal*. He appeared on CNBC the following day to say that he had been up reading WallStreetBets all night but that he had sold, sending the stock down by $33 in a minute. Palihapitiya made a $500,000 profit that he claims he donated to a charity affiliated with Dave "Day Trader" Portnoy along with his original investment.[3]

In a fiery letter released in April 2021, the hedge fund manager

David Einhorn said the two billionaires played a key role in the market mayhem.

"We note that the real jet fuel on the GME squeeze came from Chamath Palihapitiya and Elon Musk, whose appearances on TV and Twitter, respectively, at a critical moment further destabilized the situation," he wrote.

There was no love lost between Einhorn and Musk, who called the hedge fund manager "Mr. Unicorn," made fun of his firm's recently poor returns on his short positions, and mockingly sent him satin short shorts. Einhorn complained in the letter that there was "no cop on the beat" on Wall Street and that Musk had received only a slap on the wrist from regulators for manipulating his own company's shares. By contrast, he pointed out that Michael Burry, the value investor and onetime GameStop booster, had reportedly received a visit from the SEC for his market warnings and had suspended his Twitter account.

Einhorn also noted that the system of payment for order flow unwittingly made young retail investors their product. "If you want the broker to work for you, pay a commission."

One influential figure for those investors whom Einhorn didn't bother to mention was the deliberately clownish Portnoy. He had told his millions of followers on Twitter that he owned three of the meme stocks on the day that Robinhood and other brokers were forced to restrict trading. "I will hold them till the death as a reminder that @RobinhoodApp founders must go to prison," he wrote. There didn't seem to be too many hard feelings from people who followed his lead when, just three trading sessions later, Portnoy, still among the living, informed them that he had sold his shares for a $700,000 loss.[4]

Portnoy's most impressive display of influence was picking random Scrabble tiles out of a bag in the summer of 2020 until they spelled out a ticker symbol and then unleashing his "army" on the stock. On June 19, he picked out RTX, the symbol for the defense contractor Raytheon, which you might recall as the maker of the Patriot missile that starred in the first Iraq War. Trading tripled that day from its typical level, but the stock failed to achieve liftoff, dropping instead. On that occasion as well, there weren't too many hard feelings.

## The Charismatic, Prophetic Figure

Though the term didn't exist in Raskob's time, and the Silicon Valley billionaires would deny it, these men are "influencers." That status might not be explicit in the modern social media sense of Kim Kardashian or Dwayne "The Rock" Johnson, who get paid upward of $1 million for a single Instagram post. If Musk's tweets were for sale and compensating him for them directly were legal, they would fetch multiples of what people helping to hawk handbags and energy drinks receive because value can be created and turned into cash instantly in the stock or cryptocurrency markets.

That can make even inadvertent statements by Musk market-shaking events. When he made a comment on *Saturday Night Live* that Dogecoin, which he had touted, was "a hustle," tens of billions of dollars in value evaporated in the cryptocurrency market, and Robinhood's trading system was overwhelmed the next day with activity.

Even the most innocuous social media post was dynamite around the time of the meme-stock squeeze. Ryan Cohen tweeted a picture of a McDonald's ice cream cone in late February and a by-then deflated GameStop stock doubled that day on huge turnover. What did he mean by it? One person guessed it was a reference to a stock trading indicator, MACD. Another thought it was because the fast-food chain would sell food inside GameStops. A poster with a sense of humor surmised that the McDonald's ice cream machine is always broken, so the picture meant that he saw that GameStop was broken too but that he would fix it.

The most influential and well-compensated person in the GameStop saga was, of course, Gill. At his peak, he had multiplied his net worth one thousandfold, getting strangers to pile into the stock by simply broadcasting the fact that he himself kept hanging on to it. But he wasn't an influencer per se. His social media presence made him rich, but he couldn't have foreseen its impact. It was akin to catching lightning in a bottle.

By contrast, Musk, Palihapitiya, and Portnoy know that people will react to their statements and often get something out of that indirectly, beyond the psychological reward of attention. Analysts and fund managers who appear on financial television shows and whose public relations agents bombard reporters with offers to have them comment on the latest financial development would love to have just a fraction of their street cred.

People touting their expertise or making a case to buy a certain stock have been a constant of markets as long as they have existed. What made the period leading up to and around the meme-stock squeeze special, and especially prone to abuse, was the combination of many novices entering the market and new-era thinking. It is a phenomenon that repeats about once a generation. There are a legitimately novel set of technologies and a new cohort of investors who bid them up to the point that further gains have to be supported by stories rather than hard numbers. Those new to the market are much more receptive to stories than dry analysis anyway.

In the Roaring Twenties, there were cars, airplanes, and radio, plus investment trusts, an easy new way to invest. In the go-go 1960s through the early 1970s, there were microchips, space technology, conglomerates, and finally the "Nifty Fifty" stocks snapped up by star mutual fund managers that rose to what in hindsight were absurd valuations. In the early 1990s, there were dot-coms and red-hot initial public offerings. And in the run-up to the meme-stock squeeze, there were electric vehicles, social media, and blank check offerings that gave individuals immediate access to those companies before they could go through even Wall Street's usual vetting process.

One wonders how much more influential Raskob and other cheer-leaders of his era might have been if social media or even television had existed then. As recently as the early 1990s, TV executives hadn't really figured out how to make a broadcast about investments appeal-ing. The big financial program during the Reagan bull market of the 1980s was *Wall Street Week* with Louis Rukeyser, which aired on pub-lic television on weekends, when stock markets are closed, and fea-tured a rotating group of serious strategists and fund managers. The Consumer News and Business Channel, now just known as CNBC, was founded in 1989 but didn't see success until the mid-1990s under the leadership of Roger Ailes, the controversial media executive who would go on to lead the conservative powerhouse Fox News to success. Finan-cial talking heads came into their own as the tech bubble inflated. Then, as now, a few had truly outsize influence.

"The 1990s had Henry Blodget. Now we have Chamath on CNBC. It's the charismatic, prophetic figure who seems to have insider knowl-edge," says Margaret O'Mara, the scholar of Silicon Valley.

## The Right Type of Rich

When it comes to influencing the newest and most active group of investors, neither wearing a tie nor working on Wall Street is a big plus. Already being rich, which one might think is a strike against you for a generation that resents widening inequality, doesn't seem to be a problem at all. Seriously, who wants money advice from a poor per-son? In the study of billionaire wealth gains during the pandemic through February 2021, Musk was all by himself at the top with an in-crease in net worth of almost $158 billion, or 642 percent. By making his stock one of their top holdings as it climbed to levels that had more experienced investors shaking their heads and losing big as they bet the wrong way, the young generation of investors was in no small part responsible for his fortune.

Emulating rich people who happen to be self-made isn't unique to younger generations—it is quintessentially American. But then why vilify the somewhat younger Gabe Plotkin and cheer Musk?

"They benefit from the fact that hedge funds are more cartoonish villains than them," explains O'Mara. Chad Minnis, the retail investor who was incensed enough about the trading restrictions to start a registered political action committee, says that most executives and politicians leave him and his generation cold compared with no-filter Silicon Valley billionaires.

"They have that way of talking—they use a lot of words and they don't say a lot," he says. "It doesn't seem real. Elon talks to people the way that people talk to their friends."

Palihapitiya burst onto young investors' radar a bit later than Musk when he lambasted hedge fund managers and came out against aid to failing companies on CNBC as the market was plunging in the spring of 2020. "We're talking about . . . a hedge fund that serves a bunch of billionaire family offices? Who cares?" he said. "They don't get to summer in the Hamptons? Who cares?"

He gained a lot of fans that day.

"Through all the pain watching all of our portfolios go up in flames the past few weeks, this motherfucker came in and spoke for all us and really put a smile on my face," wrote a poster on WallStreetBets at the time.[5]

Later, at the height of meme-stock mania, on the day that Robinhood and others restricted purchases of certain stocks, Palihapitiya telegraphed his support for the retail traders who wanted to push GameStop to the moon, tweeting:

*In moments of uncertainty, when courage and strength are*
*required, you find out who the true corporatist scumbags are.[6]*

## "SPAC Jesus"

What is the saying about people who live in glass houses? As the spon-
sor of several SPACs, the blank check firms that were then all the rage,
Palihapitiya benefited from retail-investor enthusiasm. His barbs at
high finance were a great way to advertise his solidarity with the investors snapping up his offerings. The terms of SPACs are very favorable to sponsors like him, allowing them to cheaply control up to a
fifth of the shares if they do well.

The short seller Carson Block, who wrote an unflattering report on
one of the companies Palihapitiya brought to market through a merger,
bristles at the sanctimoniousness and derisively refers to him as "SPAC
Jesus." In his letter, Einhorn accused Palihapitiya of trying to indirectly benefit one of his own businesses by overwhelming Robinhood:

> *Mr. Palihapitiya controls SoFi, which competes with Robinhood,*
> *and left us with the impression that by destabilizing GME he could*
> *harm a competitor.*

Palihapitiya also raises a significant amount of capital from big financial institutions, and he enjoys many of the trappings of a financier's lifestyle. Like Plotkin, he is the part owner of a professional
basketball team, in his case, the Golden State Warriors.

Portnoy also was quick to be fed by the hand that he had just bitten.
Several days after his stance of solidarity with retail investors and quick
retreat, he announced that he was partnering with the exchange-
traded-fund firm VanEck to launch a fund with the ticker symbol

BUZZ designed to make a return by tracking social sentiment. It would use artificial intelligence to track fifteen million social media posts per month, according to VanEck.[7]

His fund was an immediate success, drawing in more money than almost any previous exchange-traded fund (ETF) on its debut and seeing the third-highest opening volume ever, according to Bloomberg Intelligence. The influencer was using his influence to help a Wall Street firm harness the power of social media influencers and make money by selling that influence to the people most prone to listen to it. The fund's marketing material declares:

> *Social media and mobile technology have fundamentally changed the way we engage with stocks. There's a ton of online chatter every day. Changing sentiment and our collective views clearly impact their value.*

Underscoring the importance of financial influencers in the bull market, of which the meme-stock squeeze was just the craziest part, it goes on to note that the index on which the fund was based had, in the year before its launch, appreciated by 68 percent compared with barely 20 percent for the broader stock market. The legal boilerplate about past performance not being indicative of the future was to be found down below in a smaller font.

There was some scattered skepticism among retail investors. One WallStreetBets user, in a post titled "These billionaires are not our friends," wrote:

> *They encourage us to invest and hold because they will just profit even more as the value keeps rising, they aren't doing this because they see injustice being done, they are doing this because it's in their best interest.*[8]

The replies that weren't rocket ship emojis or trading-related were far less skeptical.

"This sub likes Musk. He's made a lot of us a lot of money," read one.

"They aren't our friends but there are some that are our allies. If you piss on anyone that aligns with you just because they have a huge net worth, then you won't have anyone fighting alongside you," went another.

## The Billionaires' Clubhouse

Aside from enhancing their brands and net worth, showing solidarity with the aggrieved traders unable to buy more GameStop shares also might have been a way for Silicon Valley billionaires to avoid the pitchforks of a crowd that ultimately was upset about economic unfairness. At the peak of the meme-stock frenzy, progressive New York congresswoman Alexandria Ocasio-Cortez, known as AOC, invited Palihapitiya to a conversation on the live streaming platform Twitch. It fell through because of scheduling issues, but one wonders whether the talk would have been friendly or icy. She has called out rich men, including JPMorgan Chase chief executive officer Jamie Dimon and Amazon founder Jeff Bezos in the past.

"No one ever makes a billion dollars. They take a billion dollars," AOC said in a conversation with the writer Ta-Nehisi Coates in January 2020. A year earlier, also in a discussion with Coates, she said a society that "allows billionaires to exist" while others live in poverty is "immoral."[9]

Even seventy-one-year-old Wall Street hedge fund billionaire Ray Dalio, clearly disturbed by the vitriol against the well-to-do, seemed to attempt to endear himself to the crowd.

"What concerns me more is the general anger—and almost hate—and the view of bringing people down that now is pervasive in almost all aspects of the country," he said in an interview with the *The Washington Post*. But then he continued: "They remind me a lot of me at that age. I started investing at an early age and I was rebellious and wanted to do it my way and bring it down."[10]

Portnoy, who had established solidarity with the WallStreetBets crowd by losing a chunk of his own money, tweeted that Vlad Tenev "stole it from me and should be in jail."

He also got into a tangle with one of the richest Wall Streeters of them all. Unlike other hedge fund bosses, Plotkin's mentor Steven Cohen had a fairly impressive Twitter following of his own of about two hundred thousand around the time of the squeeze. The subject typically was the New York Mets, not investing, but Cohen made the mistake of engaging with the revolutionaries hurling insults at him after news broke of his helping hand to his protégé.

> *Rough crowd on Twitter tonight. Hey stock jockeys, keep bringing it.*[11]

When trading was curtailed by Robinhood and other brokers later in the week, Portnoy wrongly accused the sixty-four-year-old billionaire of being behind it. Cohen, who says his family received threats, suspended his account.[12]

Musk kept up the heat too. "Why couldn't people buy GameStop shares? The people demand an answer," he said in a January 30 interview on audio app Clubhouse.

One of the moderators on the panel was fellow billionaire Marc Andreessen, the early investor in Robinhood. Andreessen also was an investor in Clubhouse, which carried the talk and couldn't accommodate the crush of demand by people who wanted to hear Musk. The app had just reached a private market valuation of $1 billion. Musk's tweets that week about it sent the shares of an unrelated publicly traded company, Tongji Medical, which had just renamed itself

Clubhouse Media Group, to an even higher market capitalization of $2.5 billion for several days. Circles within circles, and everyone got richer except for the poor retail investors who were allowed to buy the wrong Clubhouse.

## "I Just Know I'm Making Money"

Reddit was the social media site that played a starring role in the meme-stock squeeze, but it isn't the only or even the predominant online source of investing information or ideas for young people. MagnifyMoney, a media firm owned by LendingTree, surveyed more than fifteen hundred people in the Generation Z and millennial demographic groups in late January 2021 and found that nearly half had consulted social media in the preceding month for "investing research." Video and images rather than boring old text seem to be the preferred medium: the largest source by far was YouTube, owned by Google, with 41 percent having consulted it. TikTok and Instagram were in second and third place, with 24 percent and 21 percent having consulted those sources, respectively. Then came Facebook groups and Twitter, with Reddit bringing up the rear at 13 percent.[13]

TikTok, owned by China's ByteDance, is popular with the younger side of the young cohort and had amassed nearly 7.5 billion views of videos with hashtags such as #FinTok and #investing by July 2021.[14] Influencers on the platform can make serious money no matter how good or bad their advice as long as they get views and followers. Steve Chen, who was a math teacher, transitioned into becoming an investing guru through his account, "calltoleap," and says he makes about $10,000 a month. His posts have titles such as "Buying calls on GME" or "Hot stocks to buy!"[15]

TikTok also is home to more cringeworthy investing advice. One video became a crossover hit, but not in a good way, garnering millions of views and many snarky comments on Twitter in January 2021. In it, @chadandjenny, a young couple, presumably Chad and Jenny, explain how they were able to stop working and travel full-time through investing income.

"I see a stock going up and I buy it and I just watch it until it stops going up and I sell it," explains Chad. "I do it over and over and it pays for our whole lifestyle."[16]

The humorist Will Rogers was about a century ahead of him: "Don't gamble; take all your savings and buy some good stock and hold it till it goes up, then sell it. If it don't go up, don't buy it," he quipped.

Chad, to his credit, rolled with the punches and used his newfound fame to launch a brand-new account, @crappywallstreetadvice.

## Are You a Bot or Not?

Speaking of which, social media is increasingly being harnessed by people with a vested interest in creating a temporary rise or fall in a company's shares, a so-called pump and dump, leaving unwitting investors holding the bag. The idea has a long and sordid history, but it took on a new dimension with the arrival of the internet and message boards dedicated to stocks. In the early days, some of the more prominent cases, or at least those that were successfully prosecuted, involved very young masterminds. There was the case of seventeen-year-old Cole Bartiromo, who bought shares of fifteen companies and then posted fake news bulletins about them on Yahoo and RagingBull message boards. Even younger, Jonathan Lebed, just fifteen at the time, was forced to disgorge gains by the SEC in a similar scheme.

Rather than teenagers, the 2021 version was likely run by people with a lot more resources and sophistication. There is widespread suspicion by many WallStreetBets users that the forum had been infiltrated by organized criminals using "bots"—algorithms or paid posters with multiple accounts—as GameStop became a front-page story. Others think that the meme-stock squeeze, or at least some elements of it, already showed signs of bot activity. Bots don't only write posts but also exploit a social media site's methodology to boost those of others to make them more visible. That certainly raises some questions about the quality of investing advice on forums such as WallStreetBets.

Take the case of a blank check company not sponsored by Palihapitiya, Churchill Capital IV (yes, there had been a roman numeral one, two, and three already). The SPAC's shares surged as high as $63.20 in February 2021 on heavy retail buying, which was very odd because it hadn't yet merged with anything and was essentially a bag of money worth no more than its initial public offering price of $10.00 a share. It soon agreed to merge with Lucid Motors, a Tesla competitor with no sales. Churchill's share price halved within days, leading to accusations on Reddit that there was a short-selling conspiracy at hand. By the end of the week, a separate subreddit to seek justice and punish the shorts had amassed more than thirty thousand members.[17]

Madmax212121 wrote on the forum: "Lucid Wall Street Bets, all longs—CCIV heavily shorted by coordinated groups and manipulators. Why can't we have a LWSB and defend. Are you IN?"

The post, made by a user who had only joined Reddit near the end of January, had nearly seven thousand comments and more than eight thousand upvotes by the next morning, including pledges to buy more and keep shares from being accessed by short sellers. But a quick check would have shown that short interest in the SPAC, which in any case had only announced but not completed the merger, was around a modest 2 percent of its shares. Either the outrage over the drop in Churchill Capital IV's price betrayed a complete misunderstanding of the situation by the posters who insisted a $10 bill was worth $60 or the outpouring of support was a sign of manipulation that tried to piggyback on the energy of the meme-stock squeeze. The following response to the initial post from Socaltexasgirl seemed off to some, for example.

*YES!!! This one I am going in all in!!! Every time I get extra*
*$$$ it goes into CCIV stocks so I can gather a bag at these*
*low prices.[18]*

More than one poster said that the syntax resembled that of someone whose first language wasn't English, comparing it to the syntax of a Russian or Chinese bot farm. The two-month-old account posted exclusively about meme stocks. When confronted, the user insisted in yet more awkward prose that she was indeed a girl who had moved from Southern California to Texas, as her username suggested. While verifying her identity would require serious detective work, the suspicion that bots, or just individuals with multiple accounts and malign intent, were active on social media seems justified. A spokesperson for WallStreetBets told CBS News that it had detected a large amount of "bot activity in the subreddit," including multiple posts with similar content.[19]

"Large amount" would be an understatement if Ben Hunt, head of the research firm Epsilon Theory, is remotely right. He looked at the subreddit for eight hours on January 29, 2021, near the height of the meme-stock squeeze, and found that 97 percent of thirty thousand posts over that span subsequently disappeared as they were removed or blocked by its moderators and filters. He says it is hard to tell how many were automated and how many were too new to the forum to post. Reddit spokeswoman Sandra Chu says that those posts that are removed before being upvoted don't gain serious visibility on a subreddit.

"What I think is important is that all of the posts made to WallStreetBets, bot or not, were intended to impact the behavior of other human readers," says Hunt, noting that they weren't trying to do research or bounce investment ideas off the group. "Automated or not, 99.9 percent of the posts are trying to add snow mass to a snowball that the author is trying to roll down the hill."[20]

Reddit cofounder and chief executive officer Steve Huffman was asked about bots at the congressional hearing about GameStop and denied that they played a "significant role," but didn't elaborate. Chu says the company defines bot activity as "content manipulation."

It seems to have appeared elsewhere at the time. A study by the cybersecurity firm PiiQ Media, which looked at Twitter, Facebook, Instagram, and YouTube, but not Reddit, found suspicious signs around meme stocks during and after the surge, including "start and stop patterns" that indicate bot activity.[21] It added that thousands of fake accounts can be bought online for a few hundred dollars.

But even very convincing bots have some heavy lifting to do if they want to manipulate the shares of larger companies. Far easier, and often very lucrative, are penny stocks. The trick is getting people to invest in the risky, lightly regulated category in the first place. Armed with zero-commission trading accounts, and often not knowing the difference between the over-the-counter market and major exchanges, retail investors certainly weren't shy around the time of the meme-stock squeeze. An incredible trillion shares of penny stocks were traded in December 2020.

## Toothless Regulators

Retail losses stemming from bot activity don't wind up with Wall Street firms—they go to manipulators often beyond the reach of the law who are usually savvy enough to cover their tracks. Wall Street is indirectly responsible, though, and not just brokers and wholesalers who make it so easy to trade. Other companies give these nefarious characters access. Privately controlled stock exchanges, hungry for fees and listings, often don't do the bare minimum to police their market. Einhorn pointed out in his letter, for example, that a company owning a single deli in New Jersey that had been closed for most of the past year was worth $100 million. It was controlled by a financier with a history of fraud accusations and a series of companies in Macao and Hong Kong located in the same offices.

News coverage often results in bursts of activity by the nation's securities regulators. Several weeks after a record jump in penny stock activity by retail investors, the SEC said that it was temporarily suspending trading in fifteen stocks because of "questionable trading and social media activity." Typical of the companies was Wisdom Homes of America Inc., which didn't appear to have a working website. Its chief executive officer also seemed to be associated with a variety of other firms, including a cannabis company, and he had recently been sued for civil fraud. The company's shares had seen an odd surge in value, and their price more than doubled from one tenth of a cent to a little over two tenths of a cent before the suspension.[22]

There are warnings about what to watch out for, but, if social media is any indication, efforts by the SEC and other bodies to warn about potential fraud, or to just steer investors away from online hype, face a serious trust and marketing problem. Take a message on the SEC's fairly active investor education Twitter feed, which has about 0.2 percent the reach of Musk's account: "Thinking About Investing in the Latest Hot Stock? Understand the Significant Risks of Short-Term Trading Based on Social Media." Virtually every response is cynical.[23] For example:

*Thinking about owning the latest hot stock? Understand we're gonna suspend / freeze it because people would dare talk about a stock and have freewill to buy / sell but billionaires shorting the stock down and only allowing sells is completely fine.*

*And they have it down to a science on how to fudge the system. And the @sec wonders why the 99 percent hate Wall Street. Because they consistently step on the little guy to get to the top*

*When the people in charge change the rules to screw people over, retail investors deserve the same bailout as the banks. You owe us a bailout.*

And so on.

The fish rots from the head, as they say. Vetting new offerings more seriously or giving more than slaps on the wrist to cool, rich influencers who might have ulterior motives would probably not be popular with the newest, youngest investors, but by refusing to do so, America's securities regulators are failing them. The government can't, and shouldn't, restrict free speech. Yet many influencers profit from access to the public markets for their own companies and either directly or indirectly from their market-moving statements delivered through social media. Tapping into the public's savings is a privilege, not a right. Silicon Valley has shaken up Wall Street in many positive ways, but its libertarian attitude toward America's capital markets and Washington's timidity have made this as dangerous an era as we have seen in decades for the ordinary people whose savings enable them to function.

# January 27, 2021

n forty-eight hours the meme-stock squeeze had gone from something you might have had an inkling about if you followed markets
closely to a major international news story. By Wednesday morning,
with GameStop on everyone's lips, traders were looking for stocks with
similar characteristics—smaller companies with high short interest—
and were buying them like they were going out of style.

A look at the big movers on the stock market seemed like a flash-
back to 2005. In addition to past-its-prime GameStop, shares of Nokia,
the once-dominant cell phone pioneer, more than doubled that morning on multiples of its normal trading volume. The stock price of the
stereo headphone maker Koss reached twenty times what its value
had been on Friday with about three hundred times the typical number of shares changing hands. BlackBerry and AMC surged too.

The day saw the most call options traded in history as retail traders, who hoped either to get the most bang for their buck or to fuel a

gamma squeeze, dove in with abandon. The most popular call option in the world was a long-shot bet that GameStop shares would reach $800 within days—more than double its closing price. Several brokerage firms experienced intermittent outages because of heavy traffic.

"We've officially broken the market," wrote one proud poster on WallStreetBets.[1]

The news story of the Reddit Revolution would get even bigger as the week wore on, but Wednesday, January 27, marked something of a crescendo on the market itself with short sellers' losses on GameStop alone topping $5 billion that day, according to estimates by Ihor Dusaniwsky of S3 Partners.[2] Many funds had only entered the short trade in the past few days as they thought GameStop's rally had gone too far. That was before Elon Musk's tweet and the impact of other influencers launched the stock into an even higher orbit.

"You had that first squeeze from the people who took the first punch," he says. "When it got close to $70, you had another huge short squeeze."

According to one school of thought, it wasn't such a big deal. CNBC's Michael Santoli observed that the market value of all stocks that had more than a fifth of their shares sold short was just $40 billion, or one tenth of 1 percent of all American public companies.[3]

Yet his employer provided round-the-clock coverage of the squeeze, effectively sucking the oxygen out of the room. And even as the meme stocks surged to values not seen since their heydays, or in some cases ever, the other 99.9 percent of the market wasn't doing so hot all of a sudden. On Wednesday, stocks had their sharpest drop in months. Some people interpreted it at the time as professional Wall Street getting spooked by the uprising. Goldman Sachs, the biggest lender to hedge funds, later came up with a more convincing explanation.

The vast majority of shorting was done by hedge funds that like it when the overall stock market goes up and wouldn't even be so upset if stocks they sold short rose a bit—as long as they went up less than the stocks they liked. But they were now losing so much money so quickly that they had to "de-gross"—to dump shares of companies they liked too. Those hedge funds' selling of stocks that Wednesday was the most since the global financial crisis, according to Goldman Sachs. What was ostensibly a revolution to help the little guy was temporarily pushing down the values of the companies that made up the vast majority of Americans' retirement savings.

Keith Gill's retirement was looking secure at least. His net worth by the end of the day had reached $47 million with almost $14 million of that now safely in cash. On that day Julia-Ambra Verlaine, a *Wall Street Journal* reporter, was speaking with Gill's mother in the suburbs of Boston after having driven up from New York in the snow.

"He always liked money," said Elaine Gill, a *Journal* reader who made sure to put the reporter in touch with her son.[4]

Other reporters were also trying to contact her, having made the connection between Gill's online personas and the man himself. Six years earlier he had dissolved a company in New Hampshire, Roaring Kitty LLC, and the name on the registration matched the photo on the website of MassMutual's financial advice division, In Good Company. It was a more corporate, clean-cut version of the now-famous but still-anonymous YouTuber. Gill had pasted a screenshot of one of his videos to a December update on WallStreetBets as DeepFucking-Value, squaring the circle. The next day, Verlaine would conduct an exclusive interview with Gill in the lobby of a Boston hotel, and that night the photographer Kayana Szymczak snapped the now-iconic photo of him in his darkened basement with a red bandana holding back his long, brown hair, the blue glow of multiple computer screens illuminating his face. Verlaine verified Gill's identity and his trading position, having him log in to his E*Trade account and also write a post on WallStreetBets as DeepFuckingValue.

Unfortunately, not every journalist was so careful. In all the excitement over ordinary people making small fortunes, the hunt was on for rags-to-riches tales—the crazier the better. *New York Post* reporter Mary K. Jacob saw the following tweet on Wednesday and took the bait:

> *Just took out a second mortgage on my parent's house while they were at work to buy more $AMC and $GME LETS GOOOO.*

Jacob privately messaged Jack West, the twenty-two-year-old behind the post, and the next day published his account of how he had taken out the mortgage by contacting the local bank via Zoom but with the video switched off. Aside from the fact that even the most careless banker wouldn't fall for such a clumsy ruse, getting the money into a trading account in two days would have been impossible. Fox News later reproduced the article before West let on that they had been duped.[5]

No doubt there were a lot of other pretenders among the reckless gamblers and overnight millionaires crowing about their big scores that week on social media. Many were real, though, as FOMO took hold, and people piled in near the top. One who took the plunge with unfortunate timing was Salvador Vergara, a twenty-five-year-old security guard from Virginia who had done a great deal right in his financial life before that. He lived with his dad, ate "a lot of rice," and drove a Honda Civic nearly as old as he was, managing to save $50,000 in index funds. But he was a WallStreetBets member, and what he read on the board convinced him to take out a $20,000 personal loan at a steep interest rate, using it to buy GameStop at $234 a share.

"I thought it could go up to $1,000. I really believed in that hype, which was an awful thing to do."[6]

Why $1,000? Because that was the value that people on the board kept mentioning. It was a big, round, aspirational number. Nobody had made a convincing case for why it shouldn't be $100 or $10,000 instead, though, or explained exactly what everyone would do with their shares of a loss-making retailer worth 250 times its recent value once evil hedge funds had been bankrupted. Vergara's investments so far had been in conservative funds that hold so many stocks that there was no need for him to have an opinion on whether something was priced correctly.

But suddenly he was confident enough to make a huge gamble with borrowed money. You can democratize finance to the hilt and throw in financial education, but most people have no business coming up with a fair value for stocks. Analysts with MBAs and years of experience are fairly awful at coming up with target prices too. They often tied themselves in knots to do so during the dot-com boom, harming many retail investors who trusted them and leading to an industry crackdown. But at least they had to come up with a projected profit that could be scrutinized. Now prices of securities or cryptocurrencies were just a number tied to a symbol or name, and the experts in suits had missed the boat again and again. GameStop and many other investments had ceased to be stocks—they were now "stonks."

# Chapter 17

# LOL, Nothing Matters

E verybody classifies it as a cigar butt and then just moves on . . .
but this isn't some horse and buggy shit," said Roaring Kitty
as he placed an unlit stogie into his mouth. "Its final puff [ex-
aggerated, hacking cough] is a legitimate opportunity to reinvent itself as a premier gaming hub."

The YouTube video by a not-yet-famous Keith Gill about GameStop
probably had fewer than fifty viewers back when it was released in
August 2020, and one has to wonder how many of them even got the
reference to the sort of down-and-out company with a little bit of life
left in it favored by Benjamin Graham, the father of value investing.
Graham's best student, Warren Buffett, dubbed his method "cigar butt"
investing.

"Though the stub might be ugly and soggy, the puff would be free."[1]

Buffett moved on from the deep-value category to make a fortune on quality companies bought at reasonable prices such as Coca-Cola, GEICO, and American Express. Gill was suggesting that, in a similar vein, the video game retailer he had by then spent more than a year following possessed appeal beyond its mere cheapness. Beer drinking, cigar chomping, and profanity aside, the August video and many others posted by Gill made as sound a pitch as any professional fund manager might to an investment committee.

Within a few months, the chartered financial analyst would amass more wealth than the vast majority of people do in an entire career as professional investors without having to wait and see if his thesis held water. Value investing often requires incredible patience, but sometimes the owner of a stock gets lucky. Gill helped to make his own luck by inspiring the forces that would push GameStop to his target price and then several times that target. The ironic thing is that he spent a year and a half making a perfectly reasonable argument about a stock, and his success wound up convincing millions of mostly novice investors to trade "stonks."

## The Rise of Stonks

The word is new enough that *Merriam-Webster* still defines *stonk* as "a heavy concentration of artillery fire" rather than a silly investment that goes up anyway.[2] It is tempting to decide whether something is a stonk with the famous line about pornography—"you know it when you see it"—and leave it at that. For a generation that had a dim view of the business of finance but had only known one long, almost uninterrupted bull market, buying a stonk and still making money—probably a lot more money a lot more quickly than you might have earned investing in something solid and conservative—let you have your cake and eat it too. It meant that you didn't need to take this investing stuff all that seriously. As *Slate*'s Jordan Weissmann put it:

*It fits the mentality of day traders who see themselves as party crashers screwing with Wall Street, make memes comparing themselves to the Joker or the Avengers, and might brag about purposely buying shares in a company just as it's about to crash, as if they were purposely getting kicked in the balls on an episode of Jackass.*[3]

The trick, though, is to sell your crazy investment before the kick is delivered. A boring old stock might earn you a nice, steady return eventually, but in 2020 and 2021, a stonk that already was worth five times what serious people with financial acumen thought it was could keep levitating until it was worth ten or twenty times that much.

"There's a group of stocks that has jumped the shark," explains Howard Lindzon, founder of social investing forum Stocktwits, former hedge fund manager, and early investor in Robinhood, holding up his smartphone. "If you put this in everybody's hands, you play a game of financial chicken."

In 2020 and especially early 2021, it was the pros with their careers and wealth at stake who were blinking first. The mostly young, mostly new investors who were helping to turn some stocks into stonks weren't monolithic, though. Some saw a number like the $1,000 price that GameStop shares supposedly were going to hit, according to so many posts on WallStreetBets, and thought that there was some basis for it that better-informed people in the crowd had figured out. Many others just saw a line going up and to the right and figured they would be able to hop on and then hop off the ride before it stopped rising— the greater fool theory. Seth Mahoney, the young Robinhood customer and longtime WallStreetBets member, fell into the latter camp. He says he would scan social media constantly in 2020 and especially in early 2021 and jump on a stock he knew almost nothing about other than the hunch that the crowd was starting to push it higher.

*Literally I would see something on Twitter and that something would double or triple—it was fear of missing out.*

Often, he said, he was too late to buy or too slow to sell and would lose money. Some stonks could defy gravity for weeks or months as long as they could keep up the momentum and avoid having the crowd move on to some new object of fascination. Eventually, though, gravity would reassert itself. With apologies to Graham for mangling his most famous quote: In the short run, the market is an episode of *America's Got Talent*. In the long run, you get kicked in the balls.*⁴

## "No Plausible Story"

Buying into GameStop during the peak of the meme-stock squeeze and believing it would somehow go to $1,000 a share and stay there long enough for everyone to make a profit certainly became a painful experience. It is likely that the trading restrictions interrupted its momentum and hastened its reversal, but it is impossible to say by how much.

At its peak of $483 a share on January 28, the retailer was worth more than forty times what even optimistic analysts reckoned, and not a single one polled by FactSet at the time had a "buy" rating on it. Aswath Damodaran, the New York University finance professor who literally wrote the book on corporate valuation and who was cited by Gill as an influence on his thinking, tried to stretch the story to its most optimistic possible version in which GameStop not only stayed in business but also doubled its sales over the following decade while earning the best profit margins in its history. Even then, he found "no

---

*What he really said was: "In the short run, the market is a voting machine . . . in the long run, it is a weighing machine."

plausible story that could be told about GameStop that could justify paying a $100 price."[5]

Likewise, there was no story to tell about how Nokia and BlackBerry could team up to invent a time machine and kill baby Steve Jobs so that Apple wouldn't dominate the smartphone business and then lend their time machine to Blockbuster Video so its executives could change their minds and buy Netflix twenty years earlier for its ridiculously cheap asking price of $50 million. The meme stocks were making some people rich, but they simply weren't very desirable businesses.

The stuffier, "institutional" part of Wall Street that is a step or two removed from individual investors isn't immune to FOMO, but careers are at stake, so it has to justify itself. It has transformed a few stonks into stocks by raising serious money for flaky companies that helped turn them into stable ones. But the meme stocks in January 2021 were a bridge too far for bankers at Goldman Sachs or Morgan Stanley to risk their reputations.

Meanwhile, that other part of Wall Street—the companies that execute trades and that get paid for routing orders, like Citadel Securities, Virtu Financial, Robinhood, and Webull—was hardly bending over backward to discourage the Salvador Vergaras of the world from taking out personal loans to buy GameStop at a nosebleed price. Order flow was order flow, and the democratization of finance was a convenient fig leaf. Even the institutional, capital-raising part of Wall Street got something out of the exuberance as blank check companies mainly bought by naïve retail investors made them a fortune in underwriting fees in 2020 and 2021.

## Good Money on Bad Stock Picks

New investors could have been forgiven for thinking that there was only the loosest connection between a company's stock price and the actual business behind it: picking winners had been deceptively easy. *Wall Street Journal* investing columnist Jason Zweig pointed out that, as of the one-year anniversary of the new bull market following the COVID-19 crash, 96 percent of stocks in the Wilshire 5000, the broadest index covering the US market, had risen. That success rate was unprecedented.

"You could have made good money even with bad stock picks," he wrote. "It was like being invited to bet on black, without limits, at a roulette wheel on which 37 of the 38 pockets were black."[6]

And, unlike in a casino, the reward wasn't identical on each of those winning roulette numbers. In the months leading up to the meme-stock squeeze, the best returns were on the worst stocks—those least likely to be profitable companies and those most likely to be sold short. For the past several months, the investments that serious financial professionals had warned them about—from joke cryptocurrencies to bankrupt car rental firms to hydrogen-powered garbage truck startups—had made a lot of people a lot of money.

It was a classic symptom of a bubble that was close to bursting, as described by the economic historian Charles P. Kindleberger in his 1978 classic, *Manias, Panics, and Crashes.*

"At a late stage, speculation tends to detach itself from really valuable objects and turn to delusive ones," he wrote. "A larger and larger group of people seeks to become rich without a real understanding of the processes involved."[7]

The pattern is self-reinforcing for a while but ultimately ruinous for the least experienced investors. And, unlike during the dot-com boom, the meme stocks rose without Wall Street's typical cheerleaders— fund managers and analysts. If anything, they became the enemy.

After certain meme stocks got a second wind in the spring and summer of 2021 and some analysts expressed skepticism, the counterarguments on social media veered into conspiracies. "They" were in the pocket of hedge funds who didn't want certain companies to succeed. Rich Greenfield, the veteran media analyst who had to go to the police because of threats directed at his family, was far from alone. Most preferred not to contradict the mob.

"Sorry. I have no desire to engage in a war of words or mathematical analysis with the apes," said one who chose to remain anonymous to CNBC. "And it's not like anyone is going to change their minds. No flexibility in their line of thought."[8]

Wall Street analysts have a deserved reputation for being bad, and often conflicted, stock pickers, but professional stock raters tend to err in the other direction. A *Wall Street Journal* study of analyst recommendations on blue chip stocks found that only 6 percent of eleven thousand ratings were "underweight" or sell recommendations. A significant part of analysts' pay is for so-called corporate access—getting the broker's clients meetings with management. That access is often tied to favorable coverage, presenting a conflict of interest. But some stocks are just too far in the stratosphere for them to recommend with a straight face.[9]

Even journalists, who have no skin in the game financially, were portrayed as part of a conspiracy to keep retail traders poor. One unfortunate technology reporter at *MarketWatch* wrote about a 30 percent slump in GameStop shares one day in March 2021, but a software glitch where the article was reproduced elsewhere printed a time stamp a few hours earlier, before the big drop. Rejecting that innocent explanation, the reporter was accused of knowing ahead of time that hedge funds would cause the stock to plunge and was harassed and chased off social media.

Even if speculators are inclined to shoot, or just ignore, the messenger, the stock market has its own self-correcting mechanisms that eventually help to turn it from a voting to a weighing machine. Lots of shares are owned by executives who have some idea what the company is worth or by fund managers who also have a number in mind. If it has suddenly reached a multiple of that, then they sell, and their selling puts pressure on the price. But there was so much retail buying in 2020 and 2021 that many stocks kept on rising anyway.

Once a stock became the sole preserve of retail investors uninterested in the business it represented, it was like a bunch of Beanie Babies enthusiasts buying and selling the once-collectible and now-worthless dolls from one another when the rest of the world thought they were silly. You could laugh, but it had no effect on the buying and selling until the price got so high that nobody was willing to pay a dollar more. Then the unlucky and naïve became "bagholders"—the people stuck owning a dropping investment. It is impossible to say when that will happen.

There is, in theory, one more brake on irrational prices—selling a stock short. At a time of extreme froth in the market, like early 2021 when many stocks were clearly overvalued, the hedge fund manager John Hempton of Bronte Capital said finding stocks to target was like shooting fish in a barrel. But suddenly, as he told interviewers at *Bloomberg*, "the fish started shooting back."[10] As stocks surged from one day to the next without rhyme or reason, it became too risky to engage in an exercise that opened you up to theoretically unlimited losses. Short sellers ran away, and there was nobody left to help prices reflect fundamental economic value.

In an environment in which stonks did so much better than stocks, and popularity trumped profitability, Dave Portnoy could say outright that he didn't know what he was doing and pick ticker symbols out of a bag of Scrabble tiles only for thousands of people to rush out and buy them anyway. It might have been funny, but it wasn't normal or healthy. Zweig commissioned a study of language on WallStreetBets showing that the frequency with which members mocked their own intelligence in posts coincided with surges in the price of meme stocks. Being a "retard" was a badge of honor.

It isn't particularly productive to lecture someone who has been trouncing older and wiser investors about how a stock is worth only the sum of its future cash flows. That might be what you read in finance textbooks, but in January 2021 many on WallStreetBets and other forums had the net worth to show you how smart they were, or they could point to others' possibly embellished big scores on social media. Success, as they say, is the worst teacher.

Even for those who had lost money, the stock market at that juncture seemed more like a casino where the pit boss was on an extended lunch break and the house appeared to no longer have the edge. Why not keep on rolling the dice until he comes back? Maybe he never will?

He always comes back. Even people who make conservative investments such as buying and holding index funds will endure some big losses in the market. It is the psychological pain of those losses and the occasionally uncomfortable volatility that make stocks such good investments in the long run—returns have to be high enough to compensate you for the stress of holding on. Novice investors who followed the recommendations of those with the funniest memes were setting themselves up for financial failure.

## Like Betting on Racehorses

At face value, millions of young people beginning to invest in the stock market in 2020 and early 2021 was a good thing. Too few save and invest for their future. But the democratization of finance would only be to their benefit if they could harness the wealth-creating power of the market over decades—without winding up as the greater fools holding a speculative stock when it finally collapsed, and without then becoming convinced that the reason they lost money was that the market was somehow rigged. That could discourage them from remaining in the shareholder class for the long term. Only 15 percent of American households own stock directly, and nearly half have no investments, contributing to inequality and a looming retirement crisis.

And there's the rub—the companies introducing them to the stock market and telling them that they were "born an investor" do what they are incentivized to do—get them to speculate. It isn't hard: potential customers of any age are already highly receptive to anything that resembles a game of chance. Defending the business that had made him immensely wealthy, Tenev wrote that "building wealth should be fun, not complex and difficult," as if the two were mutually exclusive. They aren't, but turning the market into a habit-forming video game and doing the best thing for your customers just might be. In the words of perhaps the greatest speculator of all time, George Soros: "If investing is entertaining, if you're having fun, you're probably not making any money. Good investing is boring."[11]

A brokerage firm that makes its money up front on transactions rather than through the growth of your nest egg just cares about getting you in the door and keeping you as active as possible. In a crazy bull market, retail brokers' business proposition proved far more attractive than that of companies that make their money on the back end over many years. For example, in just a single day of the meme-stock squeeze, Robinhood attracted more customers than the thirteen-year-old millennial-focused robo-adviser Betterment, which puts its clients in cost- and tax-efficient index funds.

"What these brokerages are doing is democratizing risk," says Dan Egan, vice president of behavioral finance and investing at Betterment. "They themselves are making a nice, steady return."

Less than a week after Gill, Vlad Tenev, and the rest gave their congressional testimony, Buffett's salty ninety-seven-year-old business partner, Charlie Munger, was asked about the broker at the shareholder meeting of the Daily Journal Corporation. His take was less diplomatic than Egan's.

"That's the kind of thing that can happen when you get a whole lot of people who are using liquid stock markets to gamble the way they would in betting on race horses," he said. "And the frenzy is fed by people who are getting commissions and revenues out of this new bunch of gamblers. And, of course, when things get extreme, you have things like that short squeeze."[12]

A Robinhood spokesperson was quick to take the bait.

*In one fell swoop an entire generation of investors has been criticized and this commentary overlooks the cultural shift that is taking place in our nation today. Robinhood was created to allow people who don't have access to generational wealth or the resources that come with it to begin investing in the U.S. stock market.*[13]

The release went on to call Munger's racetrack analogy "disappointing and elitist."

It would be hard to find a critic both older and richer than Munger, but finding one who is wiser wouldn't be much easier. This book could largely be filled with his insights about human folly, and whole books have been. He didn't hold back in his response.

"I hate this luring of people into engaging in speculative orgies," he said. Robinhood "may call it investing, but that's all bullshit."[14]

Another famously successful value investor, Seth Klarman, wrote a classic take on the lunacy of investing in a pure object of speculation, the parable of "trading sardines."

*There is an old story about the market craze in sardine trading when the sardines disappeared from their traditional waters in Monterey, California. The commodity traders bid them up and the price of a can of sardines soared. One day a buyer decided to treat himself to an expensive meal and actually opened a can and started eating. He immediately became ill and told the seller the sardines were no good. The seller said, "You don't understand. These are not eating sardines, they are trading sardines."*[15]

You can make ten times your money or lose 90 percent of it on either a stock or a stonk, but you have to be like the uninformed sardine buyer to mistake one for the other. Good timing or an exquisite sense of crowd psychology might just help you make money on a stonk unless, heaven forbid, you take on a quasi-religious devotion to the company, as some were starting to do at this point in the GameStop tale.

It was easy to paint the people warning about all this as curmudgeons who had missed out on a good thing. Yet even Michael Burry, who helped get the ball rolling a year and a half earlier for GameStop and made a tidy profit, was uncomfortable with what he saw. He posted and then quickly deleted a tweet during the meme-stock squeeze.

> If I put $GME on your radar, and you did well, I'm genuinely
> happy for you. However, what is going on now—there should be
> legal and regulatory repercussions. This is unnatural, insane,
> and dangerous.[16]

The defining phrase of the bull market in silly investments was borrowed from social media observations about politicians behaving badly: "LOL, nothing matters." If nothing matters, though, then problems follow.

"We're playing with something dangerous if we're going to accept that something's value is just what somebody else is going to pay for it, devoid of real value," warns the investor advocate Barbara Roper.

People can debate the value of any stock up to a point, which is why markets exist—there is a seller for every buyer and vice versa. The danger Roper alluded to is that financial markets are ultimately a way for companies to raise money and for people to invest in businesses. Investments that are just numbers tied to ticker symbols with no consideration for the health of the firms behind them threaten to make a mockery of a system that is still pretty efficient at raising money for the next Apple.

Conversely, the moment the tide of a market frenzy goes out is when companies that played fast and loose are exposed, explains the short seller Jim Chanos, who uncovered the shenanigans at Enron. It is that type of story that, in addition to incinerating a lot of money, makes ordinary savers think markets are rigged.

"Part of the outrage about all the fraud in the dot-com era is that retail investors got killed. People said: 'You see, corporate America is crooked—I'm going to put my money in real estate.'"

And we all know how that ended.

# Chapter 18

# January 28, 2021

Companies put a great deal of effort into making their marketing messages go viral, and they rarely pull it off. But when Robinhood's four-word tweet from 2016, "Let the people trade," resurfaced ironically on placards, T-shirts, and wry memes nearly five years later, its executives couldn't have been pleased.

Of course, they had much bigger things to worry about—like finding $3 billion in the middle of the night. Vlad Tenev received a phone call at 3:30 a.m. Pacific time on Thursday, January 28, from his frantic operations team. Three hours before stocks would begin trading in New York, Robinhood's clearinghouse (the organization that makes sure everyone in the business gets paid) informed the company that it needed to post that enormous amount of collateral to remain in business.

There was no way it could do that. Instead, Robinhood had to enrage its customers and make itself a political punching bag by restricting trading in the most hyped, borrowed-against, and volatile stocks, reducing the clearinghouse's collateral requirements significantly, but also dealing a serious blow to the meme-stock squeeze in the process. At first this included eight stocks: AMC, BlackBerry, Bed Bath & Beyond, Express, GameStop, Koss, Naked, and Nokia. The list would later expand to the shares and options of several more companies, but with slightly less onerous restrictions.

"We continuously monitor the markets and make changes where necessary," wrote the company in a blog post. "In light of recent volatility, we are restricting transactions for certain securities to position closing only. . . . We also raised margin requirements for certain securities."[1]

By ensuring that its customers wouldn't buy more of the main meme stocks, and by indirectly forcing some to sell or to put up more cash if they had purchased those stocks using margin debt, Robinhood reduced its immediate collateral call to $700 million. It still had to draw down its entire credit line from banks and later that day quickly raised $1 billion from its investors. It would raise billions more in the coming days. Competitors such as TD Ameritrade and Interactive Brokers were forced to enact restrictions too, but they didn't face a similar need to raise money. This was further evidence that Robinhood's customers were those most likely to have been pushing up the meme stocks and to have been doing so by using margin debt.

For those users of WallStreetBets who already had an ax to grind with a financial establishment that they saw as inherently corrupt, the broker's move was a validation of their suspicions. There were widespread but false accusations that hedge funds had intervened to force Robinhood's hand. These were repeated not just on social media, where conspiracies traditionally spring to life, but also by politicians and television personalities jumping on a story three weeks after the shocking attack on the Capitol. Here was a bad guy people could agree on regardless of their political affiliation. That evening, Dave Portnoy, who had just reached the eight-month anniversary of funding his

E\*Trade account for day-trading, was invited by Fox News host Tucker
Carlson to assess the GameStop squeeze and Robinhood's drastic move
for viewers of the network's top-rated show.

"I've never been more convinced about market manipulation and
hedge funds controlling the game than today," he said.

The fact that the asset manager Citadel had injected cash into Melvin Capital a few days earlier and that Citadel Securities processed the
largest share of Robinhood's trades stoked further conspiracies and
confusion. The two companies share a name and a controlling owner,
Ken Griffin, and the securities firm was handling huge volumes of retail stock and options orders that week. The unfairness of hedge funds'
still being able to trade while ordinary people couldn't was brought up
again and again, as if those funds were eager to buy the now grossly
overvalued meme stocks.

There were plenty of commentators like Portnoy who either didn't
understand what was happening or chose not to understand so that
they could enhance their brand by standing up for the underdog. Ob-
jective news outlets didn't amplify the conspiracies, but the overwhelming majority of articles focused on the scrappy revolutionaries and the
shocked Wall Streeters on the other side of the ledger. Those were
the stories that got clicks. Only a handful of party poopers pointed
to the fact that the revolutionaries themselves had nearly blown the
system up, and they were careful not to sound like they were blam-
ing the victim. Journalists, as they say, write the first draft of history,
and that first draft is the only one that most of the public remembers,
not the more nuanced, better-informed one that comes after the dust
has cleared. The truth is, though, that the forces behind the meme-
stock squeeze had been bubbling beneath the surface for more than
a year by that point. Social media and free trading apps had been a
potent combination, producing a windfall for Wall Street. They just
worked a bit too well during the squeeze. Even the world's most sophisticated financial system is only as strong as its weakest link, and

Robinhood simply didn't have the money or the organizational heft to harness the creature that it had helped to unleash.

The system as a whole bent without breaking, but it was a close call. And, in a sign that America has a legal system just as efficient as its financial markets, a class action suit was filed within hours against thirty-five defendants, including several retail brokers and Melvin Capital, which no longer had a short position in GameStop.

"Rather than use their financial acumen to compete and invest in good opportunities in the market to recoup the losses in their short positions, or paying the price for their highly speculative bad bets, these defendants instead hatched an anticompetitive scheme to limit trading in the relevant securities," said counsel Joseph Saveri. "It is unlikely that such a widespread ban among brokerages would have been achievable without a concerted effort in violation of antitrust laws."[2]

Even before trading was restricted, WallStreetBets users were feeling aggrieved. Late on Wednesday the subreddit had briefly gone private, an action taken by its own moderators, as they dealt with a surge of new users. Shortly after that, the group's server was taken off-line by Discord for using racial slurs following what that company said were repeated warnings—a reminder of some members' darker tendencies. Founder Jaime Rogozinski, a Jew married to a Mexican woman, cited the bigotry and homophobia on the forum as a reason for splitting with the group in the spring of 2020 in an interview published that morning.

"There were a handful of mods who were straight up white supremacists," he said.[3]

GameStop shares plunged by 30 percent in after-hours trading following the news that the subreddit had been taken off-line, yet the group gained more than a million new members overnight. On Thursday, January 28, though, even following trading restrictions, its price surged at one point to as much as $483 a share, an all-time high. It was briefly the most valuable stock in the Russell 2000 Index of smaller companies, which meant that a bunch of passive investors who would never involve themselves in an uprising to squeeze hedge funds had more than a little exposure to the meme stock through safe, boring index funds. But it wouldn't last long: in a bout of volatility rarely seen in anything but a penny stock, GameStop's price plunged within an hour and a half to $112 a share.

Keith Gill, whose name was now starting to seep out in some news reports as the man behind the pseudonyms Roaring Kitty and Deep-FuckingValue, briefly had a net worth that day well over $50 million based on the company's peak share price. By the end of the day, though, that was down to $33 million. His followers on the subreddit might have lost money that day, but nowhere near as much as he did. They were overjoyed to see that their hero had held the line:

*HIS CASH TOTAL DID.NOT.BUDGE. DFV TEACHES PATIENCE TO THE FRIGGIN DALAI LAMA.[4]*

Up until that point, the "us versus them," class-struggle aspect of the meme-stock squeeze had been mostly in the minds of some of the subreddit's members. Only Andrew Left had directly called them out, and both he and Gabe Plotkin, who had wisely stayed silent, had exited their short positions by January 26 with gigantic losses.

Right on cue, a hedge fund billionaire stepped up to play the bad guy in a "let them eat cake" moment. Leon Cooperman, the seventy-eight-year-old manager of Omega Family Office, made his comments at lunchtime Thursday to CNBC.

"The reason the market is doing what it's doing is people are sitting at home getting their checks from the government, okay, and this fair share is a bullshit concept," he said. "It's just a way of attacking wealthy people."[5]

Dallas Mavericks owner Mark Cuban, a younger and much cooler billionaire and also a frequent guest on CNBC, took the opposite tack, writing in a Wednesday evening tweet that his eleven-year-old was on the forum and made money trading stocks: "got to say I LOVE LOVE what is going on with #wallstreetbets. All of those years of High Frequency Traders front running retail traders, now speed and density of information and retail trading is giving the little guy an edge."[6]

Dan Nathan, also a CNBC personality and principal of Risk-Reversal Advisors, which advises fund managers, responded to Cuban's tweet with an astute observation about what was really going on amid all the excitement about the little guys' beating Wall Street at its own game.

> I suspect when the dust settles from the impending mushroom cloud, high-frequency traders & options wholesalers will be the real winners, they'll make money on way up & down and in vol. House always wins . . . cheers to their success, but "money ain't got no owners, only spenders."[7]

The Reddit Revolution felt like the sort of thing that cried out for government involvement, but it was hard to know what to do or say. White House press secretary Jen Psaki, asked about the new administration's views of the squeeze one week into her new job, said that President Biden's economic team was "monitoring the situation."[8] Biden himself didn't hear, or sagely pretended not to hear, the questions reporters shouted about GameStop.

The SEC, without an active head just a week after his inauguration, put out an anodyne statement:

> We are aware of and actively monitoring the on-going market volatility in the options and equities markets and, consistent with our mission to protect investors and maintain fair, orderly, and efficient markets, we are working with our fellow regulators to assess the

*situation and review the activities of regulated entities, financial*
*intermediaries, and other market participants.*[9]

FINRA, the brokers' self-regulatory organization, was oddly silent on the trading halt by companies under its purview. The following day it issued a blog post seemingly aimed at the WallStreetBets phenomenon: "Following the Crowd: Investing and Social Media."

"No matter where you get your trading insights, and whether you are following a recommendation to buy stocks, bonds, options or something else, know this: where there is opportunity, there is also risk."[10]

The SEC's Office of Investor Education and Advocacy issued a similar advisory the same day. There was nothing wrong with the guidance itself, but it was certainly no accident that both attempts to educate the newest investors came out on a day that they were losing billions of dollars in a mania that the organizations had done nothing to prevent.

"Education is a way to maintain the status quo and look like you're helping people," scoffs Jon Stein, chairman of robo-adviser Betterment, which doesn't allow clients to buy individual stocks.

The meme-stock squeeze and Robinhood's cash crunch came as a surprise to the authorities and nearly everybody else. The surge in retail activity and risky behavior was by then a year old, though. There had been dozens of news stories about mostly young investors making risky bets that many of them clearly didn't understand. Those investors were even less likely to read a company's bankruptcy filing or the 183-page form detailing the risks of options than you are to carefully scan the much shorter contract when you install the latest version of iOS on your phone.

It shouldn't have been hard for FINRA or government regulators to grasp that Robinhood's widely copied business model thrived when some of its customers were hyperactive and unsophisticated and that the hottest "trading insights" seemed to work precisely because so many people adopted them at once. If there was a time to put in some speed bumps, then it was well before the meme-stock squeeze and trading restrictions made retail traders both heroes and victims. Now the broker was being cast as the bad guy, but not for acting as an enabler to ill-advised speculation. Politicians on both sides of the political spectrum were clamoring to "let the people trade."

Asking revelers at a nightclub to keep down the noise won't win you any popularity contests. It is especially unpopular with the nightclub's owner, though. Money equals influence in America, and financial firms collectively are the largest political donors by far of any industry. It wasn't just brokers and wholesalers who were making a mint from the surge in retail trading: investment banks that hardly interacted directly with the public were too, as trading revenue surged and as offerings of blank check companies, so loved by retail investors yet with their rewards so sharply skewed to the financiers behind them, continued to be approved by securities regulators at a record clip. The first quarter of 2021 saw more SPACs issued than in all of 2020, which had itself been a record year.

After taking virtually no action, it was unclear what regulators could do in the heat of the moment other than to sound concerned. The situation was fluid, and there was no obvious wrongdoing other than possible manipulation by people or organizations that had infiltrated social media sites. Unfortunately for Robinhood, it had become the public villain in this story for an entirely different reason: not allowing its customers to keep buying the meme stocks. Tenev had an innocent explanation, but politicians saw which way the wind was blowing. Unlike regulators, they weren't shy about shooting first and asking questions later. They would mostly be the wrong questions.

# Chapter 19

# Men in Tights

They say that there's no such thing as bad publicity.

A young social media marketer may have proved that once and for all on January 29, 2021, when he hired an airplane to fly over San Francisco trailing a banner that read SUCK MY NUTS ROBINHOOD. Kaspar Povilanskas gave the pilot a bit extra to have him circle the broker's Menlo Park headquarters just south of the city a few times.[1]

Meanwhile, about one hundred thousand users egged on by social media outrage went onto the Google Play store to give the Robinhood Android app one-star reviews, tanking its overall rating. A screenshot of one of many subsequently deleted by Google read:

*Literally engaging in illegal market manipulation by blocking purchases on stocks they don't want you to purchase. Stay away from this app at all costs.*

And, in what might have been the most embarrassing episode of all, Michael Bolton—yes, that Michael Bolton—released a song on YouTube to the tune of his 1989 hit "How Am I Supposed to Live without You" about the controversial practice of payment for order flow. The message was sponsored by a much smaller competitor of Robinhood's, Public.com, that said the following Monday that it would scrap the practice and cover other brokers' account transfer fees for new customers.

"You might be thinking, how can I ever trust again," said the crooner, who topped the soft rock charts before many Robinhood customers were born. "Well, I know a thing or two about breakups."

> I could hardly believe it, what I saw on Reddit today
> Was hoping I could get it straight from you.
> They told me 'bout order flow, so I Googled, now I know.
> I think I gotta find somebody new.
> So tell me all about it
> Tell me who you sell my trades to[2]

The outrage quickly spread from online and aeronautical flaming to the courtroom. A class action lawsuit was filed the same day the trading restrictions were imposed in the Southern District of New York. "Robinhood's actions were done purposefully and knowingly to manipulate the market for the benefit of people and financial institutions who were not Robinhood's customers," it said.[3] By early the following week, there were more than thirty similar suits. Within six weeks there were forty-six, according to a regulatory filing. A separate subreddit was set up for those interested in suing, r/ClassAction RobinHood, that had more than forty-four thousand members as of late March.

Other organizations with similar names were deluged with hate mail. Robin Hood, a New York charitable foundation that happens to get much of its support from hedge funds—Gabe Plotkin's old boss Steven A. Cohen is an emeritus board member—was forced repeatedly to set people straight.[4] The World Wide Robin Hood Society of Nottingham, England, a group of ten enthusiasts of the company's legendary namesake, decided to embrace the craziness.

"We only know about old fashioned stock I'm afraid," said one tweet, referring to the medieval punishment to which retail investors wouldn't have minded subjecting Vlad Tenev.[5]

Celebrities such as the rapper Ja Rule and late-night talk show hosts lambasted the broker. Stephen Colbert riffed: "Oh, you're all for unfair capitalism unless you lose? Come on guys, there's no manipulation. It's just the invisible hand of the market extending you an invisible middle finger."[6]

Politicians immediately sensed which way the wind was blowing, often before stopping to understand what had actually happened. At a time of bitter political rancor, dunking on Robinhood, as well as evil hedge funds, was the one issue on which Left and Right seemed to agree.

"This is unacceptable," tweeted liberal New York congresswoman Alexandria Ocasio-Cortez on January 28. "We now need to know more about @RobinhoodApp's decision to block retail investors from purchasing stock while hedge funds are freely able to trade the stock as they see fit."[7]

Minutes later, conservative Texas senator Ted Cruz retweeted her post, adding: "Fully agree."

"On the face of it, it seems to favor a handful of rich, influential players at the expense of ordinary citizens and ordinary traders," he later said to reporters.[8]

Donald Trump Jr. weighed in as well: "It took less than a day for big tech, big government and the corporate media to spring into action and begin colluding to protect their hedge fund buddies on Wall Street. This is what a rigged system looks like, folks!"[9]

Back on the left, Bernie Sanders told an ABC morning talk show that weekend that the incident confirmed his dim view of high finance: "I have long believed that the business model of Wall Street is fraud. I think we have to take a very hard look at the kind of illegal activities and outrageous behavior on the part of the hedge funds and other Wall Street players."[10]

Robinhood explained in tweets and blog posts the technical details of why it had to act, stressing that it faced a huge increase in regulatory capital requirements. While it probably came at a convenient time for a few hedge funds, further unrestricted meme-stock buying would have bankrupted Robinhood and inflicted severe losses on others. It nearly did anyway.

Republican senator Josh Hawley of Missouri was one of the few not to accuse Robinhood of restricting trading to save hedge funds, though he got many facts wrong in an impassioned essay, "Calling Wall Street's Bluff," in which he lumped together conservative ire at coastal elites and social media platforms accused of being unfair to those on the right with Robinhood.

"And the elites are happy to help. Enter Robinhood—as in, steal from the rich. Robinhood was the trading platform for the little guy. No fees, no hassle. It was Big Tech, once again, allegedly democratizing another sphere of American life captured by elite control. But like the tech platforms, Robinhood wasn't really about its users. Its bread was buttered by selling the data on users' trades to the big players— the elite guys, like Citadel—to give them inside tips on where retail investors were sending their money."[11]

Misunderstandings aside, what he and almost every other critic initially failed to grasp was how dangerous Robinhood's funding crisis had been. Had the company not acted quickly, and had its clever business model not been so attractive to potential investors with a few billion dollars to spare, this book might have been about a Lehman-like market panic rather than a David and Goliath battle over meme stocks. The economist Mohamed El-Erian, president of Queens' College at the University of Cambridge and one of the most respected financial minds on the planet, said the market came very close to an "accident" that could have forced several other financial firms into distress.[12]

But correcting members of Congress, or for that matter enraged twenty-five-year-olds on Twitter, isn't wise or effective. It seemed like an utter disaster for Robinhood when it should have been enjoying its best month ever. A company that had named itself after a folk hero who stole from the rich to give to the poor was being accused of doing the opposite and short-circuiting America's capital markets to help the most despised group of plutocrats—hedge fund managers. A little more than a decade after the global financial crisis that was such a formative event for its young customers and whose ripples were still being felt in widening income inequality, Robinhood had supposedly stabbed them in the back.

## Millions of New Customers

Many users claimed on social media that they were done with Robinhood after it restricted trading of the meme stocks on January 28. There is a big difference between what people say and what they do, though. On the same day that trading in meme stocks was limited, the Robinhood app rose to the most downloaded rank on the iOS App Store for the first time ever (Reddit was number two, also for the first time, inspired by the heroics of WallStreetBets, which quadrupled its membership in a week).[13]

On Friday, January 29, just as the airplane with the rude banner was circling its headquarters and with some trading still curtailed, Robinhood hit a record 600,000 daily downloads according to JMP Securities—four times better than its best day in raucous March 2020.

For the month of January as a whole, it had 3.6 million downloads on iOS and Google combined, compared with just 93,000 for much larger broker Schwab. And cancel culture didn't trouble the company the next month either, even as Tenev was roasted in the February 18 congressional hearing: Robinhood had 2.1 million downloads during the month, a 55 percent jump from February 2020, which was itself a boom time for it and other retail brokers. Competitors serving the same young demographic such as Webull and eToro also saw a big uptick in business. For months it wasn't clear how many of those people actually signed up or how many existing customers left in disgust. In July, Robinhood put its investors' fears to rest with the news that it had added more than five million customers during the quarter of GameStop's wild ride and nearly that many the following quarter. It had quadrupled its customer rolls in just a year and a half. The excitement of the meme-stock squeeze far outweighed the negativity of the trading halt.

Even as competitors such as eToro flooded social media with ads that played up the "YOLO trader" stereotype, Robinhood could afford to be more dignified. The majority of its marketing spending was on the lottery-like element of giving a random free stock to both new customers and anyone who referred them—an extremely effective technique that paid for itself within a matter of months as new customers began trading.

Robinhood says that its warm and fuzzy Super Bowl ad, which ran just a few days after the trading halt, had been planned beforehand. Its marketing that winter and spring continued to focus on empowering people who were new to and intimidated by investing. A promo on its website from March 2021, shortly after it filed for an initial public offering, read:

> *Every investor has a story to tell. See how Robinhood has changed the way people see their finances—and themselves.*

The page showed an ethnically diverse group of clients, such as twenty-five-year-old Angelina, who said: "The investor in my head was someone who wore a suit and a tie. Robinhood *changed* that for me."

It also described thirty-year-old Kathyria, who didn't have the time for "lengthy investor education" but was able to dive in anyway: "With Robinhood, she was able to learn the basics and got familiar with managing a portfolio. After a while, she was able to ease into more sophisticated trading methods, which helped her feel more control over her finances."

The lone white male was sixty-year-old David—also the only person featured who was older than thirty-three. David wasn't a customer looking to ride meme stocks to the moon but instead used Robinhood "to learn about new businesses working towards ambitious goals to better the planet through environmental initiatives and healthy communities."

It was all very wholesome, but Robinhood's initial public offering that summer valued the company at $33 billion, or about $1,500 per customer, and it was unlikely that Angelina, Kathyria, and David were pulling their weight. The ones who did were mostly young, male, active, and confident enough to use options and margin. And if they bought stocks because short sellers had targeted them, then there was an extra bonus since Robinhood made a great deal of money lending out their shares. Those customers that signed on during 2020 were the most profitable cohort yet, producing more revenue for Robinhood than those who joined in prior years. They also were the main reason that Tenev needed to come up with a huge pile of cash in the middle of the night.

## Robinhood Robinhooded Robinhood

Robinhood takes pains to downplay the YOLO image. It said in November 2020 that 98 percent of its customers aren't "pattern day traders."[14] That is a designation common to all brokers imposed by FINRA, their own self-regulatory body. It flags and potentially suspends someone making more than four round-trip trades in a rolling five-day period if the value of those trades rises above a certain percentage of their assets.

Clearly there was at least a significant minority of Robinhood customers that was able to be hyperactive. For example, one incredible statistic from the first quarter of 2020 by Alphacution Research Conservatory shows that Robinhood customers traded forty times the number of shares per dollar held in their accounts as those with a Charles Schwab account and eighty-eight times the number of options contracts.[15]

The bigger question is whether they should even be called "customers." Most weren't, in the strict sense of purchasing a good or service from the company—trades were free, and they were buying shares from someone else out there in the market. Unless they paid margin interest to Robinhood or the $5 a month Robinhood Gold fee, they were more like someone with a Facebook or Twitter account. A social network's customers are its advertisers. Their most valuable users are the ones who engage with it the most frequently, creating content and leaving enough personally identifying information for tailored ads that they then view. Likewise, Robinhood's main source of revenue was companies such as Citadel Securities and Virtu Financial that paid it for the right to execute its trades or big investment banks that borrowed its customers' shares to lend to hedge funds like Melvin. Its most valuable users were the hyperactive ones—those most likely to move in large packs and use derivatives or borrowed money. It worked like a charm for the broker until it worked a bit too well.

The banker turned blogger Packy McCormick came up with a perfect phrase to describe it: "Robinhood Robinhooded Robinhood." It encouraged risky behavior by its clients because it profited from that behavior.[16]

But when you get more and more people to take big risks, then the market itself is affected. It creates a lot of volatility and weird price changes, and, eventually, if you encourage the use of borrowing, some of those people will get "margin calls"—forced sales to pay back that money that can leave them wiped out. If that happens to an individual Robinhood user, then it is tough luck for that person—he or she should have read the fine print. Please put up more cash, or we have to liquidate your portfolio.

But margin calls can happen to brokers too, and their creditors are more cautious—they don't wait for a broker to actually face a shortfall. That could bring the whole industry down like a row of dominoes. Robinhood itself suddenly looked like a pattern day trader during the squeeze. When too many of its users had too much riding with borrowed money on the same surging, extremely volatile stocks that they had heard about on Reddit or TikTok, alarm bells went off. It left Robinhood potentially on the hook for the inevitable reversal, and that would have affected many others if the broker blew up as a result.

## No Conspiracy

That was why Robinhood had to pull the plug on further purchases, but not sales, of shares or options in several companies and raise a bunch of cash in a hurry—so it could reduce risk enough to lower the amount of cash required for its own form of margin call. It drew down its credit lines, but the sum it needed was still much more than banks were willing to lend it. To retail traders who felt that they had hedge funds on the ropes, the halt seemed conveniently timed. The only companies it was meant to save were the ones that made it possible for them to trade, though.

Brokers route their orders to wholesalers or exchanges. They rely on a different organization, a clearinghouse, to handle the details of everyone getting paid what they are owed. To make sure that one firm's difficulties don't ever create a payment crisis, they mutualize risk—spread it across all firms using it—and ask them to set aside collateral such as cash or ultra-safe Treasury bills. As part of the reforms after the financial crisis, clearinghouses were declared to be "systemically important" and faced tighter rules.

If there are a lot of offsetting risky trades, it isn't such a problem, but if a clearinghouse sees many of a broker's customers making similar risky trades—for example, buying shares and call options of a handful of meme stocks that they are convinced will go "to the moon"—then they get worried.

The shares they have bought have often not been paid for yet. Settlement for stocks is T+2—it takes two business days to get your money. In a blog post, Tenev described the risks as a shortcoming of the system, deflecting any blame for enabling an orgy of risk-taking. He made fixing it sound like a call to cure cancer:

> The existing two-day period to settle trades exposes investors and the industry to unnecessary risk. . . . There is no reason why the greatest financial system in the world cannot settle trades in real time. I believe we can and should act now to deploy our intellectual capital and engineering resources to move to real-time settlement.[17]

Yet he understood that it was the system in which Robinhood operated. Consider what happens if a retail investor buys a GameStop share for $480 with borrowed money on Thursday morning and the price collapses to $212 on Monday before it settles. His collateral isn't sufficient, so if he can't come up with the cash immediately, then his broker has to sell the stock. In the case of the meme stocks, which obviously were headed for a huge reversal and were owned by so many of its customers, the losses could be crippling. The clearinghouse saw that.

Not everyone bought the meme stocks on margin, but Robinhood had grown tremendously over the past year, and so had its margin loans—one of the ways it earns money in the absence of commissions. A March 2021 regulatory filing by Robinhood revealed a big increase in the form of secured lending. At the end of 2020, it had nearly $3.4 billion in loans outstanding to its customers—five times as much as at the end of 2019.[18] The figure had risen by $2 billion just in the second half of the year. Then it rose by another $2 billion in just the first three months of 2021. Although margin loans are backed by stock in a customer's account, accidents happen, and traders often don't have the personal resources to top up their accounts when their brokers ask. In 2020, Robinhood wrote off more than $42 million in customer loans.[19]

As Tenev explained in another blog post, Robinhood's daily deposit requirement as determined by the clearinghouse's risk formula rose tenfold between Monday, January 25, and Thursday, January 28. To satisfy the new requirements, it suddenly needed less risk and more cash—a lot more cash. By the following week, it had secured a total of $3.4 billion in fresh capital. That was more money than Robinhood had raised in its entire history as a company. Other brokers faced increased cash needs too, but many of them are backed by larger financial firms, and none had customers as interested in the meme stocks as Robinhood. Recall that there was a heavy overlap between Robinhood and WallStreetBets. Industry-wide deposit requirements rose by only 30 percent.[20]

But all's well that ends well, right? Much to El-Erian's dismay, "the market's reaction to having avoided an accident has been to take on even more risk overall."[21] The response to Robinhood's cash call was overwhelming. Although they were angry, most Robinhood users would stick around, and many more were signing up every week. Unlike a troubled bank seeking a bailout, or even Melvin Capital, which insists its own cash infusion wasn't a rescue, Robinhood got a valuation that was no bargain for the buyers. It was a lucrative business that had just gained millions of customers courtesy of the Reddit Revolution. The fresh cash helped Robinhood rise to a private market valuation of $40 billion in the secondary market just weeks after the trading halt and a week before Tenev's congressional appearance. Its previous fund-raising round just five months earlier had valued it at $11.7 billion.[22]

## Payment for Order Flow

But none of the finger wagging in the weeks after the squeeze was about Robinhood's incredibly close call. Given all the outrage, members of Congress and journalists can be forgiven for not dwelling on an accident that didn't happen.

By the time the February 18 hearing rolled around, members of the House Committee on Financial Services were no longer fixated on the myth that hedge funds had been bailed out by the trading restrictions. Instead, they spent a great deal of energy probing the suspicious-sounding arrangement that allows Robinhood and others to offer free trading, which brought them at least one step closer to the problem. Payment for order flow went from being an arcane technical aspect of the brokerage business to a supposed smoking gun overnight when Robinhood suspended trading of the meme stocks. Surely someone very bad had come up with it. Well, that part is at least right. The practice was pioneered in the early 1990s by the late Ponzi schemer Bernard Madoff.

As recently as 2004, a prominent lawyer sent a detailed complaint to the SEC urging it to ban payment for order flow for options trading. "This practice distorts order routing decisions, is anti-competitive, and creates an obvious and substantial conflict of interest between broker-dealers and their customers," he wrote.[23] The man's employer? Ken Griffin's Citadel Investment Group. Citadel Securities, majority

Keith Gill (aka DeepFuckingValue aka Roaring Kitty) in his basement during the height of the mania. He reasoned that GameStop's shares were like a cigar that had been thrown out and still had a few puffs in it, but the incredible wave of buying he helped inspire made him almost a thousand times his money.
(Photo by Kayana Szymczak)

Reddit cofounder and CEO Steve Huffman, known by the pseudonym spez, was called to testify before Congress about the role of WallStreetBets in the squeeze. He said that the investment advice one got on the social network was "probably among the best" because thousands of people have to accept it.
(Courtesy of Reddit)

Robinhood CEO Vlad Tenev was running the hottest brokerage firm in the world. Then he got a phone call in the middle of the night asking for $3 billion in three hours and he became public enemy number one to "YOLO traders" for restricting trading in meme stocks.
(Courtesy of Robinhood)

The story of how a CEO traveled into the Jungle community. What he found was a revolution. Apes, Gorillas and Monkeys unified as one. Ready to Change the World

# GORILLAS IN THE MIST
The Adventures of Adam Aron

One of many photoshopped movie posters praising Adam Aron, CEO of AMC Theatres, who became a hero of the "apes" on WallStreetBets and was affectionately called Silverback. Aron would sell millions, and the company would sell billions, of dollars worth of AMC shares during the frenzy.

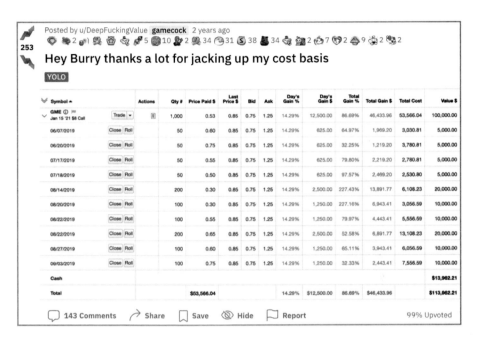

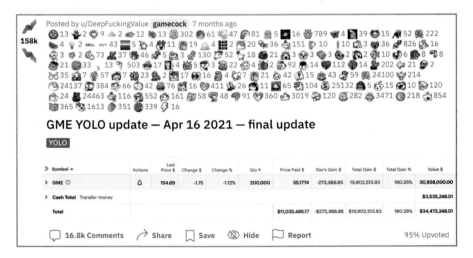

The first post by Keith Gill on WallStreetBets in September 2019.
Other users urged him to sell after he had doubled his original investment.

Keith Gill's final post on WallStreetBets. At his peak, he had made a thousand times
his money and millions were checking daily to see if he had sold or not.

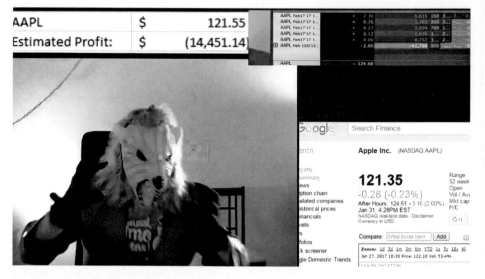

F.S. Comeau Apple earnings reaction real time

F. S. Comeau was one of the original YOLO traders on WallStreetBets. He claims to have lost most of his money on bad bets and gambled everything on derivatives that would have paid off handsomely if Apple earnings in 2017 were disappointing. Comeau livestreamed his devastating loss and apparent nervous breakdown in a wolf mask.

(Courtesy of Michael Huang)

Dr. Michael Burry was one of the heroes of *The Big Short*, but the quirky value investor's purchase of GameStop shares in 2019 got the ball rolling in a squeeze that would blow up other short sellers a year-and-a-half later. Burry made a bundle and sold. Then he called meme stock mania "unnatural, insane, and dangerous."

(Bloomberg via Getty Images)

An airplane with a banner reading SUCK MY NUTS ROBINHOOD flying over the broker's Menlo Park headquarters on January 29, 2021, the day after it restricted the purchase of meme stocks. Customers were furious, but new ones kept signing up for the app-based broker anyway.

Gabriel Plotkin was on top of the world in 2020, personally earning close to a billion dollars managing Melvin Capital Management, one of the hottest hedge funds in the world. But he would see more than half of its value evaporate in a matter of days after being targeted by the "degenerates" on WallStreetBets.

Since he started trading out of his Harvard dorm room as a freshman, everything Ken Griffin touched seemingly has turned to gold. That continued during the GameStop squeeze as his firm Citadel picked up a bargain stake in Gabe Plotkin's bloodied hedge fund and his trading firm processed a record number of retail orders during the frenzy.

Jaime Rogozinski founded the subreddit WallStreetBets in 2012 when he was frustrated by other boards' conservative approach. He would have a falling out with other moderators shortly before the forum became the epicenter of the "Reddit Revolution" that spooked but also enriched Wall Street.

(Courtesy of Jaime Rogozinski)

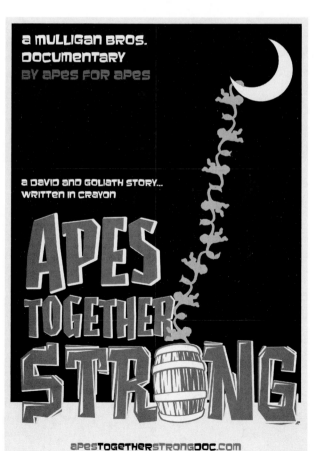

a MULLIGAN BROS. DOCUMENTARY
BY apes FOR apes

a DAVID and GOLIATH STORY...
WRITTEN IN CRAYON

APES TOGETHER STRONG

apesTOGETHERSTRONGDOC.com
ILLUSTRATED BY andreas nicolaou

Twin brothers and filmmakers Quinn and Finley Mulligan were so inspired by the achievements of retail traders on social media who took on hedge funds that they made a documentary film about the movement, *Apes Together Strong*, which was a motto of the group on WallStreetBets.

(Courtesy of Apes Together Strong LLC)

Brash short-seller Andrew Left had taken on dozens of companies over a storied career. Then he told the WallStreetBets crowd that they were "the suckers at the poker table" for betting on GameStop. It was like waving a red flag at a bull. Steep losses and harassment by the degenerates led him to cease publishing short research.

owned by Griffin, would later be the big, behind-the-scenes winner in the retail trading boom and Robinhood's greatest source of revenue.

Clearly times have changed. If the practice were outlawed today, then most of the brokerage business would be just fine, but a company like Robinhood that caters to people with tiny accounts, and relies on some of them to be hyperactive, would have a problem keeping trading "free." When SEC chairman Gary Gensler said in an August 2021 interview that banning the practice was "on the table," shares of Robinhood fell by more than 8 percent.[24] As evidence of how hard it would be for it to make money, competitor Public.com, which dropped the practice and employed Michael Bolton to poach enraged customers from Robinhood, said it would instead route its orders directly to exchanges but that it would solicit tips.

"Direct routing to the exchanges is more expensive, and therefore we're turning what used to be a revenue stream (PFOF) into a cost center and we're optimistic that the difference will be offset by the optional tipping feature," it said in a statement.[25]

The offer proved popular, with the company announcing a little over two weeks later that it had doubled its customer count to one million. Public.com says it doesn't "encourage day trading, nor do we push margin credit on new investors."

That sounds great, and discouraging day trading is commendable, but there is nothing inherently bad about payment for order flow. The problem is that it helped lower the barrier to entry so that Wall Street could attract a new group of small-dollar speculators while being able to boast that it was doing something noble by "democratizing finance." The meme-stock squeeze probably wouldn't have happened without payment for order flow, but the finger-pointing that followed wound up chasing shadows.

Orders routed to a wholesaler like Citadel or Virtu that make those payments are "dark"—orders flow into and out of their big black boxes and all you get to see are the results—whereas those that go to an actual stock exchange are "lit." The transparency of going through a lit market sounds better but often costs a bit more. If an order is routed to an exchange, then the broker's duty is to hit the "national best bid or best offer," depending on whether the customer is buying or selling. That is a term defined by the SEC and is exactly what it sounds like— the best bid or offer on an exchange. Just like a car salesman's best offer after talking to his manager, though, it isn't really the best you can get.

A modern financial market doesn't work like eBay, where people who want money and others who want stock are matched for a fee. The odds of, say, a buyer of twenty-two shares of Netflix and a seller of twenty-two shares showing up simultaneously are tiny. For a trade made via a smartphone to be filled instantly, which is what retail investors have come to expect, a market maker or wholesaler takes on a small risk each time it does so—particularly during a wild time like the meme-stock squeeze. It generally makes a profit. Citadel Securities is privately held, some 85 percent of it by Ken Griffin, so we don't know how it did during the squeeze. But a leaked presentation obtained by *Bloomberg* revealed that Citadel nearly doubled its net trading revenue in 2020 to at least $6.6 billion and that it had record earnings before interest, tax, depreciation, and amortization of $4.1 billion.[26]

Citadel and its competitors usually offer a narrower spread than the stock exchange's published best bid and offer, which is called "price improvement," and they aren't allowed to give you a worse price if the order is above a certain number of shares. Ironically, the much-scrutinized practice is the one area in which retail investors get treated better than the pros. Wholesalers are wary of giving the same prices to funds that are smart enough to take advantage and cost them money in a rapidly shifting market.

"It's a very easy marketing ploy to point a finger at something that sounds evil and is complex for most to understand," wrote Al Grujic, who founded All of Us Financial. The retail broker uses the practice of payment for order flow but rebates part of the revenue it receives from wholesalers to its users as well as other forms of revenue that brokers earn from customers, such as the money it makes from stock lending to short sellers.[27]

By routing orders directly to an exchange, Public.com is costing itself money and seeks to defray it with voluntary tips. Some small percentage of retail traders might be fine with that, but they also probably aren't the type to make thousands of trades a year. It would be fairer and more beneficial to impose a small cost on all trades uniformly through a modest fee or financial transaction tax so that people who trade more pay more.

## Invisible Pickpockets

The problem with payment for order flow is that it helps to make free trading possible and then encourages many customers to trade excessively. Each trade really isn't free because retail investors often make poor decisions, giving up a small amount of their transaction to invisible pickpockets. Opponents of a financial transaction tax point out that spreads between buying and selling prices would widen and costs increase if a small levy were imposed. They probably are right, but somebody prudently buying and selling a handful of stocks or mutual funds each year would give up a minuscule sum while less grounded investors wouldn't be as tempted to chase stonks to the moon, probably saving them money.

Naturally, that wouldn't be good for Robinhood. It notes among the risk factors in its offering prospectus that it would be affected more than others in its industry if the practice were banned. While the trading restrictions were a near-death experience and seemed like a huge black eye for the broker, the outrage might have actually been a fortuitous development. Suddenly almost every politician and social influencer was a champion of the little guys' being able to do whatever wild and crazy things they want with their money. In an interview with *The Wall Street Journal* published a day after the trading curbs were announced, Tenev summed it up perfectly:

"The irony isn't lost on me that we're in some ways having the opposite type of conversation than we typically had" with our critics, he said. "Up until about a month ago, it was, 'Are there too few barriers?' . . . Now it's all about, 'Why did you guys put these restrictions?' It's a strange situation."[28]

Chapter 20

# January 29, 2021

'm not out for anybody."

Keith Gill's interview with *The Wall Street Journal* went live just as the stock market opened for trading on Friday, January 29. The GameStop squeeze was by now a national obsession, and readers flocked to hear about the man at the center of the Reddit Revolution, lighting up the website with huge traffic for what was officially a Money and Investing story. Gill turned out to be a thoroughly sympathetic character—a middle-class, suburban family man who recorded his by-then popular YouTube videos at night in his basement to avoid waking his young daughter.[1]

But he was no revolutionary. Nor was he a manipulator, as regulators and private plaintiffs would soon allege. Nowhere in his many posts on Reddit or Twitter or in his YouTube videos did he ask people to buy a stock or even egg them on to "HOLD THE LINE" in order to squeeze short sellers, as so many others did.

In the days after the meme-stock squeeze, Gill, a former collegiate track star, posted an overdubbed video clip from *Forrest Gump* to his Twitter account. It is the scene of Gump with an overgrown beard being trailed on a bridge by microphone-toting reporters after he decides to "go out for a little run" and winds up jogging across the country for three and a half years, attracting a huge following.

REPORTERS: "Why are you buying GME? Are you doing this for world peace? Are you doing this for the homeless? Are you buying GME for women's rights? Or for the environment? Or for animals?"

FORREST NARRATING: "They just couldn't believe that someone would buy all that GME for no particular reason."

REPORTER: "Why are you doing this?"

FORREST: "I just like the stock."[2]

That he did. Gill had bet what was surely a big chunk of his net worth on GameStop a year and a half earlier. He wrote his first Reddit post about it in September 2019 to general skepticism. After doubling his investment in 2019 and then growing it thirtyfold in 2020, he multiplied it another fifteen times in January 2021. By the end of the month's final trading session, his E*Trade account had a balance of $46,043,545. At that point, Gill was the focus of so much attention and adoration on the board that buying any other stock and telegraphing the fact would have earned him another fortune—the sort of reaction even Elon Musk, Dave Portnoy, or Chamath Palihapitiya might envy. But he didn't.

GameStop shares would soar above $400 one final time during the trading session on Friday, January 29. It seems to have been a reaction to a slight easing of trading conditions by Robinhood and others as well as another round of short sellers' buying back stock to cover their bets rather than anything Gill said or wrote.

This was the fourth straight day that GameStop and WallStreetBets were dominating the headlines. The subreddit's membership had more than tripled from a week earlier, and there were hundreds of thousands of people opening and funding retail trading accounts at Robinhood and other brokers that week—many because they just wanted to be a part of something, but quite a few who believed they were getting in on a hot stock while it still had some way to run.

"Is it to [*sic*] late to buy and make profit?" read one typical response to a tweet from Gill's Roaring Kitty Twitter account at the time.

Even with that tailwind of fresh entrants, momentum became harder and harder to sustain for a variety of reasons.

First there were technical ones: GameStop was by then worth more than $20 billion, and it took a lot more cash to move the needle. Meanwhile, the percentage of shares sold short had dropped to about 50 percent from 140 percent at the start of the month, and the cost to borrow shares to initiate new short positions was starting to drop as well.

At the same time, the incredible volatility of the past several days made it extremely expensive to use options to effect a fresh gamma squeeze. As older options expired—many would on that Friday—the first thing options dealers would do was to sell the shares they had bought to protect themselves.

And then there were a couple of psychological reasons that the rally was long in the tooth. Organizing tribal behavior works when you have an enemy. The Redditors were now angrier at their main broker than at evil hedge funds. Gabe Plotkin had sought a cash infusion a few days earlier and reportedly had exited his short positions with a steep loss—it would be leaked the following day just how steep at a shocking 53 percent of his fund's assets. He was thoroughly defeated. Left bowed out too, and he even put out a YouTube video that Friday explaining that he was quitting the business of issuing short reports. From now on, he was on the same team—sort of.

"Young people want to buy stocks. That's the zeitgeist. They don't want to short stocks, so I'm going to help them buy stocks," he said.[3]

And then there was DeepFuckingValue, who was no longer some mystery man posting screenshots of his account. He was, of all things, a licensed financial professional—not someone who was trying to burn the system down.

The whole situation was paradoxical. The trading halt seemed like a slap in the face to the generation trying to stick it to the man, and now everyone—politicians, celebrities, and even their parents—seemed to agree with them. It wasn't quite an intergenerational kumbaya moment, though.

"Once you look past the vitriol, you find people who don't want to be duped or condescended to," says Quinn Mulligan, part of the duo behind the planned documentary about the meme-stock squeeze.

The newest, youngest class of traders went into the pandemic eleven months earlier angry at their generation's economic predicament and were now more pissed off than ever. Not only was their movement's most prominent, quantifiable goal, sending GameStop shares "TO THE MOON," getting harder to accomplish, but a lot of wealthy people were about to enjoy a windfall courtesy of them.

"Behind the scenes of all of this is a sense of enormous inequality," said Peter Atwater, the expert on social mood. "And capitalists found a way to monetize inequality to their own benefit."

Chapter 21

# How Not to Stick It
# to the Man

would buy magic beans on the street from a stranger if he said they had the potential to ruin a billionaire's life," explained John Motter when asked by the *Los Angeles Times* why he had invested his stimulus check in GameStop shares at the height of the squeeze. The unemployed community organizer, who remains bitter about the 2008 financial crisis, posed for a photo in a suit, top hat, and sneakers, looking like a millennial Mr. Monopoly, outside the gates of a local country club where a bronze plaque reminded members that proper golf attire was required. Motter had never owned a stock before but pledged to hang on to his position until at least the following week even if he lost money because he "didn't feel comfortable getting rich off it."[1]

He didn't. Even as Motter was mugging for the camera, though, a man who really didn't need the money was taking the opposite side of the trade.

## "Wall Street Likes Volatility"

Then seventy-six years old, Bill Gross was a retiree living in the ritzy Newport Beach enclave south of LA, where he had become a billionaire after cofounding the asset manager PIMCO. The former professional blackjack player was nicknamed the "Bond King," and for years his quirky, stream-of-consciousness essays on markets were a must-read in financial circles. "No other fund manager made more money for people than Bill Gross," said the ratings firm Morningstar when it named him bond manager of the decade.[2] Among the triumphs that would have made Motter uncomfortable: a $1.7 billion profit in September 2008 on bonds issued by the mortgage giants Fannie Mae and Freddie Mac after they were rescued by the federal government.

Gross couldn't resist coming out of retirement to pen a series of public memos during the GameStop squeeze that pointed out the futility of buying more calls after the video game retailer's shares had already risen so much and become so volatile. The options math, he explained, made it almost impossible to justify their rich premiums. He wrote that buyers "who were rooted on by several prominent investors like Elon Musk, who should know better, were the fish at the poker table, not part of an educated investment mob."[3]

Gross added that his heart was with Main Street, yet he couldn't resist taking the opposite side of the trade. He later revealed that he had earned a cool $10 million by selling call options at those inflated prices.[4] That money almost certainly came straight out of the pockets of thousands of individual investors trying in vain to keep the gamma squeeze going.

Some members of WallStreetBets insisted the whole point of the squeeze was to make money. But others—particularly among the millions who joined the forum during the last week of January 2021, tripling its ranks—clearly felt the way that Motter did: it was about sticking it to the man. When all was said and done, the revolutionaries didn't do a very good job on either count. The event that put Wall-StreetBets on the map made a lot of rich people even richer.

Not all of them, of course. Gabe Plotkin's Melvin Capital had an awful month and Maplelane Capital, another long-short hedge fund, did almost as badly, plunging by 45 percent. And Andrew Left, while coy about the dollar amount he had wagered prematurely on GameStop succumbing to gravity, said that the loss on his short bet was 100 percent. There were others that got pinched, but even the heart of the squeeze wasn't calamitous for the broad category of hedge funds like Melvin that are both long and short stocks. Analysts at JPMorgan Chase wrote that they lost only about 2 percent of their value over that Tuesday and Wednesday and that "any heavy losses in this space would most likely be confined to a few hedge funds."[5]

Many others made the same calculations as Bill Gross and earned a bundle. On January 28 alone, and just on GameStop, short sellers made a profit of $3.6 billion, according to S3 Partners. They earned another $4.7 billion combined in the first two days of February. Meanwhile, options dealers enjoyed an absolute bonanza.

The popular image of the tables being turned on America's financiers just wasn't accurate. If something stirs up the retail crowd, then it is almost always good for the industry as a whole. Take it from a man who made a fortune from the naïveté of the little guy.

"I think what the average investor doesn't understand is that Wall Street likes volatility—they make money on volatility, on volume, up or down," says Jordan Belfort, the "Wolf of Wall Street." "It's nice to have a bull market, but when volume dries up and there's no activity, that's when Wall Street suffers most."

## The Market Makers

Markets are in one sense a "zero-sum game"—your gain might be someone else's loss and vice versa—but the popular portrayal of battles of wits like those between Bobby Axelrod and Taylor Mason in the hit show *Billions* makes it seem like things happen in a vacuum. Even as Gill got rich and Plotkin became less rich on the same stock at the same time, many financial firms found themselves hoping the fight would go a few extra rounds. It was the usual situation on steroids: a big payday for Wall Street at the expense of Main Street.

There were retail traders who earned princely sums, but most did it in a reckless manner. That isn't the case for the companies that make commission-free trading possible and earn good money while doing it. Ken Griffin's Citadel Securities makes millions of small, calculated wagers that add up over time to billions of dollars in profits. In 2020, it processed almost half of all retail stock orders. It was probably even more of a force during the squeeze, with Griffin boasting in his congressional testimony that Citadel "stepped up" when its competitors were "unable or unwilling to handle the heavy volumes." He said that on Wednesday, January 27, 2021, his firm handled 7.4 billion shares for retail investors alone.

That was more retail trades than the entire US stock market saw in a typical day in 2019 before every broker moved to zero commissions. Because the figures aren't public, we don't know how lucrative the meme-stock squeeze was for Citadel Securities. Competitor Virtu Financial, which does release that information, reported the largest quarterly profit in its history. Griffin ended 2020 tied with Steven Cohen as America's thirty-seventh richest person and, as the main shareholder of both the largest wholesaler and of a $34 billion hedge fund that picked up a stake in Melvin cheaply during its moment of stress, he probably at least held his own.[6]

## Robinhood

Robinhood was in theory in the least risky position since it is just a toll taker that was paid for how many trades its customers made. Ironically, it actually came closest to going bust during the squeeze because it was too successful and couldn't handle the volume and the concentrated nature of its customers' bets. But in the end, it did more than fine, and so did Vlad Tenev and Baiju Bhatt. With the increased value of their stakes in the company, the cofounders' net worth had risen to about $2.6 billion each by July 2021.[7] When Robinhood revealed never-before-seen details of its business that month in preparation for its initial public offering, observers were taken aback by just how many new customers had signed on and how active they were despite having far less money in their accounts than customers of competitors. In just the first three months of 2021, it made almost twice as much revenue overall as it had in all of 2019. The pandemic and the meme-stock squeeze had been an amazing windfall for the company.

## Big Banks

Big investment banks were loving the Reddit Revolution too. Morgan Stanley, the broker for Gill and millions of other small fry via its "wealth management" division since buying E*Trade in 2020, doubled its net profit in the first quarter of 2021 to $4.1 billion. Speaking in February, the firm's chief financial officer, Jonathan Pruzan, gushed about results at the retail broker. "More clients, more engagement, more activity, more cash," he said, adding that the number of trades by its clients had been "off the charts."[8]

Goldman Sachs did even better than its white-shoe rival, wowing its investors. It earned $6.8 billion during the period and had its highest return on equity in twelve years. "I'd say the first quarter was an extraordinary quarter," said Chief Executive Officer David Solomon.

## The Opportunists

One huge winner from the meme-stock squeeze couldn't resist coming back for seconds. Jason Mudrick, forty-five years old at the time, seems like the sort of Wall Streeter the Reddit revolutionaries would love to hate—smart, preppy, good-looking, and very rich. Named number six in *Business Insider*'s "Sexiest Hedge Fund Managers" poll a decade earlier, Mudrick helped pay his way through Harvard Law School by teaching economics classes to undergraduates.[9]

But Mudrick briefly became something of a hero with the WallStreetBets crowd when his $3 billion hedge fund found itself on the same side of the trade as they were. The distressed-company specialist provided very expensive financing to struggling AMC in December to keep it in business, which could be converted into millions of shares. When the stock surged, he cashed them in for a nearly $200 million gain, extinguishing the debt. Yet he also was one of the hedge fund stars who jumped in and bet against the meme stocks when he thought they had gone too far, selling call options, as Bill Gross had, for an additional profit of $50 million or so. His fund, Mudrick Capital Management, wound up having its best month ever.[10]

Four months later, when AMC's shares were again sent into the stratosphere by the "apes" in an echo of the original meme-stock squeeze, Mudrick returned for an encore that wasn't taken as well. Eager to cash in on its surging share price, courtesy of several million new retail shareholders, AMC sold him $230 million in newly issued shares. Not grasping or caring that they had just had their ownership watered down, AMC shareholders pushed the stock to its highest level

in years that day, and Mudrick immediately sold the shares to the retail crowd at an estimated profit of $41 million—a highly unusual but
not illegal step.

Mudrick's sin seems to have been reportedly telling a client that he
sold because the shares were "overvalued."[11] His firm's Wikipedia entry was promptly defaced with insults and profanity. Karma would
bite him too as his fund then wound up losing money on derivatives it
used to protect itself from price moves. Mudrick had underestimated
the apes' enthusiasm and didn't expect the stock to jump.[12]

Meanwhile, other financial firms simply found themselves in the
right place at the right time. Unlike retail investors taking their cues
from fellow WallStreetBets users, there was no way they were going
to "HOLD THE LINE" after a stock rose by several thousand percent
for no fundamental reason. Senvest Management got interested in
GameStop in early 2020 and bought 5 percent of the company's shares
during September and October as Ryan Cohen arrived on the scene.
Its managers had been on the losing side of short squeezes in the past,
and they didn't hesitate to cash in their chips when this one hit, reap-
ing a profit of $700 million.[13] Must Asset Management, a South Ko-
rean hedge fund that previously owned 4.7 percent of GameStop, had
nearly perfect timing as well. It sold its shares near the height of the
frenzy for an estimated $1 billion.[14]

Even relatively sleepy mutual fund firms moved quickly when the
market handed them a golden opportunity. Fidelity Investments, which
had been GameStop's largest shareholder for a long time with a nearly
13 percent stake, sold nearly every share it owned in January 2021. The
Fidelity Low-Priced Stock Fund and the Fidelity Series Intrinsic Opportunities Fund, which generally favor dowdy but solid companies
that fast-money retail investors ignore, had been the two big holders of
GameStop shares at the giant investment firm.

Joel Tillinghast, the buttoned-down executive who manages both
funds and who joined Fidelity before most Robinhood investors were

born, wasn't mentioned a single time in the tens of thousands of messages about GameStop on WallStreetBets before he sold even as users obsessed over DeepFuckingValue, Ryan Cohen, and Michael Burry. That is a shame because Tillinghast, whose funds lagged the market in go-go 2020 but have beaten their benchmarks handily in the long run, wrote a noteworthy personal-finance book, *Big Money Thinks Small: Biases, Blind Spots, and Smarter Investing*, that spoke directly to a situation like the meme-stock squeeze. He cautioned, for example, that trying to guess "how long others will remain shortsighted" in a market frenzy is more like gambling than investing.

"If you fancy that there will be clear signs as to when the party will wind down, as most speculators do, you will surely be drawn into the thundering herd, despite knowing the inevitable result."[15]

Another nuance of the financial world that retail investors failed to appreciate is that the losses suffered by funds like Melvin weren't just on meme stocks or even on short bets. Melvin had to sell some long positions too, and the revolutionaries didn't benefit from those temporary bargains—other hedge funds did when they filled the vacuum.

## Insiders Cash Out

The bounty from the meme-stock squeeze also extended to executives and board members of the affected companies. Normally they are prevented from buying or selling shares if they know of some news, good or bad, that will affect a company's share price. That would be insider trading. But the meme-stock squeeze was an exogenous event, and many faced no such restrictions. Call it outsider trading.

For example, the activist investor Kurt Wolf of Hestia Partners agitated for months to get onto GameStop's board. When he finally succeeded in June 2020, he sounded like he was with the company for the long term.

"GameStop is a unique player in the gaming industry, and we are excited to be a part of the company's next generation of leadership," wrote Wolf in a press release. "We are optimistic that the newly reconstituted board has the right mix of people and skills to unlock GameStop's significant latent value."[16]

He was optimistic, but he wasn't *that* optimistic. Hestia's returns were 162 percent in 2020 and 223 percent in the first quarter of 2021, largely on that one lucky investment. Unlike managers of other funds, he wasn't allowed to sell his shares during the heart of the squeeze because he was on the board. Wolf resigned in April and promptly cashed in his winnings, according to securities filings.[17]

John Broderick, an activist investor who runs Permit Capital, a fund named after a hard-to-catch fish, also took a stake and pressured the company. He chose to support Wolf's taking a seat rather than asking for one himself—a concession that proved profitable. Wolf's impressive gain was like the one that got away compared with Broderick, who was able to sell all his shares closer to the peak price.

"It's sort of like after the Super Bowl when they ask someone how it feels and they say it doesn't feel real," Broderick told *The Wall Street Journal*. "I guess I can go to Disney World."[18]

Another director had less auspicious timing than Wolf. GameStop chair Kathy Vrabeck was among those who agreed to step down when Ryan Cohen and his associates were given their board seats in mid-January. She immediately sold fifty thousand GameStop shares for $1.4 million. Had Vrabeck waited just two weeks, those shares would have been worth as much as $24 million.

With Cohen pledging to remake the company, there were a number of executive departures in the months following the squeeze. Some didn't need to have their arms twisted to leave. For example, GameStop's chief financial officer resigned just weeks later with the stock still elevated. His payout was more than $15 million and reportedly might have been as high as $30 million including deferred compensation.[19] And last, but certainly not least, in the squeeze's aftermath, Chief Executive Officer George Sherman sold 263,000 shares worth in excess of $30 million and then agreed to step down in April in exchange for an acceleration of his restricted share awards in a package worth approximately $179 million at then-prevailing prices. That sort of golden parachute should raise eyebrows at any business, but it was remarkable for a company's fifth CEO in less than four years, over which time the retailer hadn't earned a dime in profit.[20]

It wasn't just GameStop. To the extent that it was legal, insiders of other suddenly inflated meme stocks cashed in too. Executives at BlackBerry, the now-struggling smartphone pioneer, dumped $1.7 million of stock during the squeeze, netting about $1 million more than they would have a couple of weeks earlier. Its chief financial officer disposed of his entire stake.[21]

Executives and board members of the stereo headphone maker Koss had excellent timing too as their stock price went from a little over $3 at the start of January to more than $127 at its peak. They sold $44 million in stock, which was more than the entire company had been worth weeks earlier. About $31 million of those sales were by members of the already well-off Koss family.[22]

## "Silverback" Takes the Crown

The most opportunistic executives by far worked for the movie theater chain AMC, which was already struggling and got crushed by the COVID-19 pandemic. Short sellers had very good reason to be skeptical about the company's survival prospects, even with vaccinations starting. Experts thought it had just months left before going bankrupt given how quickly it was burning through its cash and all the risky debt it had sold to stay afloat. During the squeeze four executives sold their shares for a total of about $3 million.[23]

Meanwhile, the private equity giant Silver Lake was in deep trouble on convertible bonds it owned in the company. These are bonds that have a sweetener—the ability to be exchanged for stock. Making the exchange is only worth doing at a certain price—the equivalent of buying a bond with a call option attached to it. That price was far out of reach in early January. But on Tuesday, January 26, the stock briefly jumped high enough thanks to retail buying and short covering. Silver Lake immediately sold its entire position for $713 million, snatching an unexpected victory from the jaws of defeat.[24]

Dalian Wanda, the Chinese company owned by the billionaire Wang Jianlin, one of China's richest men, also seized the opportunity, converting shares that gave it control of AMC to a form that was easier to sell. It sold hundreds of millions of dollars in shares, completing its exit by May.[25]

AMC itself sold more than $300 million of new shares during the meme-stock squeeze and then kept selling hundreds of millions in new shares to eager retail buyers that spring after it became the new darling of WallStreetBets for a while. Chief Executive Officer Adam Aron tried to re-create the meme-stock magic by engaging directly with the apes on social media. He complained that the company was "under attack" from short sellers, and both he and the company each made a personal $50,000 donation to save gorillas, as many on WallStreetBets had done. The subreddit's members, who were less than half his age on average, affectionately nicknamed Aron "Silverback" and rallied behind him.[26]

Aron wasn't allowed to sell the surging stock himself, but he got around that by gifting his sons five hundred thousand shares of AMC. He received these shares on the basis of a lowered bonus goal that he met only because of the meme-stock squeeze.[27] In June, his sons' shares, assuming they held on, were worth about $30 million while a company filing put the value of Aron's remaining shares and long-term grants at more than a quarter of a billion dollars.[28] Several board members dumped almost $4 million more in stock around the same time.[29] And its new retail shareholders who bought the stock? The company offered them a free large popcorn during their first visit to an AMC theater that summer.

For all of their surprising sophistication in engineering a short squeeze, the WallStreetBets crowd failed to appreciate that the torrent of stock sales by AMC and its insiders would allow short sellers to escape a trap and would instead saddle their members with loads of overvalued stock. The money the company raised from selling them so many shares went to lenders, landlords owed back rent, fund managers, executives, or board members. After AMC shares took a steep dive in June 2020 following news of board members' big stock sales, the spell was broken for some. As one poster wrote on WallStreetBets:

> Stick it to the man? Lol the AMC tards did nothing but make the "man" wealthier, all the AMC board execs sold their shares at 50+ while these tards got left holding the L. They even sold 8.5 mill shares at a discount to a hedge fund, which in turn sold it to the tards on here for a profit.

It is ironic that people like John Motter—who were justifiably incensed at bankers' being rescued with public cash and failing to suffer any serious consequences during the financial crisis—rode to the rescue of failing businesses and lenders and fund managers who had made poor choices. The meme-stock squeeze not only failed to bankrupt any millionaires or billionaires, it enriched several out of sheer, dumb luck.

When all was said and done, America's "1 percent" had a very good start to 2021. Their windfall came out of the little guy's pocket.

Chapter 22

# February 2021

Keith Gill jokingly responded, "What's an exit strategy?" when asked in December 2020 how and when he would turn his paper fortune into a real one. Despite not being a highly paid professional, he had exquisite timing in cashing in a large chunk of his long-held bet on GameStop while Gabe Plotkin, one of the financial elite, blundered into a trap. That lopsided outcome didn't translate into the results seen by the WallStreetBets crowd overall compared with Wall Street as a whole, though.

Take the gamma squeeze. While successful in blowing a huge hole in Melvin Capital, and in sending the meme stocks surging, it made the amount of money spent on the Nasdaq Whale's maneuver the previous summer seem conservative. According to Jason Goepfert, the chief executive officer of the research firm SentimenTrader, small traders had, by the end of January, spent an incredible $44 billion on call-options premium in the preceding four weeks—much of it wasted. That number had typically been around $2 billion prior to 2018.

Depending on how late people hopped onto the bandwagon, and whether they had the inclination to jump off, they were either fortunate enough to profit handsomely at hedge funds' expense or they made the equivalent of a sucker bet. A quick glance at the turnover in shares and options tells us that many fell into the latter camp.

As former blackjack shark Bill Gross explained while helping himself to some of the money in their brokerage accounts, the Reddit army had created so much volatility already that options prices had mushroomed to reflect that, and they had just a tiny chance of paying off. After their last hurrah on Friday, January 29, 2021, GameStop's shares would start to fall precipitously. On the following Monday alone, they plunged by $100, or 31 percent. A big reason was that, when a gamma squeeze unwinds, options dealers rapidly dump the shares they were forced to buy. As clever as the plan hatched by some members of the WallStreetBets community was at creating havoc for hedge funds, they had skipped over the part where everyone makes money, or at least doesn't lose much, in the process.

The revolutionaries were buying more options, but in vain. Their task was akin to rolling up a hill a snowball that had become much bigger and heavier. It took a lot more people behind it to keep it going: each new share or options contract purchased had far less bang for the buck, and, when the snowball began rolling downhill, it quickly crushed everyone who was still straining to make it move higher.

"It's literally what goes up must come down," says the derivatives expert Peter Cecchini, describing the end of a gamma squeeze.

Tuesday was even worse with a $135, or 60 percent, price drop in GameStop's share price before the shares stabilized for a day. The greatly enlarged subreddit was filled with exhortations to stop selling and naïve theories as to why GameStop shares really were falling.

According to a popular theory, the short squeeze was still on, but hedge funds were manipulating GameStop's price to make it appear as if it had ended. It held that hedge funds were engaging in something called a "short ladder attack," somehow buying and selling from one another to artificially push down the prices of the meme stocks. There is no such thing.

It is almost impossible to say how many of the millions of degenerates who participated in the meme-stock squeeze made money, but the episode made their forum hugely influential. Now WallStreetBets had to grapple with the downsides of that runaway success. It had drawn so many new members and so much attention in a week that the forum had begun to look for new mountains to conquer.

Some suspected outside manipulators when many newer members on the board began to tout silver. Starting on the Thursday of the meme-stock squeeze, the day that trading restrictions were imposed on certain stocks, a silver exchange-traded fund saw a surge in activity. The buying then spilled over to physical silver, and by the weekend several dealers of bars and coins posted notices on their sites that they had been cleaned out and couldn't accept any more orders. A member of the forum's "old guard" warned fellow Redditors not to fall for the #silversqueeze trend, writing that it was a hedge fund ploy designed to "put you on the sidelines from this righteous and glorious war we are in."

It is impossible to say who was behind the push, but it almost certainly wasn't a devious plan hatched by hedge funds as a distraction. It could have been professional speculators employing bots for a quick profit. In silver's case, though, the impetus might well have come from fellow individual investors with an ax to grind. There has long been a conspiracy theory alleging that big banks are colluding to keep down the price of silver to cheat the little guy. The idea even got a US government hearing in 2010. And, ironically, silver was caught in one of the most famous short squeezes of all time in 1980. In that case, the establishment really did circle the wagons to bring it to an end, leading to the bankruptcy of two Texas billionaires who had tried to corner the market.

As the meme stocks fell back to earth, WallStreetBets suddenly had another problem sustaining the revolution: its hero was going dark. Following a visit by the SEC, Gill posted his usual end-of-day screenshot of his brokerage account on February 3 with an added note: "heads up gonna back off the daily updates for now."

Gill had lost more than $25 million on paper in just a few days according to that day's E*Trade statement. His reversal of fortune had endeared him even more to the Reddit revolutionaries trying and failing to get enough people to "HOLD THE LINE." Every trading day that Gill had stood pat had provided inspiration, and now there would be no way to know what he was doing with his shrunken but still considerable fortune of $22 million.

"Oh man, it was definitely like 'oh shit,'" said Finley Mulligan, one of the filmmakers behind *Apes Together Strong*, remembering his reaction when seeing the update.

Even though Gill hadn't ever urged fellow members to hang on to their shares to keep the squeeze going, the fact that he might take the money and run in the absence of further updates proved disconcerting for those who had held on so far. Gill's disappearance sparked a further 42 percent slide in GameStop's share price the following day.

There was no resentment about this, and many used the occasion to tip their hats to Gill.

> *DFV made $50 million when everyone thought he was an idiot and lost $30 million when everyone thought he was a genius.*[1]

There also were several thoughtful takes about how ridiculous it was for him to be facing an investigation when members of Congress had recently been exposed for dumping stocks following confidential briefings a year earlier about the pandemic and when Treasury Secretary Janet Yellen had been paid hundreds of thousands of dollars for a series of speeches to Citadel while she was in the private sector.

> *What, are they going to go after senior citizens and high school stock clubs next? They also coordinate their moves. They may even have "secret meetings" in person so they don't leave an electronic trail.[2]*

"I don't think you understand how this works. Laws are for the little people, like you, me, and DFV. We have lovely words on a piece of paper that make it seem like no one is above the law, but you'd have to be living in a cave in Siberia to believe that. Or be young and naïve. I remember being young and idealistic. Then I got older and I realized that the government excels at two things: theft and murder."

"The SEC is probably waiting for DFV to slip up and charge him with manipulating markets. Yet no charges were brought on the senators who blatantly did insider trading when coronavirus started."

As it turned out, WallStreetBets hadn't heard the last of Gill. He resumed his updates following the February 18 congressional hearing, and in the interim he had used some of his cash to buy even more GameStop shares. He really did "like the stock." Gill's final update was posted on the day that his options expired, on April 16. He held on and converted them to even more shares, bringing his stake in the company to $30 million, with a little over $3 million in cash should things not work out.

Jaime Rogozinski, the founder of WallStreetBets, said that he was uncomfortable with the effect that a big market winner like Gill had on members of the forum by posting screenshots of his account. It certainly inspired some unwise risk-taking that mostly benefited the pros. Yet the YOLO traders weren't exactly imitating Gill, whose behavior was as rare as his performance: he developed his own thesis rather than listening either to the professionals' consensus or to random doubters on the internet, and he held on to his stake for at least a year and a half. His broker, E*Trade, probably earned very little from his millions of dollars in transactions. Win or lose, that is the sort of steadfastness that really could stick it to the man.

# The Same Old Game

A t the close of the day's business, they take all the money and throw it up in the air. Everything that sticks to the ceiling belongs to the clients."

Fred Schwed Jr.'s roasting of stockbrokers in his hilarious *Where Are the Customers' Yachts? or A Good Hard Look at Wall Street* is more than eighty years old, but much of it could have been written yesterday. Schwed worked in the business and lost much of his money in the 1929 crash. The book's title stems from an even older anecdote about someone asking that question when visiting Manhattan's financial district as he stopped to admire the fine sailboats in the marina. They were owned by brokers who worked at the stock exchange a few blocks away. Despite the promise of riches and the customers being the ones who were risking their money, a suspiciously large share of the wealth made in the market seemed to stay with the professionals rather than go to their clients.

Of course, Wall Street was a small, clubby place when Schwed wrote his book. Commissions were fixed, most Americans didn't trust the market, and you had to have a fair bit of money before a broker would bother helping himself to it. Today's boom in stock market activity and wealth can be traced back to the early 1980s when the first 401(k) plans were launched, the Reagan-era bull market started, and discount brokers like Charles Schwab really began to take off. Investing people's savings has since become a much more competitive business. Exchange-traded mutual funds give you access to hundreds of stocks costing a fraction of a percent a year, and most people pay no trading commissions. That is a wonderful development for those savers who want to grow a nest egg and keep as much of the market's gains in their pockets as possible. But is the investing business less lucrative?

A glance at the *Forbes* list of the wealthiest Americans gives us a clue. In 1982, the first year the list was compiled, not a single fund manager or broker of any type appeared in the top one hundred. The same list in 2020 had twenty-three people who made their fortunes in finance. That group includes eleven hedge fund managers, two mutual fund company owners, and two founders of discount brokerages. Ken Griffin, who made money both through hedge funds and the retail trading boom, is there too. Rounding out the list are various private equity titans. Vlad Tenev and Chamath Palihapitiya, two billionaires who profited handsomely from the rush of new investors into the market that sent GameStop to the moon, aren't in the top one hundred. Give them a couple of years.

Naturally, Americans with investment accounts have become wealthier over the last forty years too. The Dow Jones Industrial Average rose from 1,000 points in 1982 to 33,000 by the time of the meme-stock squeeze in 2021, which is significant even after accounting for inflation. The value of all those stocks and also bonds relative to the size of the economy has grown a lot, and so has turnover. A mid-2020 estimate of the average length of time a share is held fell to less than half a year from as much as eight years in the 1950s. In other words, shares changed hands about seventeen times as frequently. Each trade is less costly owing to the elimination of commissions and less of a gap between the bid and offer price, but the new crop of retail investors, including those who propelled the GameStop squeeze, might be leaving nearly as much money on the table as their grandparents. And of course a lot more of them are in the market.

## "Trading Is Hazardous to Your Wealth"

"Trading Is Hazardous to Your Wealth," a classic study of retail-investor returns by Brad Barber of the Graduate School of Management at the University of California, Davis, and Terrance Odean of the Haas School of Business at the University of California, Berkeley, looked at data from more than sixty-six thousand retail brokerage accounts in the 1990s.[1] It showed that, even without the effect of commissions, the more people traded, the less they earned on average compared with just being passively invested in stocks. The most active fifth of investors had a net return 6 percentage points less than the average market return. That is a huge difference. For example, someone saving a set amount each year between the ages of twenty-five and sixty-five would have 80 percent less money by retirement day than someone who just earned the long-run market return in an index fund.

Other studies have shown that how often people merely look at their brokerage accounts has a significant effect on returns. Michaela Pagel of Columbia Business School came up with a psychological explanation: losing money pains us more than making money pleases us—a well-known effect in behavioral finance. Because the stock market is more likely to rise over longer periods than shorter ones, more frequent observations cause us to see more losses and nudge us to trade at inopportune times. This phenomenon is known as "myopic loss aversion."[2]

It is a psychological foible that has enriched brokers for years. Smartphone-based ones catering to a generation that grew up constantly checking the devices have supercharged this tendency to their benefit and customers' detriment. An April 2021 study by Futu, a Chinese brokerage firm with a US subsidiary, found that members of Generation Z opened their trading app 8.2 times a day and traded 147 times a year on average.[3]

Where do the forgone gains of frequent traders go? Not money heaven. Some accrue to people in the market who are preternaturally patient—the Warren Buffetts of the world. He has earned 120 times the market's return since 1965. And a good deal flows to people who are the opposite of patient but happen to be pretty good at capturing short-term profits in the market from amateurs. High-frequency traders don't care about how a company is doing or what is happening with the economy. They profit by programming their computers to find a small inefficiency and then get in and out faster than a human possibly can, earning as little as fractions of a penny.

"It's akin to a casino," says Jim Chanos, the veteran short seller. "There are an awful lot of professional card players who make an awful lot from amateurs with small amounts of money."[4]

The more you play, the more you are likely to lose. Recall that Robinhood customers traded forty times as many shares for each dollar in their accounts compared with customers at more staid Charles Schwab. Even considering that huge discrepancy, there is reason to believe that being on the other side of a typical Robinhood customer is more profitable for wholesalers and slightly more corrosive to long-run success. They are two sides of the same coin.

## No, You Actually Weren't Born an Investor

The problem goes well beyond algorithms scalping tiny sums here and there. Retail investors—all of them, not just YOLO traders—simply aren't very good at picking stocks. Dispassionate stock-picking computers must have heated up their circuits with excitement when the meme-stock squeeze was going on.

One fund that showed up and then disappeared as an owner of GameStop shares according to securities filings was Renaissance Technologies. Don't ask the fund why it bought them. Not only wouldn't the secretive company tell you—it probably doesn't know. Its employees are mostly mathematicians or physicists who program computers to look for anomalies in the market. They certainly appear to have found one in GameStop. The fund's founder, Jim Simons, a renowned mathematician himself with no previous finance background, is the most successful fund manager of all time. Between 1988 and 2018, his Medallion Fund made an incredible gross annual return of 66 percent a year. That isn't a typo.

Whose money is it—or, rather, was it? In Gregory Zuckerman's fascinating *The Man Who Solved the Market: How Jim Simons Launched the Quant Revolution*, the mathematician Henry Laufer, now a billionaire thanks to his stint at Renaissance, was asked that question.

"It's a lot of dentists," he said. His point was that there is no way to extract that money from people who buy and hold stocks for years. It comes from people who think they can beat the market and who trade frequently. In the 1990s, dentists were the stereotypical retail investors who learned the hard way that they couldn't translate their general smarts to making smart investments and outwitting Wall Street.

These days, customers of Robinhood and its imitators are the new dentists—the people most likely to find themselves full of confidence yet losing against the pros and enriching middlemen like their brokers too. It is hard to say how much. Neither Robinhood nor its chief competitors would disclose average client performance.

One of the many reasons their customers probably do especially poorly is the very same phenomenon that made the meme-stock squeeze possible—paying attention to the same small subset of stocks. A newer Barber and Odean study observed thousands of "herding events" of stocks popular with Robinhood customers. If an investment fund wanted to take the opposite side of the trade, selling during a herding event and buying the stock back later, it would have made money 63 percent of the time.[5]

Don't take this as investing advice! What is true on average isn't all of the time, as Andrew Left learned to his dismay when he told the WallStreetBets crowd that they were the suckers at the poker table. He wound up getting run over by an army of apes. It is excellent advice, though, for what an ordinary investor *shouldn't* do, which is to try picking winning stocks by following the crowd.

"The stocks that the average investor buys go on to underperform after they buy them and outperform after they sell them—all the academic research shows that," says Larry Swedroe, who has studied individual-investing foibles for decades. One of his nineteen books on personal finance looked at seventy-seven errors that individual investors make. It was published a decade before the meme-stock squeeze, and he jokes that it probably could be expanded to one hundred mistakes for the WallStreetBets era.

## A Beautiful Relationship with Washington

For all the political scrutiny that the GameStop frenzy got, the evidence that retail investors pay a huge, unnecessary toll to Wall Street, in part because they are encouraged to trade so often, was barely discussed. Recall that the reason for the February 18, 2021, congressional hearing was the outcry over trading restrictions. By the time the hearing was held three weeks later, the conspiracy theory about hedge funds' engineering the halt to save themselves had been debunked. In his remarks, though, Patrick McHenry, the ranking member of the House Committee on Financial Services, decried the difficulty members of the public have hunting for the next hot stock.

"Americans are far more sophisticated, informed and capable than folks in D.C. give them credit for," he said. "We've created a world where it's easier to go buy a lottery ticket than it is to invest in the next Google. Is it any wonder why the unhealthy dynamics of GameStop happened?"[6]

Like Captain Renault in *Casablanca*, McHenry would be "shocked, shocked to find that gambling is going on" in the stock market just before being handed his winnings at Rick's. His campaign and "leadership PAC" raked in $4.7 million over just the last three election cycles from banks, insurers, and securities and investment firms. He has a beautiful relationship with Wall Street, as do many politicians in a position to regulate the industry.

According to data from the Center for Responsive Politics, the top donor by far to Washington politicians and outside spending groups was the finance, insurance, and real estate sector in the 2019–2020 period. It spent $1.969 billion—as much as energy, defense, agribusiness, the communications and electronics industries, and labor organizations combined. The sector didn't do this out of the kindness of its heart. It was to make sure that the complex rules and tax codes covering a highly regulated business allowed everyone to keep making money.[7]

And financial firms also spend heavily to make sure that, if they do run afoul of those regulations, they get a favorable hearing. Michelle Leder, one of Wall Street's favorite financial sleuths, concluded from a July 2021 search of LinkedIn that Robinhood had hired at least a dozen former regulators who had worked for the SEC or FINRA. Most prominent was former SEC commissioner Dan Gallagher, who became the company's top lawyer in May 2020 and earned $30 million during the year. Not bad for eight months' work.[8]

Washington's exasperating response to the meme-stock squeeze wasn't just about doing a favor for an old chum or not upsetting donors, though. With public sentiment firmly in favor of the underdog traders, possibly the least popular thing a politician could have said at the GameStop hearing was that maybe Congress had better things to do than investigate why some brokerage customers couldn't buy as many shares of GameStop as they wanted to on margin.

Of the six witnesses called that day, at least three must have understood that public stock market speculation enriches Wall Street. It was in neither Griffin's nor Tenev's financial interest to kill the golden goose, and even Gabe Plotkin, who had just lost more than half of his investors' money in the squeeze, generally benefited from the presence of reckless small fry. His fund would bounce back and make a fantastic 22 percent return the month of the hearing.[9]

## "A Bit of a Farce"

It was up to a handful of famous curmudgeons to puncture the "democratization of finance" fairy tale—people like the hard-drinking, sharp-tongued floor trader Art Cashin. Almost eighty years old at the time of the squeeze and still active, Cashin, who began working as a clerk at the exchange in 1959 straight out of high school, didn't hold back when asked his opinion by CNBC.

"The retail rebellion was a bit of a farce and an illusion that the financial media bought into much too readily," he said.[10]

Warren Buffett, ten years older than Cashin, addressed the Robinhood phenomenon in May 2021 at Berkshire Hathaway's annual meeting, known as "Woodstock for Capitalists."

"If you cater to those gambling chips when people have money in their pocket for the first time and you tell them they can make 30 or 40 or 50 trades a day and you're not charging them any commission but you're selling their order flow or whatever . . . I hope we don't have more of it."[11]

His even older business partner, ninety-seven-year-old Charlie Munger, called the no-fee business model "a dirty way of making money," comparing it to state lotteries.

A Robinhood spokeswoman responded, painting Buffett and Munger as plutocrats and her employer as the one working to level the playing field.

> It is clear that the elites benefited from a stock market that kept many families sidelined from participating while they amassed huge wealth from decades of investing—driving a deep wedge between the haves and have-nots. Suddenly, Robinhood and other online trading platforms have opened the doors of financial markets to everyday people, deeply unsettling the old guard who will fight to keep things the same.[12]

There really is a "deep wedge between the haves and have-nots," and a good way to narrow it is to get younger, less wealthy people to save and invest. But the notion that this would disadvantage Warren Buffett is exactly backward. He has done so well because he could buy low and sell high, which requires many people with less money than he has to do the opposite. Had commission-free trading been around decades ago, Buffett might have earned 150 or 200 times as much as the overall market. His views on Robinhood certainly weren't self-interested.

There are investor advocates like Barbara Roper's former employer, The Consumer Federation of America, that push for rules to protect investors from their gambling instincts and are critical of the free-trading model, but these organizations have a lot less money to get results in Washington than brokers and market makers. Chad Minnis's political action committee, WeLikeTheStock, represents the WallStreetBets subreddit. He says he will leave it up to the community to decide which issues to press for. He personally is open to his peer group buying speculative stocks, though he acknowledges it isn't necessarily to their benefit.

"If you take people away from buying lottery tickets they'll probably do better, but they're in a much different place than people who are about to retire."

Maybe, he says, some will learn their lessons by paying Wall Street tuition in the form of losses. Jon Stein, the founder of robo-adviser Betterment, which has many millennial customers and only allows investments in index funds, says that he made speculative and ultimately costly trades when he was younger despite being taught as an undergraduate at Harvard that it was foolish.

"I learned in college that I shouldn't do that and then I learned it again."

If Stein's Ivy League education didn't protect him—he says he bought Enron and lost money on it—then the rudimentary amount of financial education most young people receive is unlikely to have helped them avoid paying $450 a share for GameStop. The danger isn't only that they lose a small sum of money but also that they are eventually discouraged from investing at all. Moreover, because of the power of compound interest, a dollar lost early can be more costly than one lost in middle age. Stock market wealth is already very unevenly distributed by age, race, and income.

## How Not to Find "the Next Google"

Democratizing finance so that mom and pop can try to find "the next Google" makes for a great soundbite but, for far too many individuals, a lousy outcome. You might know someone who bought one of the handful of wealth-creating wonder stocks before it was discovered. Anecdotes don't add up to returns for most investors, though. The odds of finding stocks that don't merely rise but also beat the market, much less holding on through their ups and downs, are smaller than people imagine.

A guaranteed way of not finding the next Google is to buy the current Google. Robinhood's app and any social media site dedicated to frequent trading will display prominently a list of what stocks have seen big moves or unusually high turnover that day. It isn't just there to inform you—it entices retail traders to get in on the action by feeling like they are missing out. The newer Barber and Odean study shows that over a third of buying by Robinhood investors was in the top-ten stocks on any given day.

Not that the odds are so much better for obscure stocks that you heard about from your brother-in-law or on WallStreetBets. It is surprisingly hard to make money buying individual securities. People confuse the amazing, long-term wealth creation of an index like the Dow Jones Industrial Average or the share price charts of those companies that happened to have survived and prospered for decades with what their likely experience will be by acting on that stock tip. The investing industry is in no hurry to disabuse investors of the notion that they can find those needles in a haystack, though, despite the evidence.

Hendrik Bessembinder, a finance professor at Arizona State University, looked at twenty-six thousand stocks that have traded on US exchanges since the 1920s, most of which no longer do. Less than half of stocks made any money at all over their lives. The most common return for a stock over that time was to have gone to zero, and just eighty-six stocks made up half of all stock market profits—three tenths of 1 percent.[13]

But two things can be true at once: most stocks don't make money, but the stock market as a whole makes lots of it over many decades. The difference between going to the racetrack and putting your money in the market is that you can't possibly profit by betting on every horse—the house has a built-in edge. Buying an index fund that contains all the stock market's future winners and losers—the entire haystack, as it were—is a proven way to build wealth in the long run. And it costs a lot less too.

Of course, index funds make much less money for Wall Street. A $10,000 investment in a typical equity index fund will cost you about $9 a year compared with $63 a year for the typical actively managed stock fund.[14] The fund research firm Morningstar reported that in 2019 the average US mutual fund's cost had dropped over a decade by 0.42 percentage points of the amount invested annually largely because so many Americans had bought index funds. That saves investors about $100 billion a year.[15]

Naturally, some in the investment business are alarmed. A 2016 report by analysts at Sanford C. Bernstein & Company sounds almost made up: *The Silent Road to Serfdom: Why Passive Investing Is Worse Than Marxism.*[16]

"A supposedly capitalist economy where the only investment is passive is worse than either a centrally planned economy or an economy with active market led capital management," wrote the authors.

## "Showered with Compensation"

Don't fret too much about Wall Street. Whenever one part of the industry has been sent to the gulag, others have filled in the gaps. The most recent innovators are brokers that no longer charge commissions but have clients who trade more frequently.

Companies that run retail brokerages had impressive results in 2020, the first full year in which their main offering was ostensibly free. Charles Schwab, with its more conservative clientele, had close to $12 billion in revenue. Privately held Fidelity was estimated to have had about $20 billion in revenue. And, last but not least, Robinhood saw its revenue grow by 245 percent, compared with a year earlier, to nearly $1 billion.

Mutual funds earn a surprising amount of money too. Despite the popularity of index funds, tens of billions of dollars a year are still paid to poorly performing active managers, and investors compound the error by chasing the latest superstar or by pulling their money out of stock funds during turbulent times. These timing errors cost retail investors around $100 billion a year in lost returns, according to a regularly updated estimate by Morningstar, "Mind the Gap."

And then there are Wall Street money machines that cost you indirectly. Pension funds and college endowments, whose financial health affects millions of Americans, pay tens of billions a year to alternative asset managers such as hedge funds. In 2007, Warren Buffett said he would wager $500,000 with any hedge fund manager that a plain-vanilla index fund would beat their choice of top hedge funds.

"I then sat back and waited expectantly for a parade of fund managers . . . to come forth and defend their occupation," he wrote. "After all, these managers urged others to bet billions on their abilities. Why should they fear putting a little of their own money on the line?"[17]

One finally accepted. Former asset management executive Ted Seides chose five top funds whose identity he didn't reveal. Getting access to even the most exclusive one was no issue since the profits or losses were just on paper. The results were so lopsided—gains on the index fund were four times as much as those on the selected funds after fees—that Seides surrendered early. Buffett noted that it wasn't the lack of brains in the hedge fund world but the fact that managers were "showered with compensation" that they justified with "esoteric gibberish." And those performance fees don't go in reverse. The hundreds of millions of dollars that Plotkin earned in those good years and used to buy his beachfront property and his stake in the Hornets didn't have to be paid back when he lost half of his clients' money on the meme-stock squeeze.

Wall Street always seems to adapt to hardship and find new ways to make money off the public with politicians' blessings. In a disturbing development, individual investors with much less money can now more easily invest in the sorts of companies favored by sophisticated private funds, except without their own team of analysts to weed out the duds. For example, the 2012 JOBS Act, which wasn't really about jobs (it is an acronym for Jumpstart Our Business Startups), saw significant erosion of rules to protect investors. It lowered financial reporting requirements for companies with less than $1 billion in sales and made it easier for them to raise money. They are now allowed to file "confidentially" for initial public offerings—a provision used by Robinhood itself just weeks after the meme-stock squeeze—and the act expanded the types of companies that can conduct offerings without registering with the SEC.

Meanwhile, the boom in SPACs that dovetailed with the rise of millennial and Generation Z investors and influencers like Chamath Palihapitiya also made it possible to invest in less seasoned companies, bypassing much of Wall Street's typical vetting process.

The original take on the Reddit Revolution was that it had turned the tables on Wall Street and changed everything. If you just look at it through the prism of who is enriching whom, though, it is hard to conclude that much has changed. Finance is a very profitable business most of the time and especially when there is widespread public interest in the stock market. Far from a threat to their livelihoods, the meme-stock squeeze was the sort of payday that only comes around every decade or so for Wall Street.

One group of traders that was the target of vitriol on WallStreet-Bets, short sellers, might have taken a permanent hit, though, and it isn't good news at all for the little guy. Now that short squeezes can be arranged on social media, it has become much riskier to be in that none-too-popular business.

"Shorts play an incredibly important role in keeping prices efficient," explains Swedroe. "Now that they know they can be ganged up on, I think you're going to have more bubbles in the future. And who buys them? Retail investors."

It would take Fred Schwed Jr. a while to get his bearings if he were transported in a time machine to modern Wall Street: social media, zero-dollar commissions, SPACs, high-frequency traders, memes, and smartphones. But he would quickly grasp that the new boss in finance is the same as the old boss. Wall Street is still a place where customers are parted from far too much of their money—particularly when they think they can beat the house.

But there is good news too: technology and competition have made Wall Street a much friendlier and more profitable place than in the bad old days for individuals as long as they play a different, less exciting game.

# Bonus Round

Maybe you've read this far despite thinking I was too cynical about Wall Street or that I didn't give the young Reddit rebels their due. Or maybe your eyes glazed over when I tried to see the big picture, and you've only reached this point in the book because the GameStop squeeze is an incredible story. Well, at least we can all agree on that.

Wherever your sympathies lie, bear with me for one last chapter as I get to the practical part of this book. It might seem that the ups and downs of YOLO traders, hedge fund managers, brokers, and influencers are far removed from what you do with your own nest egg, but the people and companies helping you are also part of that gigantic money machine. One reason I left the lucrative world of finance twenty years ago for the less remunerative field of writing about it is because I thought I could help people navigate its shark-infested waters. To be perfectly honest, though, I mostly do this because it's a lot of fun.

Just as sports reporters often turn to writing because their athletic careers peaked in Little League, investment writers often choose their profession because it is the next best thing to being a player, and with much less chance of injury. Markets are a nonstop battle of wits involving millions of people. Instead of competing for a championship trophy or a gold medal, investors keep their score in constantly updated ledgers of dollars and cents. It's even more exciting in some ways because unexpected things like a crash can scramble the leaderboard, and ordinary people can upset the pros. Keith Gill and Gabe Plotkin started out the plague year of 2020 like some anonymous weekend golfer and Tiger Woods, respectively, yet Gill was the one who walked away wearing the green jacket.

On the day that I mustered up the courage to quit my job as a stock analyst at a big investment bank to become a writer, my boss asked me if there was some other job I might want instead. The words started to come out of my mouth, but I stopped myself. I had dreamed of working as one of the bank's proprietary traders, making calculated bets with millions of dollars of its money, sort of like an internal hedge fund. Deep down, though, I knew I probably wasn't cut out for it temperamentally—very few people are. Now I content myself with leading my team's annual investing contest at *The Wall Street Journal* in which my picks are consistently mediocre.

So you don't have to convince me of the appeal of trying to play the markets. It's intoxicating. But being an active trader is also usually a waste of time and money. About half of you are of above-average intelligence (well, you had the good taste to buy this book, and you read this far, so let's call it 70 percent). But 80 percent of you think you're above average. The same goes for your assessment of your looks, honesty, and investing ability—experiment after experiment shows this. Even most people who have just been in an accident that was their fault will rate themselves as above-average drivers.

But most people are by my definition below-average investors, and as far as I can tell, IQ doesn't help—remember all those dentists. "Average" would be just matching the passive return of an index fund that you buy and forget. If you're disciplined, then maybe the difference is just a few tenths of a percent a year. If you're not, then it's several percent. The lost potential of all those millions of portfolios adds up to hundreds of billions of dollars annually paying the salaries and bonuses of my old profession. Investing has to cost something, but active traders using "free" smartphone-based trading apps are just the newest group to buy too much of what Wall Street is selling.

Here's some great news, though: thanks to years of technological progress and fierce competition, it has never been easier to capture nearly all the market's long-run returns and to start doing so with hardly any money. Finance really has been democratized. All those charts you've seen about a dollar invested in the market a century ago turning into a fortune if left untouched are purely theoretical because there were no index funds back then, commissions were exorbitant, and even the cost of reinvesting your dividends was high. You could do the right thing as an investor and still be nickeled-and-dimed out of lots of money. Not anymore.

Progress is a funny thing, though: almost all teenagers walk around with a device in their pocket containing all the world's knowledge, yet they are no more likely to be able to tell you what the Magna Carta is than high school students were in the 1950s. We have every variety of fresh fruit and vegetable available year-round, but we eat a less healthy diet than our great grandparents did. Instagram and Cheetos don't have to work very hard to outsell Wikipedia and Brussels sprouts. An app that showers you with confetti, gives you the dopamine rush of a quick score, and lets you in on stocks that your peers are talking about online is way more fun than patiently sticking your savings in boring index funds, hiring an adviser, or letting an algorithm handle your finances.

Whenever shocking figures come out about big losses suffered by ordinary investors, the industry nods its head and stresses the need for investor education. I disagree. Studies of investing returns by profession show, for example, that schoolteachers have better personal returns than people who work in finance. Why? Because people in the latter group are conceited enough to act like they have an edge.

Aside from being aware of the ever-changing rules about taxes and retirement, the main thing you need to know is that people who get paid handsomely to choose investments and who have much better computers than you do struggle to beat the market. By far the best thing that people can do with their money is to invest it in something simple and cheap and then think about it as rarely as possible—a luxury unavailable to earlier generations.

Unfortunately, our brains have been primed over eons for action and self-preservation in a real jungle, not a financial one. It is especially hard to preach caution in a bull market like the one that prevailed in 2020 and 2021 because success, or peers' success, convinces people that active investing is easy. With younger people, who have recently been the most active yet also are the least enamored of Wall Street, a more fruitful approach than lecturing them about compound interest might be telling them how to really stick it to the man—by not playing his game.

I've pointed out repeatedly in this book that periods when the public thinks making a quick fortune is easy are the best of times for Wall Street. Still, I'm also encouraged by all the people who opened brokerage accounts around the time of the GameStop squeeze. Exposure to stocks is woefully lopsided. Stocks as a percentage of Americans' wealth hit a record in April 2021, but they accrued unevenly according to the Federal Reserve's *Survey of Consumer Finances*. The top 1 percent of Americans by net worth own 38 percent of all stocks, including those held in retirement accounts or pension funds. The bottom half own just 7 percent, mostly indirectly.[1]

That's a shame. Our governments and our employers are doing less and less to help us pay for retirement, education, and health care. The only good alternative is taking some part of our current income and letting it compound into a nest egg over decades. The best way to do that is to engage with Wall Street, which costs something. But it doesn't have to be a lot. Believe it or not, the twentysomething-year-old group of new investors has the right idea about some things that those my age mostly don't. Here are a few examples.

## Experts Are Overrated

One of the defining characteristics of the young, new class of investors has been to distrust serious people in suits dispensing financial advice, and that probably isn't such a mistake. Oddly, though, many are just as ready to accept investing tips that are either crowdsourced from social media or delivered by an influencer like a Silicon Valley billionaire. We tend to look at financially successful people and place more weight on their investing acumen despite mountains of evidence that specific stock picks aren't any good. Humans, to their detriment, are followers.

My team at *The Wall Street Journal* tried to illustrate this in a light-hearted way by tracking the picks and pans from the speakers at the closely watched Sohn Investment Conference like David Einhorn, Bill Ackman, and, yes, Gabe Plotkin and Chamath Palihapitiya. We took inspiration from Burton Malkiel's classic *A Random Walk Down Wall Street*, in which he writes that "a blindfolded monkey throwing darts at a newspaper's financial pages could select a portfolio that would do just as well as one carefully selected by the experts."[2]

Instead of paying $5,000 for a seat at the conference to hear the stars' pearls of wisdom, I walked over to the Modell's Sporting Goods store on Forty-Second Street and bought a set of darts for $9.99.

Monkeys were on back-order, so we human journalists had to fill in, taking turns by each throwing a long and short dart at the complete US stock market listing from *Barron's*, which still publishes them in print weekly. The result? Our portfolio trounced the fund managers by 22 percentage points over the next twelve months. It's all in the wrist.[3]

Our example isn't a fluke. CXO Advisory Group took a much deeper, longer look at investment recommendations between 2005 and 2012 from sixty-eight well-regarded investing experts such as *Mad Money*'s Jim Cramer, Abby Joseph Cohen of Goldman Sachs, and various investment newsletter writers. The accuracy of 6,582 verified recommendations from this august group over that time was just 47 percent, or worse than a coin toss.[4]

Now if all you did was flip a coin to make investing decisions, then that probably wouldn't be so bad. Paying someone to flip a coin for you is another matter. A fifteen-year study of stock fund managers by S&P Dow Jones Indices shows that nearly 90 percent of them failed to beat a simple, low-cost index fund over that time.[5] The reason isn't ineptitude: once you back out various fees and costs of management, fund managers as a group match the market because their combined portfolios pretty much *are* the market. As for skill, while I do believe that it exists, it is very hard to distinguish statistically from luck over just a handful of years. Not one of the five Morningstar "fund managers of the decade" through 2010 even managed to beat the market in the next ten years.

The only certainty with funds is their cost. The late John Bogle, the founder of the index fund pioneer Vanguard Group, ran the numbers on mutual funds using the example of a thirty-year-old earning $30,000 a year who saves 10 percent of her salary and gets a 3 percent annual raise. Assuming that the stock market rose by 7 percent a year, she would have $561,000 saved by age seventy in a typical actively managed mutual fund if it matched the market return before fees and other costs. She would have two thirds more, or $927,000, in a stock index fund.[6]

Of course, to actually earn those theoretical returns you have to . . .

## Be a HODLer

The best of times are the worst of times, at least for putting your savings to work. Maybe it was because the COVID-19 bear market was so short and sharp, because they had stimulus checks burning a hole in their pockets, or just because they hadn't ever suffered the trauma of losing a big chunk of their savings before, but Generation Z and millennials did the right thing in March 2020 and "held on for dear life," taking advantage of temporarily lower prices to buy stocks. According to a Morningstar study of 520,000 retirement accounts, older and supposedly wiser investors were less likely to do the same.[7]

The biggest misconception about bear markets is that they put a dent in our long-term investing goals. They are the price of admission to those gaudy long-run returns, though, and wholly unavoidable. In fact, what pinches our performance is mostly the failure to invest early enough during a rebound when things look really scary—a result of our psychologically crippling fear of financial loss. One of the core findings of behavioral finance is that losing money pains us more than an equivalent gain.

But the WallStreetBets crowd behaved differently, piling into stocks, and some of the most beaten-down ones specifically, with great results. While I don't recommend exclusively buying companies that might go bankrupt, much less ones that already have done so, like Hertz, being fully and boldly invested when times are bad is a huge boon to long-run returns.

The most profitable days to be in the market are easy to miss. J.P. Morgan Asset Management looked at the last twenty years through the end of 2020 and concluded that six out of the seven best days for the stock market were within two weeks of some of the worst days over that span and therefore at times when investors were most likely to have taken some money off the table or were the least likely to commit new savings to stocks. The second-worst day in 2020, March 12, was followed by the second-best day.

If you had just stayed fully invested in a stock index fund during this twenty-year period, then $10,000 would have turned into $42,231 by the end of 2020. Missing just the ten best days would have left you with just $19,437, or less than half as much. Missing the twenty best days would take that down to $11,474—less than you would have made in a no-risk bank savings account. And, incredibly, missing the thirty best days would see you lose money. Less than one half of 1 percent of the days made you all of your return in the stock market—if you were around for them.

That is a stylized example, but older individual investors with more substantial retirement savings cost themselves plenty through excessive caution. For example, money deposited each month into stock mutual funds has tended to peak shortly before a bull market ends when investing feels safe and then to slump when stocks have become much cheaper and are in the process of recovering. The COVID-19 panic saw the same trend on steroids with $16.7 billion invested in mutual funds in January 2020, the last full month before pandemic worries appeared. March and April of that year saw $383 billion yanked out of funds, just as the market began to surge.[8]

With the benefit of hindsight, many people reading this wish that they had done the same thing with their own savings. One way to guarantee that you buy low and sell high at least some of the time is to decide what percentage of your money you are comfortable having in the stock market and how much you want in safer investments. Circle a date in the calendar and, no matter how upbeat or scary the headlines, sell or buy some holdings to get back to that same percentage.

That sounds complicated, but this is the twenty-first century, and nothing has to be. Maybe it's time to . . .

## Welcome Our Robot Overlords

Unless you're incredibly disciplined and attentive to your savings, why not outsource the process to a computer program that can rebalance your portfolio automatically. For the younger generation in particular, who might not have a lot of money saved yet and who are more comfortable interacting with an app instead of a human, a robo-adviser is a great choice. Robo-advisers such as Wealthfront, SigFig, Marcus, Betterment, Schwab Intelligent Portfolios, and Vanguard Digital Advisor have about a quarter of a trillion in assets, which is surprisingly little. They are at least as efficient as humans, automatically rebalancing a low-cost portfolio of index funds and taking small losses to save people money on their taxes. And, because it is done by a computer, their services cost about a fourth of what a person who puts on a suit and goes to an office every day charges you.

A robo-adviser doesn't deliver the same level of excitement that a trading app does, and it deliberately puts speed bumps in a client's way when transacting, but . . .

## A Little Bit of Friction Is Good

There are a lot of businesses built around impulsive decisions, and most of them don't have a good reputation. Time-shares and car sales are two examples. Making it harder to switch around our investments, or at least forcing us to go through an extra step and think about it, can be incredibly valuable. We probably can't force app-based brokers to make their products clunkier, but we can choose one that explains the consequences of our actions and short-circuits bad decisions. For example, the robo-adviser Betterment will tell you how much you will have to pay in capital gains taxes before you sell a holding in a fund.

Humans may be more expensive when it comes to managing our finances, but they are still a lot better at one important thing: talking you off a ledge. That could pay for itself quickly. The world has come a long way from Fred Schwed's joke about the customers' yachts. Rather than a broker, who has an incentive for you to be active and to buy certain products, look for an adviser who is a fiduciary and who charges a flat or fixed fee. Your interests will be aligned.

In the bad old days, it would have been hard to find someone to handle a middle-class person's finances. Today, because of automation, a financial adviser can handle many more accounts. Some will take on the finances of a person with relatively little in assets but lots of promise down the road, dubbed a "HENRY" (High Earning, Not Rich Yet). But most of us are modest earning and not rich yet, which is why we have to worry so much about our finances. Costs really do matter in the long run. And the cheapest option of all—so cheap that investors from a few decades ago could hardly imagine it—is to . . .

## Do It Yourself

This book has warned against the dangers of free trading and free advice on the internet, both of which spurred mainly young people to be hyperactive trend chasers. That doesn't mean you have to become one by using the same tools. I once calculated the amount that I had paid my local gym over the past year, and it came out to $1.03 an hour. There is no way that it could have stayed in business with only customers like me. A gym's business model is built on people who either join because of a New Year's resolution and then never show up or pay for a lot of extras like personal training.

I am what is known as an "economic free rider," and you can be too. Robinhood and other discount brokers are like the mirror image of Planet Fitness, hoping that lots of its customers do show up and trade, but there is no requirement to do so. You can show up once a year or even less if you feel like it. And you don't have to do any research. Index funds that trade like stocks offered by Vanguard, iShares, Schwab, and others cost as little as 0.03 percent a year now for access to hundreds or even thousands of stocks. I own several through my discount broker, and buying a little bit more when I save some money or receive a dividend is (almost) free.

The price of those funds is hard to beat, but maybe you want to construct your own diversified portfolio of a couple of dozen stocks to buy and hold. There are plenty of good places to look online for advice (sorry apes, probably not WallStreetBets). For example, you might be bothered (or delighted) that Tesla is one of the largest stocks in the benchmark stock index that many funds follow and want to tweak things accordingly. Maybe you love Warren Buffett and want to own more of his Berkshire Hathaway than is in the S&P 500. The era of zero commissions makes this free as long as you pay attention to taxes and touch your portfolio infrequently.

You can even get an edge over index funds. Say you own shares of ExxonMobil and Kellogg, and they have declined in value. You can sell them at a loss to reduce your tax bill and then, to avoid triggering a tax penalty, use the money to buy shares in very similar companies like Chevron and General Mills. Rinse and repeat as necessary.

Not exciting enough? If you are of a more active bent, then at least limit the damage. Allocating only a set, small percentage of your savings to an account that lets you buy individual stocks will limit any self-harm while allowing you to channel your own inner stock market genius. And please avoid margin loans and derivatives. Go ahead and blame me if I cost you a future trade of the century by suggesting this, but . . .

## Know the Odds

As exciting as it is to read stories of people becoming rich quickly because of very concentrated wagers—Gill's one-thousand-fold return on GameStop, for example—it is hard to separate brilliance from luck, and most stock market bonanzas are the latter. There is also a sound mathematical reason for spreading your bets.

Consider some fascinating research by Victor Haghani, a name that might ring a bell for some readers.[9] He isn't only one of the sharpest minds in finance but also a man who learned things the hard way and practices what he preaches. Haghani was one of the founding partners of Long-Term Capital Management, the hedge fund staffed by Nobel Prize winners that thought it had found a free money machine by exploiting small discrepancies between the prices of nearly identical securities. It used what in hindsight seems like insane amounts of borrowed money to make its bets because it convinced the banks that lent to it that the risks it was taking were minimal.

They weren't. The fund imploded and then nearly took down the global financial system with it in 1998, as told brilliantly in Roger Lowenstein's *When Genius Failed*. Today Haghani is chief investment officer of Elm Partners, which runs portfolios of index funds for wealthy individuals, including many of his friends in high finance. These are people who have access to the best and brightest hedge fund managers. Elm, by contrast, offers low fees, uses no borrowed money, and is run by an algorithm rather than a hotshot manager with an Ivy League pedigree. It uses value and momentum to take advantage of other investors who chase bubbles or sell in a panic.

In a study, Haghani invited a group of graduate students to flip coins and win up to $250. He gave them a starting stake of $25 and a big advantage—a weighted coin that won 60 percent of the time and lost 40 percent of the time. They could bet as much or as little of their cash as they wanted per flip. The surprising thing is that 30 percent of this presumably bright bunch wound up losing all their money. They made the mistake of betting too much on certain flips.

That sounds incredible given the advantage they had. What's more, you don't have to be completely reckless and bet your whole bankroll to do poorly—just wagering half is dangerous enough. "You only live once" has become the rallying cry of a risk-loving generation of investors, but as Haghani's test subjects who went bust learned . . .

## Losing Money Early Hurts Too

Most of us have heard the example of the young person who saves part of their paycheck for ten years and the older person who saves the same amount of money for twenty years but winds up with a smaller nest egg. It is a speech many parents give to their high school or college graduates to teach them about thrift and compound interest that is promptly ignored. Wasting money on lots of peppermint mocha lattes isn't so different financially from blowing money making a YOLO bet on a meme stock when you're twenty-two.

The benign view of the Reddit Revolution is that it gave young people a good financial education when they didn't have much to lose and could bounce back. That is true for some people who then go on to be more conservative and successful investors like Betterment founder Jon Stein, who bought Enron and lost money. In many cases it isn't. The emotional toll could be worse than the financial one. If stocks are seen as speculative objects detached from underlying value, or if you are angry at your broker or at hedge funds for your own mistakes, then it is easy to get cynical about investing, and any money lost today could be a lot more costly tomorrow through failure to trust the market and build a nest egg. Instead, young investors should be more cynical about the feel-good message of profit-maximizing companies out to "democratize" investing and the cool, rich people who influence what they do with their money.

I'll return to my movie analogy in the introduction: some of you picked up this book expecting only the whiz-bang story of the GameStop squeeze, *Attack of the Clones*, and I tried to ruin it by whispering in your ear throughout the show that Chancellor Palpatine is a Sith lord, and all the heroics were for naught. That was just my geeky analogy for the events I describe, though. Wall Street isn't evil or all-powerful—it's just a collection of lucrative and not always transparent businesses. If you're at least middle-class, it's hard to avoid requiring its services, but it doesn't have to be costly or exploitative.

The force is with you.

# Acknowledgments

They say that writing a book is a lot like having a baby, and I'm even more convinced of it now that I've had my second bundle of literary joy. First of all, there's the amnesia about how tough it was the last time, without which I guess there would be a lot fewer books and people to read them. It's all very thrilling again at the beginning followed by months of wondering what you've gotten yourself into. In the end, you're exhausted but full of pride and showing it off to everyone you meet, whether they are really interested or simply being polite.

Just like a baby, you can't do it yourself, but there are a lot more people involved in a book. First and foremost, I have to thank my family. They saw very little of me for months as I worked through every evening, weekend, and vacation, conducted lots of loud Zoom interviews, and left piles of paper all over the house. But they did more than just put up with me: My son Jonah provided the spark before I knew what diamond hands were and schooled me in the ways of Reddit. Elliott asked smart questions throughout and convinced me to go on lots of walks to break up the monotony of writing. Danny organized my notes and was more excited than I was about my interview with the "Wolf of Wall Street."

My talented sister, Judy Feaster, who would rather be reading Proust in the original than my turgid prose, greatly improved an early draft; my wonderful wife, Nicole, made important suggestions and kept me caffeinated; and my mom, Veronica, supported me as she always has.

Pitching a book usually is hard, but my agent Eric Lupfer and the decision-makers at Portfolio, Adrian Zackheim and Niki Papadopoulos, immediately saw the promise in this project even as the meme-stock squeeze was still unfolding. And of course my wise and talented editor, Noah Schwartzberg, and his assistant, Kimberly Meilun, have their fingerprints on every single page. This wouldn't be half the book it is without Noah's guidance. Any shortcomings are mine alone.

My colleagues at *The Wall Street Journal*, my home away from home for the last ten years and I hope many more to come, are my inspiration. They include my editors Charles Forelle, David Reilly, and Matt Murray, my team at Heard on the Street, and the many talented reporters who produced the best coverage of and commentary on the GameStop squeeze hands down. You can see most of their names in the endnotes too, but they are Julia Verlaine, Geoffrey Rogow, Gregory Zuckerman, Telis Demos, Jon Sindreu, Dan Gallagher, James Mackintosh, Christopher Mims, Juliet Chung, David Benoit, Gunjan Banerji, Peter Rudegeair, Akane Otani, Jason Zweig, Caitlin McCabe, and Rachel Louise Ensign.

Usually this is the part of the acknowledgments when you turn to all your sources, including some who know who they are but chose to remain unnamed. I'll get to them in a second, but I also have to acknowledge the thousands of people whose real names I'll probably never know because they're hiding behind a pseudonym on Reddit like cd258519,

Stonksflyingup, and Techmonk123. They provided a real-time running commentary of how the WallStreetBets community saw the meme-stock squeeze unfold and of Keith Gill's rise from obscurity to legendary status.

As for the people whose names I both know and am able to use, I am deeply grateful to Jaime Rogozinski, Jim Chanos, Andrew Left, Peter Atwater, Jay Van Bavel, Peter Cecchini, Ihor Dusaniwsky, Jordan Belfort, Ben Hunt, Cait Lamberton, Seth Mahoney, Quinn and Finley Mulligan, Devin Ryan, Chad Minnis, Dan Egan, Larry Swedroe, Scott Nations, Howard Lindzon, Jon Stein, Keith Whyte, Barbara Roper, Margaret O'Mara, Sandra Chu, and Sean Birke.

And finally, I want to say a word about a man who might have been an "ape" if he had been born sixty years later. My dad, John Jakab, who passed away when I was a teenager, came to this country as a refugee with little more than the clothes on his back. Even before he brought my mom over and my sister and I were born, he became ob-sessed with making a fortune in the stock market. Judging from the yel-lowed Merrill Lynch statements I still have, I think he made a nice contribution to Wall Street. I don't know if he would have done better or worse with a smartphone-based app and "free" trading, but he would have loved to try.

# Notes

## Introduction

1. Burton G. Malkiel, "Are Index Funds Worse Than Marxism?" *The Wall Street Journal*, April 24, 2016.

## Chapter 1: Mr. Kitty Goes to Washington

1. Matt Levine, "GameStop Hearing Featured No Cats," *Bloomberg*, February 19, 2021.
2. Nir Kaissar, "GameStop Hearing Was a Solution in Search of a Problem," *Bloomberg*, February 19, 2021.
3. Veronica Dagher and Caitlin McCabe, "Robinhood Wants More Female Investors: So Does Everyone Else," *The Wall Street Journal*, January 7, 2021.
4. Nate Raymond and Emily Flitter, "U.S. Judge Accepts SAC Guilty Plea, Approves $1.2 billion Deal," Reuters, April 10, 2014.
5. Gregory Zuckerman and Rob Copeland, "Top SAC Capital Portfolio Manager to Start Own Hedge Fund," *The Wall Street Journal*, April 6, 2014.
6. Tom Maloney and Hema Parmar, "Coleman Leads $23 Billion Payday for 15 Hedge Fund Earners," *Bloomberg*, February 10, 2021.

7. Conrad Louis, "Achieving Success: An In-Depth Interview with Gabe Plotkin," *All That Glitters Podcast,* episode 8, July 22, 2020, www.allthatglitterspodcast .com/episodes/episode-08-interview-gabe-plotkin.

8. Bess Levin, "Hedge Fund Manager Known for Inspiring Spine-Tingling Terror in People Hopes to Lighten Things Up with Haunted House Come October," *Dealbreaker,* January 14, 2019.

9. Marcia Vickers, "Ken Griffin: Hedge Fund Superstar," *Fortune,* April 16, 2007.

10. Rob Copeland, "Citadel's Ken Griffin Leaves 2008 Tumble Far Behind," *The Wall Street Journal,* August 3, 2015.

11. Kerry Dolan, Chase Peterson-Whithorn, and Jennifer Wang, "The Forbes World's Billionaires List," *Forbes,* April 6, 2021.

12. Katherine Clark, "How Citadel CEO Ken Griffin Built a $1 Billion Property Empire," *The Wall Street Journal,* October 8, 2020.

13. Zachary Warmbrodt, "Hedge Fund King, a GOP Megadonor, Faces Off with Democrats," *Politico,* February 18, 2021.

14. Tom Maloney, "Citadel Securities Gets the Spotlight," *Bloomberg Markets,* April 6, 2021.

15. Lauren Feiner, "Reddit CEO Huffman Defends Platform's Role in GameStop Surge," CNBC, February 18, 2021.

16. Jacob Passy, "Reddit Co-founder Alexis Ohanian Compares GameStop Squeeze to Occupy Wall Street: 'This Is the New Normal,'" *MarketWatch,* January 29, 2021.

17. Don Vaughn, "Stock Market Frenzy Sentiment," survey by Invisibly, February 16, 2021, www.invisibly.com/insights/gamestop.

18. "What Is a Fiduciary?" Robinhood, accessed August 2021, https://learn.robin hood.com/articles/4tkv1OEIDNMnukYHxwzYCm/what-is-a-fiduciary.

19. Mark Schoeff Jr., "Robinhood Sues to Overturn Massachusetts Fiduciary Rule," *Investment News,* April 15, 2021.

## Chapter 2: September 8, 2019

1. Techmonk123, "Response to 'Hey Burry, thanks a lot for jacking up my cost basis,'" Reddit, September 8, 2019, www.reddit.com/r/wallstreetbets/comments /d1g7x0/hey_burry_thanks_a_lot_for_jacking_up_my_cost.

2. Jason Zweig, "Robinhood Trader's Battle Cry: 'It's All Just a Game to Me,'" *The Wall Street Journal,* March 26, 2021.

3. "Confidence Trumps Accuracy in Pundit Popularity," *WSU Insider*, May 28, 2013.

4. Interview with Seth Mahoney, conducted by telephone, May 28, 2021.

5. Interview with Jay Van Bavel, conducted by email, February 28, 2021.


## Chapter 3: Killer App

1. Packy McCormick, "Robinhood Robinhooded Robinhood," *Not Boring* (blog), February 1, 2021, www.notboring.co/p/robinhood-robinhooded-robinhood.

2. Interview with Jaime Rogozinski, conducted by Zoom video, February 19, 2021.

3. Anna Mazarakis and Alyson Shontell, "The Founders of Robinhood, a No-fee Stock-trading App, Were Initially Rejected by 75 Venture Capitalists—Now Their Startup Is Worth $1.3 Billion," *Business Insider,* July 6, 2017.

4. Interviews with Howard Lindzon, conducted by telephone and Google Meets, May 23 and May 28, 2021.

5. Rob Walker, "How Robinhood Convinced Millennials to Trade Their Way through a Pandemic," *Marker*, June 1, 2020.

6. Tom Metcalf and Julia Verhage, "Robinhood Co-founders Baiju Bhatt and Vlad Tenev Are Billionaires in a Silicon Valley Minute," *Bloomberg*, May 12, 2018.

7. Nina Zipkin, "The Entrepreneurs Behind This Multibillion Dollar Company Share Why Success Is Nothing Without a Partner You Can Rely On," *Entrepreneur*, June 14, 2018.

8. Robinhood Markets, Inc. Form S-1 July 1, 2021, available at: www.sec.gov /Archives/edgar/data/0001783879/000162828021013318/robinhoods-1.htm.

9. Aaron Levie, "The Simplicity Thesis," *Fast Company*, May 2, 2012.

10. Caitlin McCabe, "Massachusetts Regulators File Complaint Against Robinhood," *The Wall Street Journal*, December 16, 2020.

11. McCabe, "Massachusetts Regulators."

12. Interview with Barbara Roper, conducted by telephone, February 26, 2021.

13. Vlad Tenev, "Robinhood Users Come Under Attack," *The Wall Street Journal*, September 27, 2021, www.wsj.com/articles/robinhood-users-regulation-retail-investing -order-flow-access-to-capital-investing-11632776071.

14. Interview with Keith S. Whyte, conducted by telephone, May 14, 2021.

15. Susan Weinschenk, "Use Unpredictable Rewards to Keep Behavior Going," *Psychology Today*, November 13, 2013.

16. Ian Salisbury, "Meet Richard Thaler, the Man Who Just Won the Nobel Prize for Helping You Save for Your Retirement," *Money*, October 9, 2017.

17. James Choi, David Laibson, and Brigitte C. Madrian, "Plan Design and 401(k) Savings Outcomes," *National Tax Journal*, June 2004.

18. Mazarakis and Shontell, "Founders of Robinhood."

19. Joe Weisenthal and Tracy Alloway, "How Robinhood Makes Money on Free Trades," *Odd Lots Podcast*, July 29, 2020.

20. Dave Michaels and Alexander Osipovich, "Robinhood Financial to Pay $65 Million to Settle SEC Probe," *The Wall Street Journal*, December 17, 2020.

21. Dave Michaels, "Robinhood Agrees to Pay $70 Million to Settle Regulatory Investigation," *The Wall Street Journal*, June 30, 2021.

22. Peter Rudegeair, "Robinhood in Talks to Settle Finra Probes into Options-trading Practices, Outages," *The Wall Street Journal*, February 26, 2021.

23. Interview with Jay Van Bavel, conducted by email, February 28, 2021.

24. Interview with Sandra Chu, conducted by Zoom video, May 29, 2021.

25. *The Social Network*, directed by David Fincher (Columbia Pictures, 2010).

26. Katie Collins, "Reddit Slammed by Former CEO Ellen Pao for 'Amplifying' Racism and Hate," *CNET*, June 2, 2020.

27. Interview with Margaret O'Mara by telephone, March 3, 2021.

## Chapter 4: Winter of 2019–2020

1. fieldG, "Response to DeepFuckingValue post, 'GME YOLO Month end update-Feb2020,'" Reddit, February 29, 2020, www.reddit.com/r/wallstreetbets/comments/fbc49g/gme_yolo_monthend_update_feb_2020.

2. Keith Gill, Roaring Kitty YouTube video transcript, August 4, 2020.

3. David Marino-Nachison, "Here's Why Wall Street's Only Bullish GameStop Analyst Is Still Optimistic," *Barron's*, September 11, 2019.

4. FactSet.

5. Sally French and Shawn Langlois, "Meet the Millennials Looking to Get Rich or Die Tryin' with One of Wall Street's Riskiest Oil Plays," *MarketWatch*, March 30, 2016.

## Chapter 5: Race to the Bottom

1. Stephen Mihm, "The Death of Brokerage Fees Was 50 Years in the Making," *Bloomberg*, January 3, 2021.

2. Matt Egan, "This App Completely Disrupted the Trading Industry," CNN Business, December 13, 2019.

3. Lisa Beilfuss and Alexander Osipovich, "The Race to Zero Commissions," *The Wall Street Journal*, October 5, 2019.

4. "Retail Trading Barometer," provided by Robintrack, https://robintrack.net/barometer.

5. Dawn Lim, "Robinhood Draws User Ire for Repeated Outages in Volatile Market," *The Wall Street Journal*, March 9, 2020.

6. Interview with Dan Egan by telephone, April 7, 2021.

7. Caitlin McCabe, "Massachusetts Regulators File Complaint against Robinhood," *The Wall Street Journal*, December 16, 2020.

8. Svea Herbst-Bayliss, "Prominent Activist Investors Post Record 2020 Returns despite Pandemic-muted Activity," Reuters, January 6, 2021.

9. Christine Williamson, "Hedge Funds Chalk Up Decade's Best Returns in 2020—HFR," *Pensions and Investments*, January 8, 2021.

10. "Taking Stock of 2020 So Far," SoFi blog post, July 13, 2020, www.sofi.com/blog/taking-stock-of-2020-so-far.

11. u/never_noob, "Official WSB Survey Results are in!," Reddit, 2017, www.reddit.com/r/wallstreetbets/comments/52tfrg/official_wsb_survey_results_are_in.

12. Graham Flanagan, "Barstool Sports Founder Switches from Gambling to Day Trading during Coronavirus—and He Says He's Down $647,000," *Insider*, April 20, 2021.

13. Dave Portnoy (@stoolpresidente), "I'm sure Warren Buffett is a great guy, but when it comes to stocks he's washed up. I'm the captain now #DDTG," Twitter, June 9, 2020, 9:41 a.m., twitter.com/stoolpresidente/status/1270350291653791747.

14. Stephen Gandel, "Robinhood Offers Loans to Buy Stock—They Were 14 Times More Likely to Default," *MoneyWatch*, CBS News, February 5, 2021.

15. Interview with Peter Atwater via telephone, February 10, 2021.

16. Frank Van Dyke, "The Renewed Rise of the Retail Investor," Global X ETFs blog post, October 15, 2020.

17. Gregory Zuckerman and Mischa Frankl-Duval, "Individuals Roll the Dice on Stocks as Veterans Fret," *The Wall Street Journal*, June 9, 2020.

18. Dan Runkevicius, "How Hertz Fooled Amateur Investors," *Forbes*, July 1, 2020.

19. Noah Weidner, "How Well Did the Robinhood Crowd Do in 2020?" *Business as Usual*, December 21, 2020.

20. Interview with Larry Swedroe by telephone, April 27, 2021.

21. Isabelle Lee, "SPACs Are Booming 'at the Expense of Retail Investors,' and Regulators Should Take These 5 Steps to Fix the Market, Think Tanks Say," *Business Insider*, March 7, 2021.

22. David John and Curtis Dubay, "Financial Transactions Tax Would Hurt the Economy and Kill American Jobs," Heritage Foundation report, January 11, 2012.

23. Aaron Klein, "What Is a Financial Transactions Tax?," Brookings Institution report, March 27, 2020.

## Chapter 6: April 2020

1. Cd258519, "Response to DeepFuckingValue post 'GME YOLO month-end update-Apr 2020,'" Reddit, April 30, 2020, www.reddit.com/r/wallstreetbets/comments/gb3ctb/gme_yolo_monthend_update_apr_2020.

2. Jonelle Marte, "Trump Touts Stock Market's Record Run, but Who Benefits?," Reuters, February 5, 2020.

3. Kim Parker and Richard Fry, "More Than Half of US households Have Some Investment in the Stock Market," *Pew Research Fact Tank*, March 25, 2020.

4. Thomas Chua, "Why Gamestop Went to the Moon with Gamma Squeeze," *Compounding With Options* (blog), January 27, 2021, https://learnoptions.substack.com/p/why-gamestop-went-to-the-moon-with.

5. John McCrank, "Robinhood Now a Go-to for Young Investors and Short Sellers," Reuters, March 2, 2021.

## Chapter 7: Get Shorty

1. Chuck Mikolajczak, "Tesla Bears Suffer Record Short-sale Loss in 2020: S3 Partners," Reuters, January 21, 2021.

2. "Top of Mind," Goldman Sachs Global Macro Research, February 25, 2021, www.goldmansachs.com/insights/pages/gs-research/the-short-and-long-of-recent-volatility-f/report.pdf.

3. House Committee on Financial Services, "Following Recent Market Instability, Waters Announces Hearing on Short Selling, Online Trading Platforms," press release, January 28, 2021, https://financialservices.house.gov/news/documentsingle.aspx?DocumentID=407096.

4. Interview with Jim Chanos by telephone, March 2, 2021.

5. Owen Lamont, "Go Down Fighting: Short Sellers vs. Firms," NBER Working Paper 10659, August 30, 2004.

6. Leo Lewis and Billy Nauman, "Short Sellers under Fire from Investment Boss of World's Largest Pension Fund," *Financial Times*, December 11, 2019.

7. Mikolajczak, "Tesla Bears."

8. Ibid.

9. Aswath Damodaran, "The Storming of the Bastille: The Reddit Crowd Targets the Hedge Funds!," *Musings on Markets* (blog), January 29, 2021, http://aswath damodaran.blogspot.com/2021/01/the-storming-of-bastille-reddit-crowd.html.

10. Robert Battalio, Hamid Mehran, and Paul Schultz, "Market Declines: What Is Accomplished by Banning Short-Selling?" *Current Issues in Economics and Finance* 18, no. 5 (2012): www.newyorkfed.org/medialibrary/media/research/current_issues/ci18-5.pdf.

## Chapter 8: Summer–Fall 2020

1. Ryan Cohen, "The Founder of Chewy.com on Finding the Financing to Achieve Scale," *Harvard Business Review*, January–February 2020.

2. Saul Hansell, "'Buy!' Was Cry as Stock Bubble Burst," *The New York Times*, March 4, 2001.

3. hiend87, "Response to DeepFuckingValue post 'GME YOLO month start update-Sep 1 2020,'" Reddit, September 1, 2020, www.reddit.com/r/wallstreetbets/comments/ikrq8w/gme_yolo_monthstart_update_sep_1_2020/g3n848d.

4. RC Ventures LLC letter to board of GameStop filed with SEC, November 16, 2020, https://www.sec.gov/Archives/edgar/data/1326380/000101359420000821/rc13da3-111620.pdf.

5. Stonksflyingup, "GME Squeeze and the Demise of Melvin Capital," Reddit, October 27, 2020, www.reddit.com/r/wallstreetbets/comments/jjctxg/gme_squeeze_and_the_demise_of_melvin_capital.

## Chapter Nine: Cheat Code

1. Matt Stone, "Invincibility (God Mode) Cheat Demo," *GTA BOOM*, 2020, www.gtaboom.com/invincibility-cheat.

2. Mike Murphy, "Robinhood Glitch Is Letting Users Trade with Unlimited Amounts of Borrowed Cash," *MarketWatch*, November 5, 2019.

3. TheDrallen, "Response to 'Robinhood free money cheat works pretty well, 1 million dollar position on 4k,'" Reddit, November 4, 2020, www.reddit.com/r/wall streetbets/comments/drqaro/robinhood_free_money_cheat_works_pretty _well_1.

4. Lawrence McDonald, "New Vol Regime," *The Bear Traps Report* (blog), August 28, 2020, www.thebeartrapsreport.com/blog/2020/08/28.

5. Peter Atwater, "Danger, Danger Will Robinson," *Financial Insyghts*, May 21, 2021.

6. Mark Sebastian, "How Robinhood and Reddit Have Changed Options Trading— and How You Can Profit," *The Street*, March 11, 2021.

7. Peter Rudegeair, "Robinhood in Talks to Settle Finra Probes into Options- Trading Practices, Outages," *The Wall Street Journal*, February 26, 2021.

8. Interview with Peter Cecchini by telephone, March 17, 2021.

9. Theron Mohamed, "We Spoke with a Robinhood Trader Who Says He Made a 2,500% Return from Tesla's Stock Rally: Here's How He Did It," *Markets Insider*, February 6, 2020.

10. Matt Egan, "'He Would Be Alive Today': Parents Detail Son's Desperate Attempts to Contact Robinhood before He Killed Himself," CNN, February 11, 2021.

11. Summer Said et al., "SoftBank's Bet on Tech Giants Fueled Powerful Market Rally," *The Wall Street Journal*, September 4, 2020.

12. Avi Salzman, "Robinhood Filing Shows Enormous Growth in Controversial Revenue Source," *Barron's*, May 3, 2021.

13. Jeffamazon, "The REAL Greatest Short Burn of the Century," Reddit, September 9, 2020, www.reddit.com/r/wallstreetbets/comments/ip6jnv/the_real_greatest _short_burn_of_the_century.

## Chapter 10: Holiday Season 2020–2021

1. Eurekahedge Hedge Fund Database, accessed May 2021, www.eurekahedge .com/Products/Hedge-Fund-Databases.

2. "GameStop Announces Additional Board Refreshment to Accelerate Transformation," GameStop Corp. press release, January 11, 2011, https://news.gamestop .com/news-releases/news-release-details/gamestop-announces-additional -board-refreshment-accelerate.

## Chapter 11: Poking the Bear

1. "SEC Charges Marijuana-Related Company with Touting Bogus Revenues," SEC press release, March 9, 2017, www.sec.gov/news/pressrelease/2017-62.html.

2. Matt Wirz, "The Short Who Sank Valeant Stock," *The Wall Street Journal*, October 22, 2015.

3. Ben Winck, "'No longer a stock but a full casino': Palantir will lose one-third of its value by year-end after surging more than 300%, short-seller Citron Research says," *Business Insider*, November 27, 2020, https://markets.businessinsider.com /news/stocks/palantir-stock-price-target-short-selling-position-citron -research-pltr-2020-11.

4. "NIO – Citron Pulls the Plug on NIO – 2 Years After Our Controversial Recommendation," Citron Research report, November 13, 2020, https://citronresearch .com/wp-content/uploads/2020/11/NIO-Citron-Pulls-the-Plug.pdf.

5. Mo Samara, "Appeal to FINRA and SEC Enforcements to Investigate Andrew Left of Citron Research," Change.org petition, retrieved March 2021, www .change.org/p/u-s-securities-and-exchange-commission-sec-enforcement -to-investigate-andrew-left-of-citron-research.

6. Citron Research (@CitronResearch), "Tomorrow am at 11:30 EST Citron will livestream the 5 reasons GameStop $GME buyers at these levels are the suckers at this poker game. Stock back to $20 fast. We understand short interest better than you and will explain. Thank you to viewers for pos feedback on last live tweet," Twitter, January 19, 2021, 9:58 a.m., https://twitter.com/citronresearch /status/1351544479547760642.

7. NFTOxaile, "Response to 'Shitron Attacking Begins,'" Reddit, January 19, 2021, www.reddit.com/r/wallstreetbets/comments/l0lg6r/shitron_attacking_begins /gjv3z3x.

8. Truthposter 100, "Response to 'Shitron Attacking Begins,'" January 19, 2021, www.reddit.com/r/wallstreetbets/comments/l0lg6r/shitron_attacking_begins /gjutdfu.

9. Self-AwareMeat, "yeah, Melvin is small fodder. Citron is the one we want to fuck badly," Reddit, January 19, 2021. Response to "Shitron Attacking Begins," www.red dit.com/r/wallstreetbets/comments/l0lg6r/shitron_attacking_begins/gju7o8e.

10. Citron Research, "Citron Research discontinues short selling research to focus on long opportunities," YouTube video, January 29, 2021, www.youtube.com /watch?v=TPoVv7oX3mw.

11. Cre8_or, "Response to "GME The Wreckoning," Reddit, January 19, 2021, teddit .net/r/wallstreetbets/comments/l0hhqg/gme_thread_the_wreckoning.

12. Carleton English, "Tycoons Battle over Kids' $37K-a-Month Child Support Payments," *New York Post*, December 12, 2017.

13. Citron Research, "An update from Citron Research," YouTube video, January 29, 2021, www.youtube.com/watch?v=yS4yPsmaDDQ.

14. Nishant Kumar and Hema Parmar, "Short Sellers Face End of an Era as Rookies Rule Wall Street," *Bloomberg*, January 29, 2021.

## Chapter 12: January 22, 2021

1. Connor Smith, "GameStop Stock Has Soared despite Falling Sales: Reality Could Eventually Catch Up," *Barron's*, January 8, 2021.

2. "Jim Cramer: GameStop's Run Is 'Game Over' for the Shorts," *The Street*, video clip, January 13, 2021, www.thestreet.com/video/jim-cramer-gamestop-run-is -game-over-for-shorts.

3. Caitlin McCabe, "GameStop Stock Soars, and Social-Media Traders Claim Victory," *The Wall Street Journal*, January 14, 2021.

4. Roaring Kitty, "Ryan Cohen & his Chewy crew join GameStop's Board of Directors! Where does GME stock head from here?" YouTube video, January 11, 2021, www.youtube.com/watch?v=RnpoahOnLec&list=PLlsPosngRnZ1esbvs4Vbj fIOk9F5QYYXS&index=59.

5. Ibid.

6. Matthew Gault and Jason Koebler, "How Chaotic Redditors Made GameStop Stock Skyrocket (and Made Short Sellers Cry)," *Vice*, January 19, 2021.

## Chapter 13: Rise of the Apes

1. That_Guy_KC, "Stop with the ape crap," Reddit, February 6, 2021 (post deleted), archived at https://js4.red/r/wallstreetbets/comments/ldrwvl/stop_with_the_ape _crap.

2. Page statistics for r/wallstreetbets, Subreddit Stats, accessed March 2021, https://subredditstats.com/r/wallstreetbets.

3. Jack Morse, "Reddit Swoops In to Resolve WallStreetBets Moderator Drama," *Mashable*, February 5, 2021.

4. Maggie Fitzgerald, "GameStop Mania May Not Have Been the Retail Trader Rebellion It Was Perceived to Be, Data Shows," CNBC, February 5, 2021.

5. Interview with Quinn and Finley Mulligan by Zoom video, May 24, 2021.

6. Rachael Cihlar, "What Brands Can Learn from GameStop and Reddit about Social Proof and Trust," Mavrck blog post, February 8, 2021.


### Chapter 14: January 26, 2021

1. Keenfeed, "To everyone who doesn't understand GME," "Response to Deep-FuckingValue post 'GME YOLO Update-Jan 25 2021,'" Reddit, January 25, 2021, www.reddit.com/r/wallstreetbets/comments/l4xje1/gme_yolo_update_jan_25_2021/gkragzi.

2. Annie Minoff, Episode 3, June 6, 2021, in *To the Moon, Wall Street Journal* podcast.

3. Interview with Jordan Belfort via Zoom video, February 11, 2021.

4. Elon Musk (@elonmusk), "Gamestonk!!" Twitter, January 26, 2021, 4:08 p.m., twitter.com/elonmusk/status/1354174279894642703.


### Chapter 15: The Influencers

1. John J. Raskob, "Everybody Ought to Be Rich," *Ladies Home Journal*, August 1929.

2. Chamath Palihapitiya (@chamath), "Lots of $GME talk soooooo.... We bought Feb $115 calls on $GME this morning. Let's goooooooo!!!!!!!!" Twitter, January 26, 2021, 10:32 a.m., twitter.com/chamath/status/1354089928313823232.

3. Matthew J. Belvedere, "Chamath Palihapitiya Closes GameStop Position but Defends Investors' Right to Sway Stock Like Pros," CNBC, January 27, 2021.

4. Dave Portnoy (@stoolpresidente), "I own $amc $nok $nakd. I bought them with the understanding we live in a free market where people can buy and sell stocks fair and square and at their own risk. I will hold them till the death as a reminder that @RobinhoodApp founders must go to prison," Twitter, January 28, 2021, 11:42 a.m., twitter.com/stoolpresidente/status/1354832177498873860.

5. Peter Rudegeair and Maureeen Farrell, "When SPAC Man Chamath Palihapitiya Speaks, Reddit and Wall Street Listen," *The Wall Street Journal*, March 6, 2021.

6. Chamath Palihapitiya (@chamath), "In moments of uncertainty, when courage and strength are required, you find out who the true corporatist scumbags are,"

Twitter, January 28, 2021, 12:14 p.m., twitter.com/chamath/status/1354840270 064377858.

7. VanEck, "VanEck Social Sentiment ETF Overview," retrieved August 2021, www.vaneck.com/us/en/investments/social-sentiment-etf-buzz.

8. Repfam4life, "These billionaires are not our friends," Reddit, January 29, 2021, www.reddit.com/r/wallstreetbets/comments/l7sx16/these_billionaires_are _not_our_friends.

9. Eliza Relman, "Alexandria Ocasio-Cortez Thinks Billionaires Shouldn't Exist as Long as Americans Live in Abject Poverty," *Business Insider*, January 22, 2019.

10. Alan Mirabella, "Dalio Says GameStop Drama Reflects Growing Intolerance in U.S.," *Bloomberg*, January 29, 2021.

11. Steven Cohen (@StevenACohen2), "Rough crowd on Twitter tonight.Hey stock jockeys keep bringing it," Twitter, January 26, 2021, 8:47 p.m., twitter.com/Steven ACohen2/status/1354244563670601728.

12. Kevin Draper, "Mets' Cohen Deletes Twitter Account after Threats," *The New York Times*, January 30, 2021.

13. Julie Ryan Evans, "Nearly 60% of Young Investors Are Collaborating Thanks to Technology, Often Turning to Social Media for Advice," *MagnifyMoney* (blog), February 22, 2021, www.magnifymoney.com/blog/news/young-investors-survey.

14. Sophie Kiderlin, "Gen Z Investors Are Taking More Risks, Picking Up Bad Investing Habits in the Race to Get Rich Quick, Survey Finds," *Markets Insider*, June 27, 2021.

15. Laila Maidan, "Math Teacher Went from $5,000 a Month to $28,000 Thanks to 6 Strategic Money Decisions," *Insider*, March 15, 2021.

16. Justina Lee, "Robinhood couple in viral TikTok discover momentum trading, net 2,000% return in one month," *Financial Post*, January 21, 2021.

17. Will Daniel, "Churchill Capital Corp. IV Retail Investors Stung by the Steep Drop following the Lucid Motors Deal Are Banding Together on Reddit to 'Defend' the Stock," *Markets Insider*, February 26, 2021.

18. Socaltexasgirl, "Response to 'LWSB : Lucid Wall Street Bets , all longs - CCIV heavily shorted by coordinated groups and manipulators. Why can't we have a LWSB and defend . Are you IN ?" Reddit, February 25, 2021, www.reddit.com/r /CCIV/comments/lsfnhm/comment/gor6o2v.

19. Stephen Gandel, "WallstreetBets Says Reddit Group Hit by Large Amount of Bot Activity," *MoneyWatch*, CBS News, February 2, 2021.

20. Interview with Ben Hunt by Twitter Direct Message, February 27, 2021.

21. Michelle Price, "Bots Hyped Up GameStop on Major Social Media Platforms, Analysis Finds," Reuters, February 26, 2021.

22. Securities and Exchange Commission, "SEC Suspends Trading in Multiple Issuers Based on Social Media and Trading Activity," press release, February 26, 2021.

23. SEC Investor Ed (@SEC_Investor_Ed), "Thinking about investing in the latest hot stock? Don't let short-term emotions disrupt your long-term financial objectives . . . Take the time to do your homework first. Tools + resources that can help: https://go.usa.gov/xHsPD," Twitter, February 25, 2021, 2:10 p.m., twitter .com/SEC_Investor_Ed/status/1422256225207607297.

## Chapter 16: January 27, 2021

1. Anonymous, "We've officially broken the market," Reddit, January 27, 2021, original post deleted, www.reddit.com/r/wallstreetbets/comments/l662z0/weve _officially_broke_the_market.

2. Interview with Ihor Dusaniwsky by telephone and email, April 6, 2021.

3. Michael Santoli, "It's Likely Going to Take a Constant Stream of Excited Buyers to Keep the GameStop, AMC Rally Going," CNBC, February 1, 2021.

4. Julia Verlaine and Gunjan Banerji, "Keith Gill Drove the Reddit GameStop Mania: He Talked to the Journal," *The Wall Street Journal*, January 29, 2021.

5. Reed Richardson, "NY Post Deletes Story after Getting Duped by Post by Random Twitter User Who Pushed Absurd Story about Buying GameStop Stock," *Mediaite*, January 28, 2021.

6. Rachel Louise Ensign, "GameStop Investors Who Bet Big and Lost Big," *The Wall Street Journal*, February 15, 2021.

## Chapter 17: LOL, Nothing Matters

1. Berkshire Hathaway Inc., 2014 Annual Report, 26.

2. *Merriam-Webster*, s.v. "stonk (*n*.)," accessed April 1, 2021, www.merriam-webster .com/dictionary/app.

3. Jordan Weissmann, "What We Talk about When We Talk about Stonks," *Slate*, January 28, 2021.

4. Quoted in Berkshire Hathaway annual letter to investors, March 1, 1994, www .berkshirehathaway.com/letters/1993.html.

5. Aswath Damodaran, "The Storming of the Bastille: The Reddit Crowd Targets the Hedge Funds," *Musings on Markets* (blog), January 29, 2021.

6. Jason Zweig, "Robinhood Trader's Battle Cry—'It's All Just a Game to Me,'" *The Wall Street Journal*, March 26, 2021.

7. Charles P. Kindleberger, *Manias, Panics, and Crashes: A History of Financial Crises,* 3rd ed. (New York: John Wiley and Sons, 2011), 14.

8. Sarah Whitten, "AMC's Apes Gave It a Lifeline: Now Its CEO Wants to Use the Meme Frenzy as a Springboard for Growth," CNBC, June 1, 2021.

9. Serena Ng and Thomas Gryta, "New Wall Street Conflict: Analysts Say 'Buy' to Win Special Access for Their Clients," *The Wall Street Journal*, January 19, 2017.

10. Joe Weisenthal and Tracy Alloway, "John Hempton on Greensill, Archegos and What It's Like to Short Right Now," *Odd Lots* (*Bloomberg* podcast), April 18, 2021, www.bloomberg.com/news/articles/2021-04-19/john-hempton-on-greensill-archegos-and-what-it-s-like-to-short-right-now.

11. Colin Twiggs, "Good Investing Is Boring, George Soros," *Patient Investor* (blog), July 1, 2019, https://thepatientinvestor.com/index.php/2019/07/01/good-investing-is-boring-george-soros.

12. Alex Veiga, "GameStop Is Surging Again, but Why?" Associated Press, February 25, 2021.

13. Caitlin McCabe and Jason Zweig, "Charlie Munger Renews Robinhood Criticism," *The Wall Street Journal*, February 25, 2021.

14. Ibid.

15. Seth A. Klarman, *Margin of Safety: Risk-averse Value Investing Strategies for the Thoughtful Investor* (New York: HarperBusiness, 1991), 60.

16. Heejin Kim, "Michael Burry Calls GameStop Rally 'Unnatural, Insane,'" *Bloomberg*, January 27, 2021.

## Chapter 18: January 28, 2021

1. Robinhood, "Keeping Customers Informed through Market Volatility," blog post, January 28, 2021, https://blog.robinhood.com/news/2021/1/28/keeping-customers-informed-through-market-volatility.

2. Joseph Saveri Law Firm, "Short Squeeze Stockbrokers and Hedge Funds Face Proposed Antitrust Class Action," press release, February 1, 2021, www.saverilawfirm.com/press/short-squeeze-stockbrokers-and-hedge-funds-face-proposed-antitrust-class-action.

3.  Akane Otani, "WallStreetBets Founder Reckons with Legacy amid Stock Market Frenzy," *The Wall Street Journal*, January 28, 2021.

4.  Theseyeahthese, "Response to GME YOLO Update-Jan 28 2021," Reddit, January 28, 2021, www.reddit.com/r/wallstreetbets/comments/l78uct/gme_yolo_update_jan _28_2021/gl5dab8.

5.  "Billionaire Chamath Palihapitiya on GameStop Surge and Rise of Retail Investors," *Halftime Report*, CNBC, January 27, 2021, www.cnbc.com/video/2021/01 /27/billionaire-investor-chamath-palihapitiya-on-gamestop-surge-and-rise-of -retail-investors.html.

6.  Mark Cuban (@mcuban), "I got to say I LOVE LOVE what is going on with #wallstreetbets. All of those years of High Frequency Traders front running retail traders,now speed and density of information and retail trading is giving the little guy an edge. Even my 11 yr old traded w them and made $," Twitter, January 28, 2021, 9:14 p.m., twitter.com/mcuban/status/1354613692239925249.

7.  Dan Nathan (@RiskReversal), "I suspect when the dust settles from the impending mushroom cloud, high-frequency traders & options market makers will be the real winners, they'll make money on way up & down and in vol. House always wins . . . cheers to their success, but 'money ain't got no owners, only spenders,'" Twitter, January 27, 2021, 9:59 p.m., twitter.com/RiskReversal/status/1354625 166270197760.

8.  "White House Monitoring Situation Involving GameStop, Other Firms," Reuters, January 27, 2021.

9.  "Joint Statement regarding Ongoing Market Volatility," SEC press release, January 27, 2021, www.sec.gov/news/public-statement/joint-statement-ongoing -market-volatility-2021-01-27.

10. FINRA, "Following the Crowd: Investing and Social Media," blog post, January 29, 2021, www.finra.org/investors/alerts/following-crowd-investing-and-social-media.

## Chapter 19: Men in Tights

1.  "Banner High above San Fran Headquarters . . . 'Suck My Nuts,'" *TMZ*, January 31, 2021.

2.  Michael Bolton, "Michael Bolton: Break Up With Your Brokerage: Public.com," YouTube video, updated February 23, 2021, www.youtube.com/watch?v=xiu MuvqCoXA.

3. Nadia El-Yaouti, "Robinhood Revolt: App Faces Lawsuit after Halting Trade on GameStop and Other Securities," *Law Commentary*, February 1, 2021.

4. Spencer Jakab, "Will the Real Robin Hood Please Stand Up," *The Wall Street Journal*, January 28, 2021.

5. James Hookway, "Angry Robinhood Traders Take Aim at the Wrong Robin Hood," *The Wall Street Journal*, February 8, 2021.

6. Clemence Michallon, "Stephen Colbert tears into Wall Street Traders: You're all for unfettered capitalism unless you lose!" *Independent*, January 29, 2021.

7. Alexandria Ocasio-Cortez, "We need to know more . . . ," Twitter, January 28, 2021, https://twitter.com/aoc/status/1354830697459032066.

8. Jordan Fabia, Erik Wasson, and Daniel Flatley, "Ocasio-Cortez Urges Scrutiny of Robinhood Curbs on GameStop," *Bloomberg*, January 28, 2021.

9. Kathryn Krawczyk, "Donald Trump and Alexandria Ocasio-Cortez Agree on This 1 Thing," *The Week*, January 28, 2021.

10. Egberto Willies, "Senator Bernie Sanders and Politics Done Right Agrees: The Business Model of Wall Street Is Fraud," *DailyKos*, February 1, 2021.

11. Josh Hawley, "Calling Wall Street's Bluff," *RealClear Politics*, February 3, 2021.

12. Mohamed El-Erian, interview by Sara Eisen, *Closing Bell*, CNBC, February 2, 2021.

13. Sarah Perez, "Robinhood and Reddit top the App Store as trading apps surge following GameStop mania," *TechCrunch*, January 28, 2021.

14. Bob Pisani, "Attention Robinhood power users: Most day traders lose money," CNBC, November 20, 2020.

15. Paul Rowady, "Alphacution Press: New York Times and Robinhood," Alphacution press release, July 8, 2020, https://alphacution.com/alphacution-press-new-york-times-and-robinhood.

16. Packy McCormick, "Robinhood Robinhooded Robinhood," *Not Boring* (blog), February 1, 2021, www.notboring.co/p/robinhood-robinhooded-robinhood.

17. Vlad Tenev, "It's Time for Real-Time Settlement," Robinhood blog post, February 2, 2021, https://blog.robinhood.com/news/2021/2/2/its-time-for-real-time-settlement.

18. Robinhood Form X-17 A-5, full year 2020.

19. Stephen Gandel, "Ahead of IPO, Robinhood Expands Risky Stock Market Lending," CBS News, March 25, 2021.

20. Annie Massa, Viren Vaghela, and Yalman Onaran, "What's the DTCC and How Did It Stop GameStop Mania?," *Bloomberg*, January 29, 2021.

21.  Mohamed El-Erian, "Market Insouciance Means the Reddit Rebellion Will Be Back," *Financial Times*, February 4, 2021.

22.  John Detrixhe, "Robinhood shares are soaring just like the stocks that trade on Robinhood," *Quartz*, February 11, 2021.

23.  Jonathan G. Katz to SEC, "Competitive Developments in the Options Markets," April 13, 2004, www.sec.gov/rules/concept/s70704/citadel04132004.pdf.

24.  Avi Salzman, "SEC Chairman Says Banning Payment for Order Flow Is 'On the Table,'" *Barron's*, August 30, 2021.

25.  Public.com, "Aligning with Our Community," *Medium*, February 1, 2021, https://medium.com/the-public-blog/aligning-with-our-community-300885799d03.

26.  Tom Maloney, "Citadel Securities Gets the Spotlight," *Bloomberg Markets*, April 6, 2021. Tom Maloney and Sally Bakewell, "Citadel Securities Reaps Record $6.7 Billion on Volatility," *Bloomberg*, January 22, 2021.

27.  iainclarke7, "Mythbusting: Payment for Order Flow & Tipping," All of Us blog post, March 13, 2021, www.allofusfinancial.com/post/mythbusting-about-payment-for-order-flow-tipping.

28.  Peter Rudegeair and Orla McCaffrey, "Robinhood Raises $1 Billion to Meet Surging Cash Demands," *The Wall Street Journal*, January 29, 2021.

## Chapter 20: January 29, 2021

1.  Julia Verlaine and Gunjan Banerji, "Keith Gill Drove the Reddit GameStop Mania: He Talked to the Journal," *The Wall Street Journal*, January 29, 2021.

2.  Roaring Kitty (@TheRoaringKitty), video, Twitter, March 9, 2021, 10:21 a.m., twitter.com/TheRoaringKitty/status/1369307339568873473.

3.  Gregory Zuckerman and Geoffrey Rogow, "After GameStop Backlash, Citron Research Will Stop Publishing Short-Seller Reports," *The Wall Street Journal*, January 29, 2021.

## Chapter 21: How Not to Stick It to the Man

1.  Daniel Miller, Suhauna Hussain, and Hugo Martín, "GameStop Investors' Motives: Take a YOLO Bet: 'Ruin a Billionaire's Life,'" *Los Angeles Times*, January 29, 2021.

2.  John Gittelsohn, "Bill Gross, the Bond King That Racked Up One of the Longest Winning Streaks of Any Money Manager, Retires," *Financial Post*, February 4, 2019.

3. Bill Gross, "Bill Gross Releases Investment Outlook: Game(Stop), Set, Match," PR Newswire, January 29, 2021.

4. Bérengère Sim, "How Billionaire Bill Gross U-turned and Made $10m Shorting GameStop," *Financial News*, March 17, 2021.

5. Telis Demos, "GameStop Stock Frenzy May Not Be So Bad for Wall Street," *The Wall Street Journal*, February 1, 2021.

6. Kerry Dolan, Chase Peterson-Whithorn, and Jennifer Wang, "The Forbes World's Billionaires List," *Forbes*, April 6, 2021.

7. Ari Levy, "Fintech Keeps Minting Billionaires as Robinhood Co-founders Prepare for IPO," CNBC, July 19, 2021.

8. Elizabeth Dilts Marshall, "Client Activity on Morgan Stanley's E*Trade Is 'Off the Charts': CFO," Reuters, February 25, 2021.

9. Leah Goldman and Dina Spector, "The Sexiest Hedge Fund Managers Alive," *Business Insider Australia*, December 23, 2010.

10. Katherine Burton and Katherine Doherty, "Mudrick Capital Gains $200 Million on AMC, GameStop Bets," *Bloomberg*, February 2, 2021.

11. Katherine Doherty and Bailey Lipschultz, "Hedge Fund Flips 'Overvalued' AMC, and Shares Keep Surging," *Bloomberg*, June 1, 2021.

12. Katherine Doherty, "Mudrick's AMC Bet Backfires after Meme Frenzy Wrecks Hedges," *Bloomberg*, June 11, 2021.

13. Juliet Chung, "This Hedge Fund Made $700 Million on GameStop," *The Wall Street Journal*, February 3, 2021.

14. Tomi Kilgore, "GameStop Shareholder Sells Off Stake Valued at over $1 Billion," *MarketWatch*, January 30, 2021.

15. Joel Tillinghast, *Big Money Thinks Small: Biases, Blind Spots, and Smarter Investing* (New York: Columbia University Press, 2017), 31.

16. Connor Smith, "Activist Investors Join GameStop's Board: What That Means for Investors," *Barron's*, June 12, 2020.

17. Svea Herbst-Bayliss, "Exclusive: GameStop's Strong Stock Performance Triggered Board Director's Exit," Reuters, April 8, 2021.

18. David Benoit, "Two Small-time Investors Were Buying GameStop Stock before It Was Cool," *The Wall Street Journal*, February 2, 2021.

19. Nina Trentmann and Mark Maurer, "GameStop CFO Resigns Weeks after Reddit-fueled Stock Market Frenzy," *The Wall Street Journal*, February 24, 2021.

20. Jessica DiNapoli, "How a Sweetheart Deal Gives GameStop CEO a $179 Million Goodbye Gift," Reuters, April 21, 2021.

21. Stephen Gandel, "Corporate Executives Reap Millions from Reddit Stock Frenzy," *MoneyWatch*, CBS News, January 30, 2021.

22. Robert Frank, Nick Wells, and Pippa Stevens, "Koss Family and Company's Execs Cash in $44 Million in Stock during Short Squeeze Frenzy," CNBC, February 4, 2021.

23. Ed Lin, "AMC Executives Sell Large Amounts of Stock," *Barron's*, January 29, 2021.

24. Joshua Franklin, "Silver Lake Cashes Out on AMC for $713 Million after Reddit-fueled Rally," Reuters, January 29, 2021.

25. Rebecca Davis, "China's Dalian Wanda Sells Remaining AMC Stake for $426 Million," *Variety*, May 21, 2021.

26. Sarah Whitten, "AMC CEO Adam Aron Raved about Its New Investors Who Are at Odds with Wall Street," CNBC, May 7, 2021.

27. Rachel Layne, "AMC's Meme Stock Soared into Orbit: So Did CEO Aron's Wealth," CBS News, June 7, 2021.

28. Kelly Gilblom, "AMC CEO's Stock Gift to Sons Balloons to More Than $30 Million," *Bloomberg*, June 2, 2021.

29. Tomi Kilgore, "AMC Board Members Sold Nearly $4 Million Worth of Stock This Week," *MarketWatch*, June 10, 2021.

## Chapter 22: February 2021

1. Anonymous, "Response to DeepFuckingValue post, 'GME YOLO Update-Feb 3, 2021 – heads up gonna back off the daily updates for now,'" Reddit, February 3, 2021, www.reddit.com/r/wallstreetbets/comments/lbykxg/gme_yolo_update_feb_3_2021_heads_up_gonna_back/gmb06of.

2. Ibid.

## Chapter 23: The Same Old Game

1. Brad M. Barber and Terrance Odean, "Trading Is Hazardous to Your Wealth: The Common Stock Investment Performance of Individual Investors," *Journal of Finance* 55, no. 2, April 12, 2000, doi.org/10.1111/0022-1082.00226.

2. Michaela Pagel, "A News-utility Theory for Inattention and Delegation in Portfolio Choice," *Econometrica* 86, no. 2 (March 2018): 491–522.

3. "Futu: Generation Z to Dominate Investment Landscape for Foreseeable Future," PR Newswire, April 7, 2021.

4. Interview with Jim Chanos by telephone, March 2, 2021.

5. Brad M. Barber et al., "Attention Induced Trading and Returns: Evidence from Robinhood Users," *SSRN Electronic Journal*, July 27, 2021, https://papers.ssrn.com/sol3/papers.cfm?abstract_id=3715077.

6. David McCabe and Sophia June, "GameStop Hearing Centers Around Robinhood," *The New York Times*, February 18, 2021.

7. Lobbying Data Summary, Opensecrets.org, accessed April 2020, www.opensecrets.org/federal-lobbying.

8. Michelle Leder, "Can $30 Million Solve Robinhood's Legal Issues," *Bloomberg*, July 19, 2021.

9. Svea Herbst-Bayliss, "Melvin Capital Gained 21.7% Net of Fees in February—Source," Reuters, March 3, 2021.

10. Quoted by CNBC host Carl Quintanilla (@carlquintanilla), "CASHIN: ".. everything we read confirms what we said from the very beginning. The 'retail rebellion' was a bit of a farce and an illusion that the financial media bought into much too readily," Twitter, February 8, 2021, 8:31 a.m., twitter.com/carlquintanilla/status/1358770450025881601.

11. Maggie Fitzgerald, "Warren Buffett Says Robinhood Is Catering to the Gambling Instincts of Investors," CNBC, May 2, 2021.

12. Jacqueline Ortiz-Ramsay, "The Old Guard of Investing Is at It Again," Robinhood blog post, May 3, 2021, https://robinhood.engineering/the-old-guard-of-investing-is-at-it-again-a8b870fbfd49.

13. Hendrik Bessembinder, "Wealth Creation in the U.S. Public Stock Markets 1926 to 2019," *SSRN Electronic Journal*, February 13, 2020, https://papers.ssrn.com/sol3/papers.cfm?abstract_id=3537838.

14. Investment Company Institute, "60th Edition Investment Company Institute Fact Book," 2020, www.ici.org/system/files/attachments/pdf/2020_factbook.pdf.

15. "U.S. Fund Fee Study," Morningstar, 2019, www.morningstar.com/lp/annual-us-fund-fee-study.

16. Alliance Bernstein, "Active-Passive Debate: The Public Policy Angle," blog post, September 8, 2016, www.alliancebernstein.com/library/active-passive-debate-the-public-policy-angle.htm.

17. Berkshire Hathaway letter to shareholders, February 25, 2017, www.berkshire hathaway.com/letters/2016ltr.pdf.

### Bonus Round

1. Federal Reserve Board 2019 Survey of Consumer Finances, accessed April 2021, www.federalreserve.gov/econres/scfindex.htm.

2. Burton G. Malkiel, *A Random Walk Down Wall Street: A Time-Tested Strategy for Successful Investing* (New York: W. W. Norton, 2007), 24.

3. Spencer Jakab, "Making Monkeys Out of the Sohn Investing Gurus," *The Wall Street Journal*, May 6, 2019.

4. CXO Advisory Group, "Guru Grades," retrieved June 2, 2021, www.cxoadvisory .com/gurus.

5. Murray Coleman, "SPIVA: 2020 Mid-year Active vs. Passive Scorecard, Index Fund Advisors," Index Fund Advisors blog post, October 7, 2020, www.ifa.com /articles/despite_brief_reprieve_2018_spiva_report_reveals_active_funds _fail_dent_indexing_lead_-_works.

6. John Bogle, "The Arithmetic of 'All-in' Investment Expenses," *Financial Analysts Journal* 70, no. 1 (2014): https://doi.org/10.2469/faj.v70.n1.1.

7. Larry Swedroe, "Older Investors Handled Last Year's Volatility Worst," *The Evidence-Based Investor*, April 9, 2021, www.evidenceinvestor.com/older-investors -handled-last-years-volatility-worst-morningstar.

8. Investment Company Institute database, accessed March 2021.

9. Victor Haghani and Richard Dewey, "Rational Decision-Making under Uncertainty: Observed Betting Patterns on a Biased Coin," *SSRN Electronic Journal,* October 19, 2016, http://dx.doi.org/10.2139/ssrn.2856963.

# Index